The Vivid Flavors Cookbook

the

Vivid
Flavors

cookbook

International Recipes
from Hot & Spicy
to Smoky & Sweet

By Robert Wemischner

Library of Congress Cataloging-in-Publication Data

Wemischner, Robert.
    The Vivid Flavors Cookbook : international recipes from hot and spicy to smoky and
    sweet / Robert Wemischner.
        p. cm.
    Includes index.
    ISBN 1-56565-152-9
        1. Cookery, International.   I. Title.
TX725.A1W376 1994
641.59—dc20   94-10987
                                                                     CIP

Lowell House books can be purchased at special discounts when ordered in bulk for premiums and special sales. Contact Department VH at the address below.

Requests for such permission should be addressed to:
Lowell House
2029 Century Park East, Suite 3290
Los Angeles, CA 90067

Publisher: Jack Artenstein
General Manager, Lowell House Adult: Bud Sperry
Director of Publishing Services: Mary D. Aarons
Project Editor: Janice Gallagher
Text design: Nancy Freeborn

Manufactured in the United States of America
10 9 8 7 6 5 4 3 2 1

Acknowledgments

To all my family, friends, and colleagues who have unfailingly supported me in the long but pleasurable task of writing this book

A special thanks to Nancy Berkoff, friend, colleague, and registered dietician, whose idea it was to include the nutritional data on the recipes and who did the work to make it happen

And a warm and big thank-you to Janice Gallagher, my editor, who from start to finish has offered nothing but encouragement

With love and thanks to Leslie, my wife, and our children, Lauren and Chad, who have lent me their patience as well as their palates.

Contents

Vivid Flavors

From my vantage point behind the counter as chef-proprietor of two gourmet-to-go and catering establishments, I constantly heard the clamor for "flavor" from a varied public. Deciding between one salad, prepared entree, or side dish and another, my customers would unfailingly ask, "Which one has more flavor?" And I would unfailingly answer, "They all have flavor, but it depends on what *kind* of flavor you are looking for"—and I would enumerate the adjectives: "piquant, pungent, bittersweet, intense, smoky. . . ." Over the course of almost twenty years in gourmet food retailing (which is nothing if not the romancing of flavors), my overwhelming quest has been to create dishes that would reveal the quintessential flavor of their starring ingredients. Therein lies the impetus for this book. But I am getting ahead of myself in the story.

It's difficult to chart particular moments in an idiosyncratic culinary journey that put me on the path to writing this book. But surely I can credit a few epiphanies that stand out: a mile-high fresh apple pie crowned with a thick thatch of whipped cream at Chandler's (New York City) after a Broadway matinee with my parents; the glistening exotica in Fauchon's Paris windows, which promised a feast for the eyes and delivered impeccable quality to the palate; my first handmade chevre at a dairy farm in Burgundy; the grilled polenta at Al Fogher (Rome); the pristine fennel and arugula salad, simply dressed with fine olive oil, at Trattoria da Alfredo (New York City).

What ties all of these memories together? I can think of only one word: *honesty*—the honesty of cultivation, manufacture, and preparation that went into these foods. *Simple, bright, direct,* and *vivid* are other words that spring to mind.

THE TASTES

Technically speaking, the taste buds can perceive only four categories of flavors: salty, bitter, sour, and sweet. But the well-traveled palate tells a different story. How then to account for the exquisite subtlety the palate senses when confronted with a flood of complex flavors that transcend the basic four?

What about the puckery, pungent, sweet-sour, intense, and smoky qualities and all the multidimensional flavors in between? It's not within my province to explain the physiology of taste or the finer points of how the taste buds register these complex and wonderful flavors. Instead, in this book I will be focusing on dishes that exemplify a broad gamut of unforgettable flavors within these five roughly defined basic categories. My goal is not to explain *why* something tastes the way it does but merely *how* to achieve that taste. For this task, I have taken my inspiration from many shopping and tasting expeditions to ethnic and farmer's markets, always scouring the shelves for a new hot pepper sauce or raiding the produce displays for an as-yet-untasted vegetable or varietal I may have missed on a previous go-round. Broadly defined, my cooking is a fusion of time-honored preparation techniques from one cuisine with the most direct and memorable flavors of another.

In most of the recipes, my objective has been to put a new spin on classic flavor combinations found principally in the cuisines of France, Italy, the Middle East, Southeast Asia, China, and the Americas. The resulting recipes fall into four distinct categories.

In the first category, I deliberately wed the ingredients of one cuisine to the techniques of another. For example, Dark and Dusky Chicken, page 128, combines a staple from the Oriental pantry, dried shiitake mushrooms, with the French method for stuffing boned chicken thighs.

In the second group, I have heightened a particular flavor by simply using a key ingredient or two in an unorthodox manner. My Bittersweet Bouquet (page 27) borrows pomegranate syrup from the Middle Eastern pantry to counterbalance the bitterness of the greens but adds its own pleasant tartness to the dish in the process. Porcini

Mushroom Soup au Gratin (page 205) borrows chapati, the thin flatbread from India, tops it with melted French cheese, and floats it like a raft on a bubbling bowl of richly scented soup.

Overall, my goal has been to remain faithful to the spirit, if not the letter, of authentic ethnic flavors. In some cases, native dishes serve as springboards to the recipes; in other cases, I have chosen to deconstruct a classic recipe, examine its main constituents, and use them in a novel way to arrive at new taste sensations, to make the "exotic" accessible, while always remaining grounded in sound culinary principles. No mere novelty for novelty's sake has been allowed to creep in to trivialize the adventure.

In the third category, I have chosen to combine ingredients from dissimilar cuisines to achieve an entirely new flavor; for instance, Dark Greens with a Bright Flavor (page 160) features stir-fried greens in a strongly Asian-accented sauce topped with a new twist on good old-fashioned Southern cornbread.

The last group grew out of weekly trips to farmer's markets but has no multiethnic correlative unless you consider the ethnic diversity of the growers themselves (which, in Los Angeles, where I live, is considerable). Inspired by impeccably fresh local produce—often organically grown, brought directly from farmer to market (a welcome national trend), picked and sold at its peak—these dishes offer compelling reasons to encourage small-scale farmers to continue their pursuit of biodiversity and excellence.

Intended to honor the passionate commitment of small-scale farmers to bring quality back to the table, Seurat's Cauliflower (page 88), for example, gives a sweet and sour treatment to the freshly picked, creamy white vegetable and then showers it with freshly snipped chives. Similarly, Golden Melting Moments (page 144) depends for its impact on the quality and freshness of its main ingredients and celebrates the twin glories of yellow tomatoes and yellow bell peppers in a late-summer soup.

Shopping a farmer's market in the morning and getting on a first-name basis with the farmer who grew and picked what will grace your dinner table that night adds a dimension to the cooking and eating experience that cannot be underestimated. Nameless, faceless multinational agribusiness simply cannot deliver a head of cauliflower or a tomato or raspberry with flavor equal to those lovingly tended by a small-scale grower.

THE RECIPES AND BEYOND

The main recipes are grouped subjectively by their overall taste profile: puckery; pungent; sweet-sour/hot-sour/hot-sweet; intense; or smoky. Within each is a selection of Starters, smaller dishes designed to be served as appetizers or as part of a procession of dishes on a buffet (in larger portions these can function easily as entrees); Sides, highly flavored accompaniments to main dishes; and entrees themselves, denoted as Stars. Twenty Not-So-Sweets that lie beyond the specific taste categories, run the gamut from custards, cakes, and pastry to fruit-based treats, with a chapter to themselves.

To facilitate menu planning, most of the recipes conclude with Serving Suggestions to help you structure pleasing and provocative juxtapositions of dishes for any occasion, from an elegant New Year's Eve supper for 8 to a beer-tasting bash for 30 anchored by a buffet of robust stand-up and dig-in fare whose origins encompass several continents at least. Whether you are searching for just the right side dish to set off an old family favorite or looking for a startlingly refreshing ending for a meal, this collection of widely diverse recipes will allow you to find just the flavors to suit your mood.

Featuring many readily available ingredients from the pantries of the Middle East, Southeast Asia, China, Mexico, Central and South America, and more, the recipes are designed to allow the everyday cook to create dishes marked by brilliant and satisfying flavors. My intention is to take you and your taste buds on a journey avoiding all of the dull and bland byways and "throwaway" dishes that lend nothing but calories to a meal. Create a meal using a puckery Starter, and then move on to a pungent main dish chosen from a constellation of Stars. Pair these with an aromatic vegetable dish (see Sides) and then end the meal on an intense but Not-So-Sweet note.

In the Back-of-the-Book Recipes, you will find a subset of basic preparations (most doable in advance) used in the other recipes. These are noted by page number in the ingredient lists of the recipes where used. And to prove that healthful eating and satisfied palates need not be mutually exclusive, I have placed many of the recipes into the following four categories: low fat, low sodium, low calorie, and high fiber, as defined by the FDA's 1994 Labeling Act. To help in menu planning, I have further categorized the recipes by course (Starter, Star, Side, and Not-So-Sweet).

Finally, there is a short list of Superb Sources offering foods whose uniqueness recommends them for use in some of the recipes (French epicures would honor these vendors-craftsmen-producers with the word *artisanal*, and justifiably so). All of these sources cheerfully and reliably handle mail orders.

Beside some of the recipes are Flavor Flashes!, where you will find miscellaneous ramblings on some of my favorite foods, quick bites of culinary fact, notes on salient ingredients adjacent to the recipes that feature them, short recipes, and just plain opinion, collected from my years of traveling, cooking, catering, and creating, during which I have nourished myself (and hopefully others) in more than the literal sense.

Whether your schedule allows only a half hour to get a weeknight dinner on the table or the better part of a weekend day to produce a multicourse feast, you will encounter a balanced collection of time-saving and time-consuming recipes from which to choose. In both cases, be assured that no steps are wasted in the preparation. Every move counts. Every ingredient is carefully calculated to play its part in contributing to the overall taste impression. But ultimately the most important ingredient is you. Trust your own innate creativity and your instinct. Taste as you go. Make notes for future reference. Using the recipes merely as a road map, feel free to veer off on your own taste detours, substituting an ingredient here, amplifying one seasoning or toning down another there, as you wish. Cooking, whether a solitary or collaborative activity, after all, should remain fun and reflect *your* personality and mood; sticking your finger into a sauce to taste its progress, or offering that taste to someone else in the kitchen should not be off-limits; these are all parts of the overall sensual experience.

Along the way I hope to reawaken taste buds blunted by a long procession of foods that have had all their inherent flavor bred or manufactured out of them. Think of it as a return to essences and Old World flavors. This is food painted with a bold palette of flavors, gleaned from a finite list of often underused yet accessible key ethnic ingredients, using basic, easily mastered techniques borrowed from a number of world cuisines. Although working in an ephemeral medium, the cross-cultural cook layers flavors in much the same way the painter wields a richly hued palette of colors, building complexity, contrast, depth, and interest with each brushstroke.

I hope you enjoy the ongoing taste trip as much as I continue to do, nourishing yourself and others as you go.

But before embarking, here are a few notes to embolden you.

How to overcome fear of "exotic" ingredients

As a goad and a guide to your culinary inspiration, at the beginning of the first five chapters you will find eclectic (however subjective) lists of Key Ingredients. You will also find recommendations for brand names as well as the country of origin for the best versions of many of these items. (Where appropriate, I have included common substitutes for the authentic foods of each cuisine from which I borrow.) The more common ingredients stand alone as mere entries in the lists with no need for further explanation. The rest, some of which may be new even to well-seasoned cooks, are buttressed with bits of background information to aid in identifying and purchasing the ingredients in question.

Some items on the lists, like dried spices and bottled hot sauces, are shelf-stable basics that you might consider adding gradually to your multiethnic pantry as you encounter them in the recipes. Once you have made space for them in your pantry and on your palate, I am sure that you will reach for many of these as readily and reflexively as you do your everyday seasonings. I like to place these front-and-center on my shelves to encourage frequent, constant, and creative use. I urge you to do the same.

I have included certain seasonal fresh produce among the Key Ingredients simply to spotlight marvels that are only briefly in the markets and cry out all the more loudly to be used in recipes designed to celebrate them. And celebrate them I do, especially in the purely vegetarian Sides and fruit-based Not-So-Sweets.

Still others, like special cheeses, smoked meats, and seafood, are perishable and must be fresh to be good. Hunt down good local sources (some wholesalers who supply the better restaurants in your town may be willing to sell in retail quantities). Simply put these items on your shopping list on the day you plan to make the particular dish that includes them.

Not wishing to play favorites, I have arranged the items in each list in alphabetical order. Keep in mind that I have not intended to be exhaustive in these classifications. You won't find a heavy representation of the staples of Russian or German or Scandinavian cooking (among others), which fall outside of my purview.

Moreover, you will also find items on the lists that do not appear in the recipes at all. I have included these as added inspiration for daring cooks who wish to explore other ingredients to produce overall taste impressions that roughly parallel those shown in each chapter. Once you gain a measure of comfort with the recipes, you will soon find that the possibilities for transcending them are endless and endlessly exciting. But a limited *batterie de cuisine* will help to send you on your way and, when properly chosen, will keep you well equipped for a long time to come.

The tools of the trade

Beyond good knives and a few wire whisks, there are two electric appliances that, over time, have proved to be indispensable to my culinary pursuits. First, a heavy-duty food processor; this kitchen wizard makes fast work of many an otherwise laborious task. Next, an electric coffee grinder does double duty perfectly as a spice grinder to yield the burst of bright flavor that only freshly ground, just-roasted spices can give to a dish. (I have two such grinders, each a different color and dedicated to its own special use; one is reserved for the morning java and the other for the aforementioned spices.)

I have found that it's impossible to live without a small selection of heavy-weight sauté pans (8" and 10"), one old-fashioned 12" cast-iron skillet, a few saucepans (1-, 2, and 4-quart capacity), and a 10- or 12-quart stockpot with steamer basket and a tight-fitting lid. Also make room in your kitchen cabinet for a cast-iron, ridged skillet for effective stovetop grilling for those times when outdoor cooking is out of the question. All of these are subordinate to my favorite cooking vessel of all, a stainless steel wok with steamer rack, tight-fitting lid, and its accompanying long-handled tools, including a skimmer, a shovel-like scoop, and tongs. An accurate kitchen scale (up to 11 lbs., marked in ounce increments) is a joy to have on hand, as are a large metal colander with feet and a few large and small fine-meshed sieves. Keeping all these recommendations in perspective, however, I am constantly reminded that memorable food can (and often does) emerge from kitchens that are doggedly primitive, small, or both. The inspiration fueling the person behind the stove is infinitely more important than the quality of the kitchen space or what kinds of pots or pans are in it.

Assembling the cross-cultural pantry

From coast to coast, America is changing. We are a nation becoming increasingly more multiethnic, particularly in and around our major metropolitan centers. That means that cooking enthusiasts are beneficiaries of abundant sources for obtaining the ingredients required to explore most of the world's great cuisines at home without compromise of authenticity. And mail-order sources are a good alternative in areas where local retail supply is spotty or nonexistent (see Superb Sources).

During the 1950s and 1960s, the greatest concentration of immigrants came from Italy, Great Britain, Germany, and the West Indies. The '70s and '80s saw a sharp increase in immigrant populations from Mexico, Central America, India, and China (both from the mainland and Taiwan), with Vietnamese, Thais, Filipinos, and Koreans comprising the bulk of non-Chinese Asians entering the United States during that same period. In our current decade, Mexicans, Central Americans, Caribbeans (the latter mainly settling on the East Coast—more than 500,000 in Brooklyn alone), and non-Chinese Asians (largely Filipinos) continue to arrive in considerable numbers. The statistics are staggering. In Los Angeles County alone, the school system has over 80 different languages spoken. The cumulative impact of these waves of immigration on the culinary life of our country can't be overestimated.

Just 25 years ago, something now as commonly available as fresh basil was scarce, if not impossible to find unless you grew it yourself or cajoled the maverick Italian grocer to part with some of his homegrown stash (as I used to when I first ventured into an "ethnic" food store).

Today, staples like rice and noodles of many kinds, fresh and dried herbs and spices, fresh and frozen imported fish, special cuts of meats and poultry, and formerly exotic produce are becoming increasingly available thanks to the surges of migration to these shores over the last 40 years or so.

Now the adventurous cook can easily choose to venture beyond the chain supermarkets into the realm of ethnic groceries that range from mom-and-pop stores to units of multinational conglomerates, which are changing the commercial profile of our major cities. Once-tentative gropings to recapture a bit of their homeland away from home have led some immigrants to open sparkling American-style hypermarkets to meet the growing demand. Take, for example, the Yaohan Supermarket chains in California, Illinois, and New Jersey or the 99 Ranch chains in California, where ingredients from China, Japan, Korea, and Southeast Asia are displayed abundantly and seductively.

No matter which type of store you visit, the array of merchandise can be bewildering. But once you've become addicted to the pleasures of shopping in an ethnic market, it's tough to return to your garden-variety supermarket (somehow the international aisle in the local chain store just doesn't take the place of the real thing). An important rule of thumb: The best place to buy "ethnic" ingredients is in an "ethnic" store; there you can be assured of the best price and quality. It stands to reason that the greater the volume sold, the better the price and the fresher the merchandise. As demand has increased, so has the supply and its breadth.

Notwithstanding first impressions to the contrary, generally speaking, the range of merchandise in these stores is organized in a logical, consumer-friendly fashion. In some of the smaller shops, you may often stumble over bargain-priced cases of at-their-peak seasonal fruits and vegetables piled prominently by the front door. Beyond these attention-grabbing displays, you most likely will confront aisles chock-a-block with noodles and rice (and noodles made from rice). Venture farther and you may find shelves fairly brimming with bottled condiments, spice mixes, and tinned or preserved vegetables and fruits. Next you may find well-stocked refrigerated cases of dairy products (particularly yogurt and cheese in the Middle Eastern stores), fresh noodles, colorful displays of perishable vegetables and fresh herbs, soybean curd, and jarred chile pastes grouped by degree of hotness. The Middle Eastern and Indian stores will often feature bulk displays of grains and dried legumes of all kinds which are a staple in Iran, Egypt, Israel, Greece, Turkey, Saudi Arabia, Morocco, and the Indian subcontinent.

Freezers in Asian markets are apt to be full of imported whole fish and seafood, staples like coconut meat and milk, exotic fruits and vegetables, and leaves used as wrappers for steamed foods. Spices and dried herbs and packets of dehydrated mushrooms are generally grouped together in their own corner. Sweets ranging from baklava and flaky pine-nut fingers in the Greek markets to coconut-scented rice puddings and technicolored gelatinous sweets in the Thai stores are usually displayed separately from other prepared foods designed to be eaten as is, or taken out to be reheated or to stage an impromptu picnic. In some stores you will find a rather comprehensive display of beverages, both alcoholic and non-, ready to lend an added authentic touch.

Allow frequent unhurried visits, confining your explorations to one specific area of the store at a time. Don't hesitate to point at an inscrutable jar or package and inquire about its contents. The way to learn is simply to ask. It's indeed worth the gesticulating to get on friendly terms with the wonders within your local Middle Eastern bazaars, Hispanic *mercados,* and Asian supermarkets.

Some store clerks may endure your questions with withering condescension. But if you're fortunate as I have been, you will catch the ear of a friendly store clerk or customer who will satisfy your eagerness to learn and appreciate your efforts at gaining an insight into their culture through its food.

In addition to retail stores, there is a welcome proliferation in our cities and suburbs of family-owned and -operated restaurants dishing up authentic and often highly distinctive versions of the street foods of Bangkok, Manila, Calcutta, Oaxaca, and Seoul, among others. Keeping your mind and palate open to new taste sensations when dining out, you will undoubtedly be gratified.

Through the recipes, I urge you to take the exciting next step: recapture and transform those diverse and vivid flavors in your own kitchen.

CHAPTER 1

Pleasantly Puckery

ALL TARTED UP

D rawing selectively from among others the diverse pantries of Southeast Asia, the Middle East, China, and the Mediterranean for inspiration, the dishes featured here have one thing in common: a pronounced but pleasant mouth-filling tart-ness tempered by a more mellow ingredient. I like to think of these as flavors that fairly sing with exuberance, especially welcome when the sun doesn't shine. Just imagine the pucker of freshly squeezed lemonade, or the pleasant tang of creamy Bulgarian feta cheese, and your palate will be attuned to the specialties that await you.

These are foods that owe the acidic edge in their sauce, dressing, or marinade to a relatively circumscribed miscellany of ingredients: It's a short list that includes vinegar, citric fruits, a few tart-tasting vegetables, some sharp spices, and foods containing the active milk cultures that give their pleasant tang to yogurt, buttermilk, and cheese. Dishes such as White Bean Potage with Sorrel Swirl (page 33) and Fennel-Orange Salad (page 18) are sure to convert even those who continue to cling to the primitive notion that sweet flavors prevail and sour (or even tart) tastes are to be avoided.

Key Ingredients

These ingredients produce flavors that are astringent, bracing, sharp, acidic, and tart.

ALLSPICE—also known as pimento (not to be confused with pimiento, the red pepper, often sold in brine); derived from a tropical tree belonging to the myrtle family—see Flavor Flash, page 15)

APRICOTS—dried, fresh, or glaceed

CANDIED LEMON (or other citrus) **PEEL**—homemade is best (see Back-of-the-Book Recipes, page 275)

CAPERS—the immature flower buds of a Mediterranean shrub, available in jars, salted, or in vinegar brine, tiny or colossal

CARDAMOM—seed pods from a cousin of ginger, with husks that are green, white, or black, sold whole (hulled or not) or ground

CINNAMON or **CASSIA**—bark from two members of the same family, the first considered true cinnamon, the second an impostor; available ground or in quill-like sticks

CLOVES—a relative of allspice; the dried flower bud from a tropical myrtle

FETA CHEESE—Bulgarian, Sardinian, French, Danish, and, of course, Greek are the most common varieties ranging from creamy to firm; Italian ricotta salata makes a fine-flavored, if drier, substitute

FIVE-SPICE POWDER—Chinese spice mix consisting of ground star anise, cinnamon, cloves, fennel, and Szechwan peppercorns

GREEN TOMATOES—an end-of-summer treat, suitable for relishes, chutneys, vegetable side dishes; do *not* substitute Mexican green tomatoes (tomatillos)

KAFFIR LIMES—highly aromatic, small, round limes with pitted skin, used in Thai cuisine; dried form is used in Persian cuisine to flavor long-cooked stews

KAFFIR LIME LEAVES—fresh or dried, traditionally used in Southeast Asian cooking, particularly in the green and red curries of Thailand and Cambodia

LEMON LEAVES—unsprayed, fresh or dried in powdered form (fresh is better)

LEMONGRASS—a tropical grass used in Vietnamese, Thai, and other Southeast Asian cooking, also known as citronella (buy some, root in water and then plant in soil)

LIME JUICE—fresh

LINGONBERRIES—Scandinavia's answer to the American cranberry; tart, ruby-colored and most commonly bottled as a sweetened conserve

OLIVES—with their purplish black color and sharp and tangy flavor, Greek Kalamatas for me reign supreme; these are harvested ripe, incised with a slit, and pickled in brine

PERSIMMONS—a tart seasonal marvel, favored in China and Japan, a great source of vitamins A and C and potassium; also available dried; the slightly flattened fuyu variety may be eaten when hard like an apple; the heart-shaped hachiya variety develops its sweetness and flavor when completely ripe, soft to the point of squishy, with its skin often blackened in spots

PLUMS, SOUR DRIED—yellow Bukhara prunes, a Middle Eastern favorite; not to be confused with the Japanese *umeboshi,* which are often pickled or salted

POMEGRANATE—fresh or in bottled juice or syrup; the deep garnet-colored pomegranate concentrate sometimes known as pomegranate molasses (no sugar added)

QUINCE—a staple in Middle Eastern cooking, often used in combination with meats and poultry

RHUBARB—fresh, it's a spring sensation; also available frozen

SEVILLE ORANGES (NARANJA AGRIA)—juice used in Caribbean cooking, especially Cuban; also used in orange marmalade (see page 24 for substitutes)

SORREL—an herb with succulent acidic-tasting leaves, favored in French sauces and some Middle European soups

SZECHWAN PEPPERCORNS—the berries of the prickly ash tree with a slight lemony undertone and a subtle hotness; also known as anise pepper, or sansho, a Japanese pepper

TAMARIND—beanlike fruits of the tamarind tree, available in a block of compressed pulp, dried pods, and concentrated juice; commonly tasted as a component of Worcestershire sauce

VINEGARS—a seemingly limitless array, ranging from those based on wine, rice, and palm-leaf and sugarcane juice to those infused with fruit essence

YUZU—Japanese citron, its juice is available bottled; its peel is sometimes available dried in powdered form; the fruit itself is rarely available outside of Japan

Broiled Trout Aegean

STAR

Serves 4

The ubiquitous farm-raised trout benefits immeasurably from this uncommon treatment. With its sweet flesh, firm texture, and (when properly cooked) incomparably crispy skin, this relative of salmon is the perfect foil for a highly flavored rough chop of roasted red peppers and green olives. Here the signature flavors of Greek cuisine, dill and lemon, play key roles in elevating the commonplace to the nearly sublime. Brush the fish with a bit of fruity olive oil just before broiling for an extra-special treat.

From early fall through spring, an alternate but no less beguiling topping for the fish might consist of a roasted fennel bulb (standing in for the red peppers) heightened by a generous helping of fresh thyme or oregano with a scattering of capers for an acidic zing.

4 whole trout (10–12 oz. each), boneless
Salt and freshly ground black pepper
2 tbsp. fruity olive oil, for brushing the fish before broiling (optional)

THE ROUGH CHOP:
1 cup balsamic vinegar
1 tsp. sugar
½ lemon, minced (rind, pith and all, seeds removed)
1 large red bell pepper, roasted, cut into ⅓" cubes (about 1 cup)
¼ cup chopped green olives
2 tbsp. roughly chopped fresh dill (if unavailable, use fresh mint)

ALTERNATE ROUGH CHOP:
1 medium bulb fennel, halved and cored
Fruity olive oil
Few sprigs fresh thyme
2 tbsp. capers, drained
Freshly ground black pepper

THE GARNISH:
½ bunch fresh dill, feathery part only
1 lemon, cut into wedges

1. Adjust broiler rack to a position about 3" or 4" from the heat source.

2. Wash the trout and pat dry. Salt and pepper the fish inside and out. Brush the skin with the olive oil.

3. Prepare the rough chop as follows: In a heavy 1-quart saucepan, bring the balsamic vinegar, sugar, and lemon to a boil. Cook over high heat until the mixture is reduced by half. Add the red pepper and reduce again by half. The mixture should be thick but not completely evaporated. Do not allow the mixture to burn. (If too much of the liquid has cooked out, simply add a bit of water.) Mix in olives and dill and set aside.

   To make the alternate rough chop, preheat oven to 350°. Brush the fennel lightly with the oil and place on a heavy baking sheet. Bake for about 25–30 minutes, or until tender. Turn the fennel occasionally during baking to ensure even browning. When tender, remove from oven and chop into rough ½" pieces. Chop the thyme and add to the fennel. Add capers and black pepper and proceed with recipe.

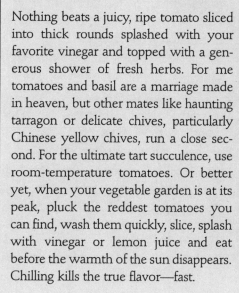

Flavor Flash!
Summer Tomatoes

Nothing beats a juicy, ripe tomato sliced into thick rounds splashed with your favorite vinegar and topped with a generous shower of fresh herbs. For me tomatoes and basil are a marriage made in heaven, but other mates like haunting tarragon or delicate chives, particularly Chinese yellow chives, run a close second. For the ultimate tart succulence, use room-temperature tomatoes. Or better yet, when your vegetable garden is at its peak, pluck the reddest tomatoes you can find, wash them quickly, slice, splash with vinegar or lemon juice and eat before the warmth of the sun disappears. Chilling kills the true flavor—fast.

4. Preheat broiler and broil the trout for 12–15 minutes, carefully turning once with a long metal spatula. Check for doneness by pressing lightly on the fish. When done, the fish should feel firm to the touch. Remove to heated plates and spoon the rough chop over the fish. Garnish with additional dill and lemon wedges.

SERVING SUGGESTIONS: Some crisply roasted red potatoes in their jackets sparked with garlic and rosemary, or a side dish of orzo flavored the same way, and a chilled salad of watercress, orange, radish, and feta would bring a bit of summer to the dinner table no matter what the season. Oven-crisped triangles of fresh lavosh would be the perfect bread to wipe the plates clean.

Pale Perfect Poached Celery

Serves 4

Celery, that humble cousin of parsley, is most often subordinated to supporting role status. Here, however, it's thrust into the spotlight and does a star turn as a Starter or Side salad that is almost Japanese in its understatement. In fact, two of its key ingredients are staples in the Japanese pantry.

Less is indeed more in this strikingly simple dish. Pale inner stalks of celery are poached slowly in a highly flavored broth of honey, Japanese citron juice, and Root Stock, heightened with flecks of a piquant Japanese pepper mix with lemony undertones. The dried and crushed berries of the prickly ash (*aka* Szechwan peppercorns or anise pepper) are the source for this sensational seasoning. Garnished with a scattering of fresh basil and oregano leaves and a confetti of diced red pepper, this is a quiet dish for all seasons that fits as comfortably on a multicultural buffet as on a more formal dinner table where fat-free and full flavor are synonymous.

Tender pale inner "heart" of 1 bunch celery

2 cups Root Stock (page 258)

2 tsp. strongly flavored honey, such as lavender or lime blossom

2 tsp. yuzu, Japanese citron juice (available bottled)

½ tsp. kona sansho, Japanese pepper mix

Salt to taste

THE GARNISH:

1 tbsp. thinly slivered fresh basil leaves

1 tbsp. finely chopped fresh oregano leaves

2 tbsp. finely diced fresh red bell pepper (¼" pieces)

1. With a small sharp knife or swivel-bladed vegetable peeler, remove the stringy outer layer from the celery stalks. Cut the celery into pieces 2" long and set aside while you prepare the poaching broth.

2. Bring the Root Stock, honey, and citron juice to a boil in a 2-quart saucepan. Add celery and reduce heat to a simmer. Cook for about 10 minutes, or until celery is tender but still a bit crisp. Remove the cooked celery and arrange on a serving platter. Continue cooking the broth until it is reduced to a glaze. Let cool slightly.

3. Nap the celery with the reduced broth and sprinkle with the Japanese pepper mix, salt to taste, basil, oregano leaves, and the red pepper.

SERVING SUGGESTIONS: This light but highly flavored salad would be a perfect opener for a dinner featuring Petti di Pollo Semiamaro (page 108) accompanied by a side of lemon-scented risotto or lightly garlicked orzo.

Thai-Dyed Seafood Soup   STARTER
Serves 4

Whether the mercury is approaching 90 degrees and your goal is to get out of the kitchen fast, or it's a chilly autumn night and you crave some comfort food, this simple, satisfying soup with its unmistakably Thai accent is at once filling, light, and positively addictive. What's more, despite its limited list of ingredients and utterly unfussy preparation, it boasts a beguiling complexity of flavors.

Cubes of rich, moist salmon (added at the last moment) play against the almost austere, briny sweetness of scallops. A small handful of fresh Kaffir lime leaves provides just the right citrusy note (fresh lime peel is an adequate stand-in for the leaves, in a pinch). Used with a judicious hand, a dose of moderately hot jalapeño peppers turns up the heat a notch. If you're feeling a bit bold, a squeeze of Thai chile paste (look for Sriracha brand) will turn the whole thing a flamingo hue and transform a subtle, relatively tame concoction into a bowl of red worthy of its name. This is soup in no Thai'*mmm* flat.

6 cups water

6 fresh Kaffir lime leaves, halved (or peel of 2 fresh limes, green part only)

2" piece gingerroot, peeled, cut into thin slices

1 bunch scallions, sliced into thin rounds

½ medium-sized lemon, sliced into paper-thin rounds

2 medium-sized jalapeño peppers, ribs and seeds removed, diced fine

1 lb. bay scallops

Salt and freshly ground white pepper

½ lb. fresh salmon fillet, skin removed, cut into ½" cubes

THE GARNISH:

¼ cup fresh basil leaves, sliced into long strips

Palm vinegar to taste (ordinary white distilled vinegar will do)

Red chile paste to taste (optional heat enhancer)

1. Bring the water, lime leaves, gingerroot, scallions, lemon slices, and jalapeños to a boil. Reduce the heat and simmer for 5 minutes. Add the scallops and simmer for 3 minutes more. Add salt and pepper to taste. Just before serving, add the salmon. Simmer for an additional minute, just until the salmon loses its raw color. Do not overcook.

2. Ladle into heated wide shallow bowls. Garnish with basil. Serve with palm vinegar and chile paste as desired.

SERVING SUGGESTIONS: I like to serve this as a lead-in to Southwest by Southeast Saté (page 57), skewered boneless dark meat of chicken coated with an unorthodox but hauntingly memorable spice paste of roasted fennel seeds, cuminseed, and curry powder. End on a creamy tropical note with Sticky Rice Snowballs with Coconut Sauce (page 250).

Flavor Flash! *Palm Vinegar*

A staple of the Philippine pantry, this somewhat opaque vinegar is derived from the fermented juice of the nipa palm. It has a mellow, milder taste than most other white vinegars. A must in adobo, the national dish of the Philippines, palm vinegar adds the requisite tartness to a marinade for meat or poultry in which garlic, soy, and sometimes sugar also figure prominently.

   Where modern refrigeration is still not taken for granted, especially in remote parts of the islands, this vinegar is the preservative of choice. Like the proverbial chicken-and-egg dilemma, it is not clear which came first—the need to preserve foods or the predilection for tart flavors.

Rally of the Dals

Serves 4

STARTER or SIDE

On one of many aromatic browsings through my local Indian bazaar, I succumbed to a visually seductive display of bagged dried beans and bought one bag of each— yellow, green, red, and white. Laden with pounds of colorful dried lentils, chickpeas, and pigeon peas and an urge to invent a new use for all this protein and carbohydrate, I created this dish. With an appreciative nod to the intricately spiced classic dals of India (served hot as an almost-sauce or accompaniment for rice), this room-temperature salad brings together a mix of carefully cooked dried beans and imbues them with the clear and direct flavors of the Indian subcontinent along with those borrowed from the Mediterranean and the Middle East.

The busy cook can be grateful that this perfectly portable picnic fare is best made two days in advance of serving. (The dried beans are soaked overnight before they are cooked and dressed. Then allow for an essential overnight stay in the refrigerator for the cooked beans to absorb the full aroma and savor of the dressing and become properly tender in the process.)

With its rainbow of yellow, green, salmon, and white beans and bright vegetable accents, this dish is a feast for the eye as well as the palate. If you're dining alfresco, don't forget to bring along the sherry wine vinegar for the last-minute splash that truly makes the flavors of this dish come alive.

½ cup chickpeas or split pigeon peas

½ cup red lentils

½ cup green split peas

½ cup pigeon peas

1 medium white onion, finely chopped

½ cup diced sweet red bell pepper (seeds and ribs removed, cut
    into ¼" dice)

½ cup diced ripe red tomato (peeled, seeded, and cut into ¼" dice)

1 cup diced English hothouse cucumber (cut into ¼" dice)

THE DRESSING:

Juice of 1 lemon

¼ cup fruity olive oil

1 tsp. cuminseed

½ tsp. turmeric

½" piece gingerroot, peeled and finely chopped

1 clove garlic, crushed and minced

1 tbsp. chopped fresh mint leaves

1 tbsp. chopped fresh basil leaves

Salt and freshly ground black pepper

THE GARNISH:

¼ cup sliced fresh basil leaves, cut into long, thin strips

Sherry wine vinegar (add just before serving)

1. Keeping the four varieties separate, drain and wash the beans well to remove any dirt or other foreign matter. (Be on the lookout for the occasional tiny pebble or twig lurking among the beans.) Soak the dried legumes in water in four different bowls overnight.

2. Cook the chickpeas at a simmer in enough water to cover just until the beans are tender, but not disintegrating, about 1 hour. Add the red lentils, green split peas, and the pigeon peas after ½ hour. In this way, these and the chickpeas will be finished cooking at about the same time. It's hard to give exact cooking times; they vary depending on the types of beans used, length of presoaking time, and heat of the cooking liquid. Check frequently to avoid overcooking since the dressing will tend to soften the beans somewhat with time. When cooked sufficiently, drain the beans of any excess cooking liquid and place in a large mixing bowl.

3. Add the onion, red bell pepper, tomato, and cucumber and mix gently into the beans with a spoon, being careful not to break up the beans.

4. Toast the cuminseed in a small, dry, heavy sauté pan just until fragrant, about 1 minute, stirring constantly. Grind in an electric coffee or spice grinder, or by hand in a mortar and pestle. Set aside.

5. To make the dressing, in a small bowl whisk the lemon juice into the oil. Add the cuminseed, turmeric, gingerroot, garlic, mint, and basil and whisk to combine. Pour this mixture over the beans. Refrigerate covered overnight, stirring once or twice. Taste for salt and pepper and adjust seasoning as needed. (I like this mixture to speak authoritatively of freshly ground black pepper.)

6. Bring to room temperature. Just before serving, splash with the sherry wine vinegar. Garnish with basil leaves.

SERVING SUGGESTIONS: I like to serve this as a vibrant accompaniment to a boneless breast of chicken or salmon poached in a perky gingery broth. A sharp side of Bitter Greens in a Honey-Lemon Drizzle (page 25) would bring just the right edge to the menu. A cinnamony fruit crisp made from the best the season has to offer would end the meal on a comforting, mellow note.

Flavor Flash!
Rainbow of Peppers

Dried legumes aren't the only foods that appear in a rainbow of colors. Bell peppers, both imported and domestic, are increasingly appearing in a wide spectrum of colors.

For a perky appetizer that truly wakes up the palate at the start of any meal, choose any three contrasting colored peppers: the orange, green, and yellow varieties tend to retain their color best after roasting. Roast them in a preheated 350° oven until the skins are uniformly blackened, usually in about 12–15 minutes. When cool enough to handle, peel them, removing seeds and ribs. Slice into bands ¾" to 1" wide. Arrange attractively on a platter in a stripe pattern, splash with unseasoned rice vinegar and a brightly flavored accent of grated lemon rind. Allow to marinate for as long as an hour at room temperature. Just before serving, sprinkle the platter with your choice of fresh herbs (dill and mint are my personal favorites here). This is a symphony of flavors in miniature, with the sweetness of the peppers providing a counterpoint to the pleasantly eye-opening tang of the vinegar.

To serve 4 as an appetizer salad, I use 3 large peppers, ¼ cup rice vinegar, the grated zest of 1 medium lemon, and ½ cup chopped herbs. Experiment until you find just the right proportion of vinegar to lemon to suit your palate. Dieters take note: No sugar, salt, or oil comes between the pure flavors of the peppers and their marinade.

Flavor Flash! *Thai-talian Peppers*

Serves 6 as appetizer or side dish

For another (albeit not oil-free) pan-ethnic variation on the same theme, try these peppers. Geography notwithstanding, Thailand meets Italy in a quick marinade. The heat, sweet, and tang from the Thai flavor palette softened with a pair of Italian standbys, fruity olive oil and balsamic vinegar, produce an unexpectedly harmonious marriage of flavors. Each bite of meaty charred pepper is finely nuanced. Clear as a bell, ginger, garlic and lime, in rapid-fire succession, announce their presence against the bass notes of olive oil and vinegar. A few slivers of long, thin Thai hot peppers are laced throughout to make matters just that much more complex and addictive: let the tasters beware.

2 large red or green bell peppers, halved, seeds and ribs removed

THE MARINADE:

½ cup balsamic vinegar

2 tsp. fruity olive oil

Juice and zest of 2 limes

2 cloves garlic, peeled and crushed

3" piece gingerroot, peeled and sliced into very thin slivers

1–2 fresh Thai chile peppers, roasted, peeled, seeded, and slivered

Pinch sugar

Salt and freshly ground black pepper

THE GARNISH:

Wedges of 2 limes

1. To make the marinade, in a small stainless steel or crockery bowl whisk together the vinegar, oil, lime juice and zest. Add garlic, gingerroot, and chile peppers. Add sugar, salt, and pepper to taste.

2. In a 350° oven, roast the peppers on a heavy baking sheet for about 25 minutes, or until evenly browned. Peel and then slice into large blocks. Place in a stainless steel or crockery bowl. There should be about 2 cups. Pour marinade over peppers, turn

to coat, and cover. Marinate at room temperature for one hour. Serve immediately or, if time allows, refrigerate overnight before serving.

3. If refrigerated, allow to come to room temperature before serving. Taste again just before serving and adjust sugar, salt, and pepper if necessary. Garnish with lime wedges.

Gilded Chicken with Lemon Confiture

STAR

Serves 4

I never tire of the sunny warmth of this dish. With a largely Mediterranean palette of main ingredients, literally bursting with lemon both inside and out, the humble roast chicken takes on new meaning. In its pan sauce, the pucker of lemon is balanced by the sweetness of slow-roasted garlic. A light rub of ground allspice on the skin endows the bird with a subtly Caribbean flavor. Piny rosemary needles and aromatic bay leaves lend an herbal note to a honey-sweetened lemon jam that serves as the gilding on the lily. (Incidentally, this mellow marmalade of sorts is a wonderful spread for thick slices of rustic sourdough toast at a lazy weekend brunch.) Chunks of multicolored pepper, batons of celery, and wedges of red onion, added halfway through roasting, lend flavor and color to the final dish. Lightly caramelized, they also make a toothsome wreath for the bird when presented on a grand platter.

1 fryer chicken, about 3 lbs.
Salt and freshly ground white pepper
2 tsp. ground allspice
2 medium-sized lemons with bright yellow skin, well scrubbed
2 sprigs of fresh rosemary, 4" long
2 large bay leaves
10 cloves garlic, peeled
2 red bell peppers, seeds and ribs removed, cut into 2" chunks
2 yellow bell peppers, seeds and ribs removed, cut into 2" chunks
6 stalks celery, peeled, cut into pieces 3" long
2 medium-sized red onions, tough outer layer removed, cut into quarters

THE LEMON CONFITURE:

    2 medium-sized lemons with bright yellow skin, well scrubbed

    Fragrant honey to taste (lavender would be first choice, followed by

        lime blossom or raspberry)

    1 2" long sprig of fresh rosemary

    1 bay leaf

    1 cup freshly squeezed orange juice

    2 cups Root Stock (page 258) for deglazing roasting pan

1. Preheat oven to 425°. Wash and dry the chicken well. Salt and pepper it inside and out. Rub the ground allspice on the skin.

2. Slice 1 lemon into paper-thin slices and stuff into the cavity of the bird along with the rosemary and bay leaves. Slice the second lemon thinly and place slices under the breast skin of the chicken as evenly as possible. Place chicken in an ovenproof and stovetop-proof roasting pan just large enough to fit snugly but still accommodate the garlic, peppers, celery, and red onions to be added later.

3. Place in oven and roast for 15 minutes. Reduce the oven temperature to 375° and continue roasting for approximately 45 minutes longer, or until juices run clear when a fork pierces the thickest part of the thigh. After 30 minutes, add the garlic cloves, peppers, celery, and red onion. While the chicken is roasting, make the Lemon Confiture.

4. To make the Lemon Confiture, cut the lemon into paper-thin slices. To remove the excess bitterness, blanch in a quart of boiling water. Continue boiling for 3 minutes more. Drain and wash in cold water. Return to a pot of fresh boiling water and boil for another 3 minutes. Drain again and wash the lemon in cold water. Set aside.

5. In a heavy 1-quart saucepan, combine the honey and orange juice and bring to a boil. Add the lemon slices, rosemary sprig, and bay leaf and simmer over low heat until the jam thickens. Remove the rosemary and bay leaf and taste for sweetness. Adjust with either freshly squeezed lemon juice or more orange juice, as you prefer. If you add any juice, cook further to return the jam to its original thickness. Remove to a sauceboat and set aside.

6. When chicken tests done, transfer it to a cutting board, reserving the garlic cloves. Place the roasted vegetables around the outer edge of an oval serving platter and keep warm, covered, in a 200° oven.

7. Add the Root Stock to the roasting pan and place on stovetop burner. Cook over medium heat, scraping with a wooden spoon to dislodge any browned particles that cling to the bottom of the pan. (This is known as deglazing). Transfer the pan juices to a heavy saucepan. Mash the reserved garlic to a smooth paste and set aside. Remove all visible fat from the pan juices, add the mashed garlic and cook over moderate heat to reduce until the sauce lightly coats a spoon. Adjust salt and pepper to taste.

8. Divide the chicken into 4 serving portions and place on the heated serving platter. Pour the sauce over all, and serve with the Lemon Confiture.

SERVING SUGGESTIONS: As a side dish, this needs nothing more than the Ovenroast of Jumbled Grains with Tomato-Chile Coulis (page 73), which includes pearl barley, quinoa, and buckwheat. Proceed to a post-entree salad of tender butter lettuce with a splash of your favorite vinegar and a plate of perfectly ripe goat cheese surrounded by the best fruit of the season. Then take your bows.

Flavor Flash!
Allspice

During his exploratory travels through the West Indies in 1493, Columbus ignored the spice-giving potential of the allspice tree, an evergreen belonging to the myrtle family. Later Spanish explorers found the spice but mistook it for a species of pepper and called it Pimienta, hence its name pimento (not to be confused with the blocky sweet red pepper that in a vinegar brine, is used to stuff green olives). However, it took nearly two centuries before this kissing cousin to cloves took hold as a culinary spice of any significance. In fact, it got its name because its flavor was considered a convincing amalgam of cloves, cinnamon, and nutmeg.

Gorgeous Georgian Chicken

STAR

Serves 4

T hat other state of Georgia, in the south of what was formerly called the USSR, has a cuisine marked by a warm blending of spices (fenugreek and coriander the two standouts among them) and, like Iran, its not too distant neighbor to the south, a heavy reliance on walnuts, particularly in its main dishes. Inspired by the traditional Georgian dish called *Satsivi,* this enlightened version features spartan steamed chicken breasts (instead of boiled and shredded) and a luxurious toasted walnut sauce thickened with yogurt (instead of eggs). True to the spirit if not the letter of the original, this rendition also features the requisite catalog of spices with one addition: fresh dill here adds a clear herbal note to the intricate blend. Steaming the chicken over a generous bed of dill yields moist, fragrant meat, which in turn provides the showcase for a sauce of subtle suavity. Lemon peel and yogurt provide a puckery counterpoint to the dish. In warm weather, served cold on a bed of highly flavored jewels of chicken aspic, this dish makes for perfect picnic fare.

1 bunch fresh dill (about 2 cups)

Zest of 1 large lemon

4 chicken breast halves (about 8 oz. each), skin removed

2 cups Gingery Chicken Stock (page 258)

1 tbsp. fruity olive oil

4 cups finely shredded white cabbage

Salt and freshly ground black pepper

1 tsp. ground fenugreek

1 tsp. ground coriander

1 tsp. cayenne

½ tsp. turmeric

4 cloves garlic, crushed and finely minced

1 whole ancho or serrano dried chile pepper, freshly ground

1 tbsp. hot paprika (Szeged brand from Hungary is best)

Salt and freshly ground black pepper

2 cups shelled walnuts, toasted and finely ground

1 cup Thickened Yogurt (page 265)

¼ cup coarsely chopped cilantro

THE GARNISH:

    8 thin lemon slices

    8 large walnut halves

    ½ bunch dill, stems removed (about 1 cup)

1. Make a bed of dill and lemon zest in the top of a steamer basket. Place the chicken over it. Bring enough water to a boil to produce a generous amount of steam. The water, however, should not come in contact with the chicken during the steaming. Cover the pot and steam for about 25 minutes, or until the chicken feels firm to the touch. Remove from the steamer and allow to cool, basting occasionally with a bit of the stock. When cool enough to touch, remove the bones and any visible fat. Cover and keep warm in a 200° oven.

2. Heat the oil in a heavy sauté pan and cook the cabbage over high heat, stirring until tender and slightly browned. Salt and pepper to taste. Set aside.

3. To prepare the sauce, bring the remaining stock to a boil and cook over high heat to reduce by half. Add fenugreek, coriander, cayenne, and turmeric and cook over medium heat until the stock is fragrant, about 5 minutes. Add garlic, chile, hot paprika, and salt and pepper to taste and cook for another 5 minutes. Allow to cool to lukewarm.

4. Add the ground nuts and the yogurt and stir just to blend. Taste again for salt and pepper and adjust seasonings if necessary. Blend in chopped cilantro.

5. Create an island of cabbage in the middle of a large decorative platter. Arrange the chicken breasts around the cabbage. Nap each breast generously with the sauce. Place 2 lemon slices and 2 walnut halves alongside each breast. As a final touch, garnish with some feathery dill.

SERVING SUGGESTIONS: The warm, toasty flavor of wild rice echoes and absorbs the rich nuttiness of the sauce beautifully. If you wish, round out the plate with some caramelized turnip or sweet potato and pour your favorite dry spicy Gewürztraminer.

Fennel-Orange Salad

STARTER

Serves 4

Fennel is one vegetable that you either love or leave alone. But this treatment, which combines the flavors of sweet licorice with bittersweet orange, may convert even those who find the unaccustomed anise-like note jarring in a vegetable. When sliced into long thin spears, fennel at first glance may look like a kind of *faux* celery. After an initial sniff and the first bite, however, you'll know its true identity.

When it comes to this pale green bulb, I can never get too much of a good thing. Believing that if one texture is good, two are better, I place crisp, raw matchsticks of the vegetable on a base of twice-cooked, "melted" fennel and drizzle the whole delicate pile with a vinaigrette infused with Seville orange marmalade, fresh juice, and dried tangerine peel. Two ways with fennel and three ways with citrus in one dish prove that more is sometimes more.

2 large fennel bulbs, with feathery tops attached (about 2 lbs. total)

THE "MELTED" FENNEL:

2 cups dry white wine (or 1 cup dry vermouth and 1 cup wine)

2 bay leaves

2 large cloves garlic, crushed

Zest of 1 medium-sized lemon

2 hot dried chile peppers (ancho or serrano will do)

6 whole allspice

1 tbsp. fruity olive oil

THE FENNEL MATCHSTICKS:

Juice of 1 lemon, to prevent fennel from darkening

THE VINAIGRETTE:

2 tsp. Dijon mustard

1 tsp. white wine vinegar

½ cup freshly squeezed orange juice

Juice of medium-sized lime (about 2 tbsp., or more to taste)

3 tbsp. Seville orange marmalade

½ cup fruity olive oil

1 tsp. dried powdered tangerine peel or orange peel (store-bought, or homemade,
    see page 276)
Salt and freshly ground black pepper

THE GARNISH:
    Feathery tops of fennel, chopped
    1 large orange, peeled and sectioned, membrane and pits removed
    ¼ cup oil-cured black olives

1. To make the poaching liquid, bring the wine, bay leaves, garlic, lemon zest, chile peppers, and allspice to a boil. Reduce to a simmer.

2. Remove the stalks and feathery tops from the fennel bulbs. Save the feathery tops for the garnish. Set aside one fennel bulb. Roughly chop the other one and cook in the poaching liquid at a simmer until tender. Remove from the poaching stock and set aside. (Save the poaching liquid, sieved, for a soup base, if desired.)

3. Heat the oil in a small heavy sauté pan and add the poached fennel. Cook slowly, stirring occasionally, until the fennel is very soft. Remove from pan. With a heavy knife, reduce to a rough puree. (You may use a food processor or blender here, but do not overprocess.) Set aside.

4. Slice the reserved fennel bulb into thin strips, about ½" wide by 2" long. Toss with the lemon juice and cover while you make the vinaigrette.

5. To make the vinaigrette, whisk to combine the mustard, vinegar, and orange and lime juices. Add the marmalade and whisk to blend. In a thin stream, whisk in the oil gradually. Add the dried tangerine powder and salt and pepper to taste. The vinaigrette should have a slightly biting edge. Adjust the lime juice accordingly.

6. Center equal portions of the fennel puree on each of 4 plates. Pile the fennel matchsticks on top and dress with some of the vinaigrette. Garnish with fennel tops, orange sections, and black olives. Serve the remaining vinaigrette in a sauceboat.

SERVING SUGGESTIONS: A broiled striped bass or other firm but delicate fish is my favorite follow-up entree. Keeping within the Mediterranean palette of flavors, I would suggest, as alternates, either Gilded Chicken with Lemon Confiture (page 13) or, more simply, a quick-cooking paillard of chicken (breast meat pounded thin) served with a mere spritz of lemon juice, a slick of olive oil, and a scattering of capers. A dry Greek white wine, well chilled, would place these sunny flavors into clear focus.

Grilled Turkey Paillard
with Honeyed Rhubarb Ginger Sauce   STAR

Serves 4

When rhubarb appears in markets like clockwork each spring, I am always inspired to invent new dishes that make the most of its rosy, earthy tartness. Unlike its usual pairing with the first strawberries in early summer for a pie or compote, here rhubarb shows its vegetable side in an easy sauce for turkey. (Only the stalks are used; the leaves, when eaten in large quantity, are toxic!)

Combined with a rough chop of peeled and seeded tomato and a hint of honey for mellowness, and powered by a richly flavored reduction of Root Stock and Gingery Chicken Stock, rhubarb proves to be a potent though difficult-to-identify presence.

Think "undercooking" when you grill the thin turkey cutlets to preserve their fragile moisture. When you present this dish to guests, they are sure to be beguiled but hard pressed to recognize just what that indefinably lush flavor is. Keep its name secret until after it has been devoured.

THE SAUCE:

2 cups Root Stock (page 258)

2 cups Gingery Chicken Stock (page 259)

1 lb. fresh rhubarb with bright pink or red color, cut into 1" lengths

3 tbsp. honey

1 cup cubed peeled and seeded tomato ($1/4$" cubes)

Salt and freshly ground white pepper

1 tsp. olive oil for brushing the turkey

$1\frac{1}{2}$ lbs. turkey breast, skin removed, thinly sliced and pounded

THE GARNISH:

2 tbsp. finely diced crystallized ginger

1 tbsp. finely chopped parsley

1. Combine the stocks in a heavy saucepan. Bring to a boil and reduce by half over high heat.

2. Add the rhubarb and honey and cook over medium heat, stirring occasionally, just until the rhubarb disintegrates. Pass through a fine sieve, pressing hard on the solids. Discard the solids and return puree to pan. Add the tomato and cook for another 2 minutes. Salt and pepper to taste. Keep warm until ready to serve.

3. Brush the turkey on both sides with olive oil and set aside. Heat a stovetop grill with a ridged surface, or oven broiler. Cook the turkey for about 4 minutes, turning after 2 minutes.

4. Nap some of the sauce on each of 4 warmed plates. Fan several slices of the turkey on each. Drizzle the turkey with the remaining sauce. Sprinkle with the ginger and parsley.

SERVING SUGGESTIONS: An Ovenroast of Jumbled Grains with Tomato-Chile Coulis (page 73) and some first-of-the-season steamed asparagus would be the perfect partners for this dish. On the creamier side, Four-Way Bulbs (page 71), a pale quartet of melting onions zinged with a bit of horseradish, would provide an earthy contrast.

You Don't Have to Chiu This Chow   STARTER or STAR
Serves 4

This dish is in some ways a translation of a translation with its roots in traditional Chinese cooking deeply buried. The Chiu Chow Chinese who can claim the original version of this dish are comprised of mainland Chinese who left their homeland and dispersed throughout all of Southeast Asia. In the 1980s and early '90s many emigrated to America, bringing with them hybridized styles of cooking influenced by the cuisine of their adopted country. In so doing, the best of Thai, Vietnamese, Cambodian, Laotian, Indonesian, and Malaysian flourishes and flavors have found their way into this Chinese-accented cooking. In restaurants, this kind of soup is served with an array of condiments to enable the diner to doctor the brew to taste at the last minute. Most commonly, an assortment of hot peppers (liquid hot sauces, dried pepper flakes, chiles in vinegar or in oil), ground white pepper, rice vinegar, soy sauce, and sugar are offered at the table.

In addition to these, in my translation I have prescribed a hefty pour of mellow homemade Tropical Vinegar to provide the right tartness to counterbalance the seeming richness of the dish. Wishing to keep fats in check, I use a mere ¾ pound of lean beef to serve 4 and have substituted cornstarch-thickened nonfat milk perfumed with coconut essence for the coconut milk often found in the original version, with no sacrifice of flavor or body. Using a defatted Gingery Chicken Stock instead of one based on beef streamlines the fat profile even more.

    1 tsp. peanut, safflower, or soybean oil
    1 large onion, thinly sliced (about 2 cups)
    6 cloves garlic, finely minced (about 2 tbsp.)
    2 tbsp. Curry Blend (page 264)
    1 large carrot, peeled and sliced on the bias into thin rounds (about 1½ cups)
    2 quarts Gingery Chicken Stock (page 259), plus any needed to thin the soup
    ½ recipe Mock Coconut Milk (page 267)
    ½ lb. fresh or dried wide rice noodles (known as gwaytio in Thai)
    ¾ lb. boneless rib eye beef, well trimmed of fat and sliced paper thin, cut into 1"
        roughly square pieces
    4 tsp. Tropical Vinegar (page 271)
    Salt and freshly ground pepper to taste (keep in mind last-minute additions of soy
        and hot pepper sauces at the table)

THE GARNISH:
    ½ cup cilantro leaves
    ½ cup scallions, thinly sliced, green part only
    Array of hot pepper sauces, Chinkiang vinegar (see page 44), soy sauce, sugar,
        shallot and garlic slivers fried in oil until golden, as desired

1. In a medium saucepan, heat the oil and cook the onion until tender but not browned. Add the garlic and Curry Blend and cook, stirring, until the mixture is fragrant, about 1 minute. Add the carrot and cook, stirring over low heat, for 2 minutes more.

2. Add the stock and simmer for about 10–15 minutes until the onions almost disintegrate.

3. Blend Mock Coconut Milk into the soup. Cook about 2 minutes more, stirring constantly, until the mixture coats a spoon and loses the raw starchy taste. Add the noo-

dles and cook gently just until tender (fresh rice noodles only require heating through; the dried noodles will require 7–10 minutes of cooking). Thin the soup with more stock if needed.

4. Add the beef and cook just until it loses its bright red color. Add the vinegar, salt and pepper to taste, and serve immediately in wide deep bowls, garnished with the cilantro and scallions.

SERVING SUGGESTIONS: This constitutes a light but filling one-pot meal when followed by a Toss-Up of Red and Yellow Peppers with Crisp Water Chestnuts (page 175). Finish with some crisp, sweet Asian pears or persimmons, whichever look best in the market.

Pan-Grilled Pressed Cornish Hens, Cuban-Style   STAR
Serves 4

In midwinter when the bitter Seville orange, *naranja agria*, turns ripe, Cuban cooks combine its puckery juice with large amounts of garlic and hints of cumin and oregano and marinate whole chickens overnight in the resulting liquid. When served, the roasted meat with its cracklingly crisp skin is doused with a garlicky benediction of the tart citrusy glaze (after it is boiled down to concentrate its flavor) and then topped with a tangle of raw onion for added zing. Without doubt, there's no better choreographed dance of flavors and textures in the Cuban repertoire.

Here, Cornish hens stand in for the larger fryers, and borrowing from the pan-fried chicken *tabaka* of the Caucasus, weights are applied to the cooking bird to ensure close contact with the pan's surface. In that way, the hens are evenly bronzed. The intense blast of heat also helps to cook the meat in its own juices in no time.

If the time and place are not right for the fresh fruit, substitute a mixture of freshly squeezed sweet orange juice cut with enough fresh lime or grapefruit and lemon juices to produce a pleasantly acidic blend (recommended proportions are given below). I have tried and rejected the artificially flavored bottled versions of the marinade that are often available in Latin markets. One bit of advice: Don't stint on the garlic here.

THE MARINADE:

1 tsp. cuminseed

2 cups freshly squeezed Seville orange juice (about 15 oranges), or 1½ cups freshly
squeezed sweet orange juice and ½ cup freshly squeezed lime juice;

or, for another fair approximation of the Seville orange juice:

1 tbsp. plus 1 tsp. grated grapefruit zest

¾ cup freshly squeezed sweet orange juice

¾ cup freshly squeezed grapefruit juice

½ cup fresh lemon juice

Cloves from 1 head garlic (about 2 oz.) peeled and crushed

1 tsp. dried oregano leaves

1 tsp. salt

2 Cornish hens, about 1½ lbs. each

Salt

Freshly ground black pepper to taste (I opt for generous amounts)

Fruity olive oil to brush hens before pan-grilling

Granulated sugar to sweeten the sauce to taste

THE GARNISH:

1 medium-sized yellow onion, peeled, sliced into paper-thin rings

Wedges of orange and lime

Bouquet of parsley

1. Over medium heat, toast the cuminseed in a small, heavy sauté pan, stirring constantly until fragrant, about 1 minute. Grind in an electric coffee or spice grinder or by hand in a mortar and pestle. Set aside.

2. To make the marinade, combine the citrus juice, garlic, cumin, oregano, and salt in a crockery or stainless steel bowl large enough to hold the hens.

3. Wash and dry the hens. Cut through the backs, discard the wing tips, and flatten the birds by breaking the breastbone. Salt and pepper. Place in the bowl to marinate overnight, covered and refrigerated. Turn occasionally to be sure the hens are marinated evenly.

4. Remove hens from marinade and pat dry. Refrigerate the marinade and reserve. Brush the hens lightly with olive oil. (The dish can be prepared to this point earlier in the day and then completed just before serving.) Preheat oven to 450°.

5. When ready to serve, heat a 10" heavy skillet until a drop of water flicked into the pan evaporates immediately. Place hens, skin side down, in the skillet. Place a 3–4 lb. weight on top of them (a clean stockpot half filled with water will work). Allow to cook for about 7 minutes on this side before turning. Check to be sure that the hens are not sticking to the pan and that they are well-browned before turning. Remove the weight, turn the hens over and place in the oven for about 15 minutes more, or until they test done (a meat thermometer inserted into the thigh should read 190° and the juices that flow from the thighs, when pierced, should be yellowish or clear). Remove to a heatproof serving platter. Reduce the oven temperature to 200° and place the platter, covered with aluminum foil, in the oven to keep warm while the sauce is made.

6. Skim off any visible fat left in the pan. Pour the marinade into the pan and use a wooden spoon to loosen any browned bits that cling to the pan. (This is called deglazing.) Bring the liquid to a boil, stirring occasionally. When it has the consistency of a glaze, remove any traces of fat and place in a blender or food processor to puree until smooth. If the glaze is too thick, add water gradually to thin to a light coating consistency. Adjust salt and pepper to taste. Add sugar if needed. Pour the glaze generously over the hens, and then garnish with the onion rings, citrus wedges, and parsley.

SERVING SUGGESTIONS: Instead of steamed rice, soupy black beans, and fried plantains tradition dictates, serve with Bitter Greens in a Honey-Lemon Drizzle (page 25), finishing with an icy coupe of Prickly Pear Sorbet (page 248), which rivals the hot magenta of a Caribbean sunset.

Bitter Greens in a Honey-Lemon Drizzle   SIDE

Serves 4 generously

Loaded with minerals and full of fiber, the *Brassica* family of leafy greens, including mustard, kale, and collards, makes a sturdy combo that can easily stand up to many highly flavored entrees. Against an otherwise plain main dish, this melange places an often overlooked trio centerstage where it belongs. (Not fully keeping it all in the family, I sometimes like to include dandelion greens to add an extra kick to the mix.)

Frequently smothered in pork fat and robbed of their green delicacy through over-cooking, these greens take on a new, delicate guise here. Sliced into thin, quick-cooking shreds, the greens are merely wilted in a scant amount of fruity olive oil, preserving both their color and subtlety of flavor. Their tantalizing, slightly bitter edge is then softened with a honeyed lemon drizzle. This deep green chop makes a forceful but not over-powering backdrop to grilled chicken and fish. Even without their sauce, they become a luscious crown atop of mound of thin pasta such as spaghettini or angel hair.

1½ lbs. mixed bitter greens (choose among kale, collard greens, mustard greens, turnip greens, watercress, dandelion—whatever the season brings)

1 tsp. (approx.) fruity olive oil

2 large cloves garlic, crushed and finely minced

Salt and freshly ground white or black pepper

THE HONEY-LEMON DRIZZLE:

1 cup Root Stock (page 258) or chicken stock (as a last resort, water will do)

Juice of 1 large lemon (about 3 tbsp.)

2 tbsp. highly perfumed honey (lavender, acacia, raspberry, lime blossom, buckwheat)

2 tbsp. Thickened Yogurt (page 265)

THE OPTIONAL GARNISH:

1 tbsp. chopped Candied Lemon Peel (page 275)

1. Wash and dry the greens, removing any tough stems. Roll the leaves into tight cigar-like cylinders and cut into strips ½" wide.

2. Heat the oil in a large heavy skillet. Add the garlic and greens, stirring lightly to cook evenly. Cook for about 5 minutes. Salt and pepper to taste, and remove to a warmed serving platter. Keep warm in a 200° oven.

3. Make the drizzle by bringing the stock to a boil in a small saucepan. Add the lemon juice and honey and cook to reduce by half, watching carefully to avoid burning. Swirl in the yogurt and stir to blend. Pour over the greens and serve immediately. Garnish with Candied Lemon Peel, if you wish.

Bittersweet Bouquet–Sweet-and-Sour Greens with Quince and Pomegranate

SIDE

Serves 4

Huge leaves of collard greens, and their cousins mustard greens and kale, take on a completely new shading when served with a glistening sauce of pomegranate syrup and vinegar. Drawing from a dim memory of having once tasted creamed spinach pureed with a bit of sweet ripe pear to substitute for the cream, I conceived this dish of a different texture, which conceals under its mound of barely wilted greens a cache of rosy, tender cubes of cooked quince, fragrant with cinnamon, nutmeg, and cloves.

1 lb. assorted bitter greens, including collards, mustard greens, and kale

1 tbsp. fruity olive oil

2 tsp. finely chopped shallots

3 cloves garlic, crushed and finely minced

1 large ripe quince, peeled, cored, and quartered

THE COOKING SYRUP FOR THE QUINCE:

⅓ cup granulated sugar

Water to cover the quince in the saucepan

1 large cinnamon stick

½ tsp. ground nutmeg

6 whole cloves

THE SAUCE FOR THE GREENS:

¼ cup pomegranate concentrate (also known as pomegranate molasses)

3 tbsp. Tropical Vinegar (page 271) or white wine vinegar

THE GARNISH:

Olive oil

¼ cup thinly julienned red bell pepper

1. Wash the greens well. Remove any woody stems. Pile the leaves of each kind separately. Roll them into compact cylinders and slice crosswise into thin shreds. Set aside.

2. Make the cooking syrup for the quince by combining the sugar, water, and spices in a small saucepan. Bring to a boil. Add the quince, reduce to a simmer, and cook over

low heat for about 12–15 minutes, or until the quince is tender but not mushy. (Quince is actually quite forgiving of overcooking.) When done, remove the quince, cut into ½" cubes, and mound in the center of a heated serving platter. Keep warm, covered, in a 200° oven. Sieve the syrup, discarding the solids, and set aside.

3. Heat the oil in a heavy skillet until hot. Reduce heat to medium and add the garlic and shallots. Cook, stirring constantly, for about 2 minutes or until they are tender but not browned. Add the greens and cook, stirring, until they are just wilted but bright green, about 2 minutes. Remove the platter from the oven and arrange the greens over the quince.

4. Add the pomegranate concentrate and the vinegar to the quince syrup and boil until the liquid lightly coats a spoon. In a small sauté pan coated with a film of oil, stir-fry the red pepper just until slightly wilted. Pour the sauce over the greens and garnish with the pepper shreds.

SERVING SUGGESTIONS: This complements any crisp-skinned broiled fish or poultry. I like it especially well with grilled turkey or chicken burgers when served with a starter of Muncha Buncha Mungs—Crisp Bean Sprouts in a Lime-Ginger Marinade (page 162).

Grilled Chicken Piccata with Lemon Times Three   STAR
Serves 4

In the language of any cuisine, timing is everything when grilling chicken. Exposed to intense heat, the boneless white meat can easily be overcooked, robbed of its juicy savor if allowed to languish a mere 30 seconds too long on the grill. Properly timed, however, this leanest part of the bird can be a wonderfully delicate thing suffused with the subtle char of the grill. This is a dish that at its best captures the elusive flavor imprint of the grill in the same way as the most accomplished Chinese cooking captures the taste of the wok.

Here, stripped of its fat-laden skin, then given a tenderizing short soak in an intensely lemon-flavored marinade, the breast emerges refreshed and ready for a few-minutes-only stay on a superheated grill. (A top-of-the-stove ridged, cast-iron grilling pan works beautifully here and is a worthwhile investment for those times when, even weather permitting, firing up the outdoor barbecue seems a daunting task.)

Fresh lemon juice, lemon rind, and fragrant stems of that Asian staple, lemongrass, figure prominently here. Adding an overlay of flavor is fresh rosemary, whose strongly scented piney sprigs are added at the last second to perfume the chicken further. With its balanced melding of clear flavors, this is a dish that in its utter simplicity packs a puckery punch greater than the sum of its parts.

> 4 boneless chicken breasts (about 8 oz. each), skin removed, pounded between sheets of parchment or plastic wrap to a thickness of approximately 1/3"
> Salt and freshly ground white pepper
> 1 tbsp. fruity olive oil to brush the chicken before grilling (this will prevent the chicken from sticking to the surface of the grill)
> 4 fresh rosemary sprigs

THE MARINADE:

> 1 cup freshly squeezed lemon juice
> Zest of 2 medium lemons, grated
> 2 stalks fresh lemongrass, crushed to release their aroma
> 2 cloves garlic, crushed and finely minced
> 1 cup Root Stock (page 258) or Gingery Chicken Stock (page 259)

THE GARNISH:

> Thin slices of onion, drizzled with a bit of olive oil and broiled until well browned (or almost black)

1. Wash and dry the chicken breasts. Prepare the marinade by combining all of the ingredients. Place chicken in the marinade up to 1 hour before cooking (longer may result in an unappealingly mushy texture).

2. Remove the chicken from the marinade and pat dry. Reserve the marinade. Salt and pepper the chicken lightly. Sieve the marinade, discarding the solids, and reduce by half over moderate heat in a small heavy saucepan. Reserve and keep warm. Broil onions for garnish and set aside.

3. Brush the chicken lightly with olive oil and prepare the grill. (If using an outdoor barbecue, allow enough time for the coals to become almost uniformly white-hot before cooking the chicken. If using a stovetop ridged grill, heat until a drop of water evaporates instantly when dropped onto the surface.)

4. Carefully place the chicken on the grill and cook for exactly 2 minutes per side, turning once during cooking. Add the fresh rosemary sprigs to the coals or the pan during the last 30 seconds of cooking. When done, the chicken should feel slightly springy to the touch. Remove the chicken to a serving platter and keep warm, covered. Strew the caramelized shreds of onion around the chicken and serve a sauceboat of the reduced marinade on the side.

SERVING SUGGESTIONS: I like to juxtapose this with Heavenly Scented Couscous with Crisped Chapati (page 63), which combines a starch and vegetable in one dish and would lend another texture and a contrastingly warm, spicy resonance to the sharply citric tones featured here.

Nutty Chiffonade of Crunchy Cabbage   SIDE
Serves 4

Take some garden-variety cabbage, accent it with a shred of its purple relative and the somewhat more delicate white Chinese Napa, and top it off with some irresistible candied walnuts, and the transformation from lowly vegetable to sparkling side dish is complete. These sturdy cruciferous vegetables can stand up to the fast, high-heat wilting given them here and retain their character even under the glaze of a strongly lime-scented, chilied vinegar dressing.

    1 cup walnut halves
    1 egg white, lightly beaten
    Oil to coat baking sheet
    Confectioners (or powdered) sugar to coat the nuts heavily before candying
    Coarse granulated sugar or crystal sugar to coat nuts after roasting

THE CHILE DRESSING:
    2 fresh jalapeño chiles, halved
    2 Thai red chiles
    ¼ cup rice vinegar
    ¼ cup freshly squeezed lime juice

Zest from 1 lime, bruised to release its essential oils
1 tbsp. honey
4 large cloves garlic, crushed and roughly chopped
½ tsp. salt
2 tbsp. walnut oil or fruity olive oil

1 small head green cabbage, core removed, thinly shredded
1 cup thinly shredded red cabbage leaves
1 cup thinly shredded Napa cabbage leaves
Freshly ground black pepper

1. Preheat the oven to 350°. Coat the walnut halves in the egg white thoroughly, allowing any excess to drip off. Place the nuts on a lightly oiled heavy baking sheet. Dredge
   heavily with a coating of the confectioner's sugar. Bake for approximately 15 minutes, or until the nuts look evenly browned and the sugar has melted, turning the
   nuts over with a metal spatula halfway through the roasting process. Watch carefully during the last few minutes of roasting to avoid burning. Remove from the oven,
   release the nuts from the pan onto a plate of granulated sugar. Roll the nuts in the
   granulated or crystal sugar to coat evenly. Place on a cooling rack to dry. Set aside.

2. Make the chile dressing by combining chiles, vinegar, lime juice and zest, honey, garlic, and salt and allow to steep for 15 minutes before serving. Sieve out solids. Taste
   carefully for heat and salt. (If too hot, dilute with more lime juice, vinegar, or water,
   or a combination of the three. Adjust salt accordingly.) Blend in oil with a whisk and
   set aside.

3. In a large heavy skillet, heat the oil and cook the cabbage in batches just until slightly wilted. Place in a decorative bowl. Pour the dressing over the cabbage, toss lightly, and garnish with the candied nuts. Top with a generous grinding of freshly
   ground black pepper.

SERVING SUGGESTIONS: Try this with Village Baked Chicken (page 150) for an
assertively heartwarming meal on a wintry night. To cap things off, pursue a course of
least resistance and serve store-bought almond cookies lifted beyond the ordinary with
a Kumquat Dipping Sauce (see page 234).

Roots Revisited

STARTER

Serves 4

It's no secret that vegetables grown underground often taste more intensely of the earth than those that take their nourishment directly from the rays of the sun. Here a trio of truly earthbound terrestrials are given an initial searing in a hot wok to seal in their juices and then are finished in a slow oven for a flavor-deepening roast. They are served all tarted up under a versatile honey-lemon-olive oil dressing spiked with a prepared Indonesian spice paste and finished off with a delicate shower of finely shredded bitter greens.

When shopping for this one, try to select the smaller specimens of these roots as they tend to be less woody at the core (and faster cooking), although their flavor is in no way diminished. Save the peelings to flavor a stock or soup.

Salad oil such as canola, safflower, or peanut to coat the wok

1 lb. parsnips, peeled and cut into rough chunks

1 lb. parsley root (usually sold with leafy tops attached), peeled and cut into rough chunks

1 lb. celery root, peeled and cut into ½" chunks

Salt and freshly ground black pepper

THE DRESSING:

Juice of 1 large lemon (about ¼ cup)

1 tbsp. honey

1 tbsp. sambal kachang, Indonesian spice paste (usually a blend of galangal, ginger, chile paste, and curry, often found in the freezer of Southeast Asian markets; a mild Thai curry paste may be substituted)

2 tbsp. fruity olive oil

Salt and freshly ground black pepper

½ lb. escarole or chicory, well washed, finely slivered

THE GARNISH:

1 small red jalapeño (or other medium-hot chile pepper), seeded, finely chopped

1 sweet red bell pepper, finely chopped (about ¾ cup)

1. Preheat oven to 325°. Drizzle enough oil into the wok to coat it lightly. Heat until almost smoking and quickly toss-fry the prepared root vegetables, stirring frequently to brown evenly. Remove to a roasting pan. Salt and pepper lightly and roast in the oven for approximately 35 minutes, or until the vegetables are fork-tender. Stir occasionally during roasting. If they are browning too much, cover lightly with foil until tender.

2. Make the dressing in a small bowl by first dissolving the honey in the lemon juice. Add the sambal and whisk to blend well. Whisk in the oil in a thin stream. Add salt and pepper to taste.

3. Mound the vegetables on a decorative platter, pour the dressing over them, and top with the shredded greens. To garnish, combine the jalapeño and red bell pepper and sprinkle over the greens.

SERVING SUGGESTIONS: Serving Pepper-Crusted Turkey Steak (page 65) with this would keep things hot and light. Any squash of your choice, simply steamed, would add a creamy, cooling contrast to the plate.

White Bean Potage with Sorrel Swirl   STARTER
Serves 8

Here's a protein-rich bowl to nourish the body as well as the soul. Taking its cue from the Tuscans, whose *zuppa di fagioli* starts many a meal, this vegetarian version plays the soft flavor of long-cooked Great Northern beans against the sharp tartness of fresh sorrel, with fruity olive oil creating a link between the two. To add some contrasting crunch, I like to top the soup with well-crisped croutons of caraway-studded pumpernickel.

1½ lbs. dried Great Northern beans
4 quarts Root Stock (page 258), plus additional for thinning the soup as
    needed
6 whole cloves
4 bay leaves

1 tsp. juniper berries

1 tsp. dried oregano

½ tsp. dried thyme

Fruity olive oil

1 large onion, roughly chopped

6 cloves garlic, crushed and finely minced

1 medium-sized bulb celery root, peeled, roughly chopped

2 large carrots, peeled, roughly chopped (about 2 cups)

Salt and freshly ground black pepper

4 cups pumpernickel croutons, about ¾" square, made from crustless fresh bread

Olive oil to coat baking sheet

THE SORREL SWIRL:

1 bunch fresh sorrel leaves, well washed, stems removed, about 2 cups lightly
    packed (lacking these, fresh watercress leaves would produce an equally tart
    puree, with a somewhat different personality)

1 to 2 cups (approx.) cooking liquid from the beans

THE GARNISH:

Fruity olive oil

1. Soak the beans overnight at room temperature in water to cover.

2. Drain beans and discard the soaking liquid. Over low heat, simmer the beans in the stock with the cloves, bay leaves, juniper berries, oregano, and thyme until tender, about 1½ hours. Add water as needed to keep the beans floating freely as they cook. Remove and discard the bay leaves. Remove 2 cups of the cooking liquid and reserve.

3. In a large heavy skillet over medium heat, sauté the onion, garlic, celery root, and carrots in enough olive oil to lightly coat the bottom of the pan. Stir frequently and continue cooking until the vegetables are tender but not browned. Add the cooked vegetables to the beans and simmer for about 30 minutes, stirring occasionally. Puree in a blender or food processor until smooth, thinning with additional stock as necessary to coat a spoon lightly. Add salt and pepper to taste. Keep the soup warm while the croutons are being made.

4. Place the croutons on a baking sheet lightly coated with olive oil. Toast in a pre-heated 350° oven until crisp, about 10 minutes. Set aside.

5. Make the Sorrel Swirl by combining the sorrel leaves with enough of the reserved cooking liquid to make an easily pourable mixture.

6. Divide the soup among 8 shallow, wide, heated serving bowls. Spoon a circle of the sorrel mixture over the soup. Scatter some of the croutons on each serving. Serve with a cruet of olive oil.

SERVING SUGGESTIONS: This is filling enough to become the centerpiece of a meal. Follow it with a salad of mixed greens with a Rainbow of Peppers (page 11) on the side.

CHAPTER 2

Perfectly Pungent

KEEPING THE HOME FIRES BURNING

From the peppery bite of fresh young arugula to the mouth-searing intensity of Middle Eastern *harissa* sauce, the pungent panoply of dishes in this chapter is proof that heat perceived by the palate comes in as many forms as degrees of hotness. A quick glance at the Key Ingredients that form these dishes makes it clear that each cuisine contributes its own brand of fire. A leisurely browsing down the seasonings aisle of any comprehensive Asian market will reveal the astonishing variety available. Note that some of the chile pastes from China are strongly garlicked, while those from Korea are enriched with soybean paste. The blistering *belado* of Indonesia has a clear vinegary undertone, while the hot mustard oil of India owes no debt to chiles at all for its mellow heat. The cross-cultural dishes you will meet in this chapter range from Syrian Fire (page 59), an addictive and ineffably delicious dip patterned after *mouhammara*, a brick-red blend of red peppers, walnuts, and *harissa*, to Four-Way Bulbs (page 71), a gratin of onion that smolders with the slow burn of horseradish. (Its low-fat relative, Onion Crème Brûlée (page 69), also in this chapter, relies on Tabasco for its heat.)

Particularly when you're in the mood to break out the beer, build the fire with dishes with this high flavor profile. Always used cautiously and sometimes sparingly, the heat unleashed in these recipes serves to underline other flavors in the dish; not as the star, but rather as an able supporting player. You can never have enough shelf space in your pantry for the incendiary bottlings of *Capsicum frutescens*. There's always one more fiery friend out there waiting to be encountered.

Key Ingredients

These announce their peppery presence in everything from a whisper to a shout.

CARDAMOM—seed pods from a cousin of ginger, sold whole (hulled or not) or ground—green, white, or black

CHILE-SPIKED OIL—see Back-of-the-Book Recipes, page 268

CHILES, CANNED—my personal favorite are fire-roasted **CHIPOTLE** chiles in a tomato-based *adobo* sauce, for a smoky searing hotness, available in most Hispanic markets

CHILES, DRIED WHOLE—I like to pulverize these just before using to ensure freshness, but beware when opening the grinder

CHILES, FRESH—of variable hotness with most of the heat contained within the ribs and veins close to the seed heart; the mild varieties include the long green Anaheim and the blackish-green heart-shaped pasilla (*aka* ancho or poblano); up a notch in hotness are the yellow wax and Hungarian hot yellow wax; hotter still are the short tapering green or red Fresno, cylindrical jalapeño, and short, slender serrano varieties; at the top of the hotness scale are tiny green or red pequins (used in vinegared hot sauces such as Tabasco and in cayenne powder), Asian varieties including Thai bird peppers and *prik khi nu*, tiny green varieties (translated as "rat droppings" due to their size); stretching the hotness envelope even farther are the fiery pale orange habanero or Scotch bonnet peppers, reputedly the hottest chiles

CURRY POWDER—what comes out of a bottle premixed gives only a lame inauthentic idea of the real thing; curry powder is not the product of a single spice but rather a balanced, fragrant amalgam of spices that are first carefully roasted and then ground. Traditionally, the mix includes some or all of the following: cardamom, cloves, cuminseed, fennel seeds, dried ginger, and black or white pepper. Amounts of each constituent spice vary depending on the level of heat desired. See page 264 for my own favorite Curry Blend

DAIKON—Japanese white radish

GALANGAL, FRESH—aromatic relative of ginger with mentholated edge (see Flavor Flash!, page 42)

GARAM MASALA—a mixture of fragrant spices, usually cinnamon, cardamom, and cloves, ground just before using for the best effect, and usually added to dishes at the last moment since the volatile oils in these spices are quickly dissipated if exposed to prolonged high heat. A feast for the nose

GINGER, CRYSTALLIZED—This is where hot and sweet come together in one pleasantly chewy mouthful; the best comes from Australia where the ginger is picked when young and then candied, resulting in a ready-to-eat confection that is tender with none of its feisty hotness diminished (see Superb Sources, page 291)

GINGER, DRIED POWDERED—for the best flavor, use whole dried pieces of gingerroot and grind in an electric coffee grinder just before using

GINGERROOT, FRESH—now commonly available in most supermarkets; look for the pale, creamy-colored young and slender "hands" with a thin papery skin; these are the least fibrous and easiest to mince

HARISSA—Moroccan hot pepper paste, flavored with garlic, coriander, and caraway; look for the convenient recloseable tubes

HORSERADISH, FRESH—a gnarly tuber that's brown on the outside and creamy beige inside; this sinus-clearing root brings tears to many eyes when prepared; peeled and freshly grated, mixed with a bit of vinegar, water, salt and a pinch of sugar, in a dressing or a sauce, this radish enlivens salads, cold roasted meats or poached fish served hot or cold; moderate its heat and add a ruby blush with a puree of tender cooked beet

JALAPEÑO-INFUSED VINEGARS—See Back-of-the-Book Recipes, Sweet Chile Vinegar, page 272

KOREAN PEPPERS—varying degrees of hotness; sold dried and powdered, and in a paste as *gochujang,* a milder, slightly salty form

LIQUID HOT SAUCES—from Indonesia to Jamaica, and Louisiana to Thailand (save a whole shelf in your pantry for these if you dare)

MUSTARD, PREPARED—smooth or grainy, herbed or plain, sweet or pungent

MUSTARD OIL—an infused oil used in Indian cuisine, prepared from roasted black mustard seeds, pungent when raw, but mellow and almost fruity when heated

MUSTARD POWDER, DRIED—Chinese or English will be equally fiery; the English often has cracked seeds as well

PAPRIKA, HUNGARIAN HOT—Szeged is a good brand name

PEPPERCORNS—white, whole, or ground; black, whole, or ground; both are best freshly cracked and dispensed from a peppermill just before using (see Flavor Flash!, page 53)

PEPPERCORNS, SZECHWAN—also known as anise pepper

RADISH, BLACK OR WHITE—looking like escapees from some Grimm's fairy tale, these are usually larger than the common red varieties and boast dense, sometimes bitingly hot flesh; irresistible when sliced thinly into a simple green salad, or served on buttered rustic bread; when julienned or shredded, these make a provocative addition to cole slaw or potato salad; they also take well to Indian spicing in a vegetarian casserole

RADISH, FRESH—red, pink, or French butter (pinkish with white tips)

SANSHO—an aromatic Japanese pepper with lemony undertones, made from the dried crushed berries of the prickly ash tree, sold in Japanese markets, also known as Szechwan peppercorns or anise pepper; partially dried and salted sansho berries are sometimes available in Asian stores

SHICHIMI TOGARASHI—sold in small bottles, a blend of seven spices including Japanese red pepper flakes, green laver (edible seaweed), black and white sesame seeds, dried citron (*yuzu*) peel, rapeseed, and sansho; highly aromatic, this packs a terrific wallop

WASABI—dried Japanese green horseradish powder

WATERCRESS—a member of the mustard family notable for its sharp, almost peppery flavor and small tender leaves; as its name implies, it is grown near or slightly submerged in water

Sumatran Salmon with Honey Glaze   STAR

Serves 4

Indonesian food is some of the hottest in the world. Many fish, poultry, and vegetable dishes of the region owe their heat to *sambal oelek,* a fiery, Day-Glo-colored chile paste edged with vinegar, available at most Asian and Southeast Asian markets. In this dish, which owes its inspiration to one of many visits to my local Indonesian-Dutch market, the *sambal* is used sparingly, almost as a tincture, in a haunting honey glaze for oven-roasted salmon. With cilantro as an accent, this dish should make a convert out of the most stubborn chile hater. Here the hotness of the fish is balanced by relatively bland, pan-fried wide Thai rice noodles (known as *gwaytio,* in Thai), with further interest added by crisply fried shards of fresh galangal and garlic. A fine scattering of chopped peanuts lends a welcome crunch.

1 tsp. oil to brush the baking dish

THE HONEY GLAZE:

1 tsp. sambal oelek (or less, to taste)

Juice of 1 large lemon, sieved

½ cup honey

2 lbs. center cut fillet of fresh salmon, bones and skin removed

½ lb. fresh red, ripe tomatoes, skinned, seeded, and excess juice removed

2" piece of fresh galangal, peeled and sliced into paper-thin strips (substitute fresh gingerroot if necessary)

2 large cloves of garlic, peeled and cut into thin slivers

2 tbsp. cooking oil (preferably soybean or peanut)

¼ cup raw skinned peanuts

1 lb. Thai wide rice noodles (gwaytio)

THE GARNISH:

1 bunch fresh cilantro, leaves only

1. Preheat oven to 450°. Brush baking dish with oil. Make the glaze as follows: In a small bowl, dissolve the sambal oelek in the lemon juice. Add the honey, whisking until blended.

2. Place salmon in oiled baking dish and pour half of the glaze over the salmon. Bake for 10 minutes. Remove from oven and sprinkle tomatoes and remaining glaze over the fish. Return to the oven for an additional 10 minutes, or until the fish tests done. Do not overcook. The fish should have a good brown caramelized exterior. If not, run under the broiler briefly until the surface is glazed.

3. While the salmon is cooking, fry the galangal shreds (or fresh gingerroot) and garlic slivers in 2 tsp. of the oil. Drain on absorbent paper and set aside. Roast the peanuts in a 350° oven for about 7 minutes or until they are fragrant. Chop finely and set aside for the garnish.

4. Pour boiling water over the rice noodles in a bowl to cover. Let soak until just barely softened. Drain well. Heat the remaining oil in a heavy skillet and pan-fry the noodles until lightly browned and heated through, taking care not to break them up with too much vigorous stirring.

5. Spread the noodles over a wide platter. Center the fish over the noodles. Scatter the fried galangal, garlic, and peanuts over the fish. Garnish with a wreath of cilantro leaves.

SERVING SUGGESTIONS: A perfectly steamed medley of zucchini, pattypan, and yellow crookneck squash or wheels of steamed butternut squash would round out the plate nicely.

Flavor Flash! *Galangal*

When in an Asian market, be sure to look for fresh galangal (also known as *galanga, galingale,* or *laos* (Indonesia), *lengkuas* (Malaysia) or *kha* (Thailand). This creamy beige relative of ginger has a flavor faintly reminiscent of fresh gingerroot with all of its bracing astringency but little of its pesky stringiness. It's great as a last-minute addition to your favorite homemade chicken soup or, when deep-fried, as the finishing touch on a plate of cold sesame or peanut noodles, Oriental style, or broiled or roasted fillets of fish. Avoid the powdered version, which is but a pale imitation of the genuine fresh article. In a pinch, fresh gingerroot may be substituted; however, it's worth the search for the real thing. Wherever used, galangal lends an inimitable, almost perfume-like savor.

Chilled Chinese Crunch

SIDE or STARTER

Serves 4

Inspired by the wonderful steamed Chinese broccoli served commonly at dim sum breakfasts, this cold version will jazz up even the most pedestrian grilled turkey or chicken burger and make even the most diehard coleslaw and potato salad fans resist the temptation to succumb to the tried and true. Here the crisply cooked vegetable (commonly called *gai lan* or *choy sum* in Asian markets) is enlivened by a pungent sauce that gets its punch from dry Chinese mustard powder. It's not only convenient but advisable to make the sauce a day in advance of serving to allow the mustard flavor to "open up" and mellow as its flavor marries with those of the other ingredients.

When buying Chinese broccoli, pick those that are bright green and perky. Avoid any that are yellowed. In a pinch, ordinary broccoli will do.

1 lb. Chinese broccoli, lower 2" of the stems peeled

THE DRESSING:

2 tsp. Chinese mustard powder

1 tsp. Chinkiang vinegar (balsamic vinegar may be substituted)

1 tbsp. hoisin sauce

1 tbsp. dark molasses

1 tsp. honey

¼ cup soy sauce

1" piece of fresh gingeroot, peeled and minced

1 clove garlic, crushed and minced

THE GARNISH:

½ bunch scallions, chopped

2 tbsp. pine nuts, toasted in 350° oven until golden brown, about 5 minutes

Chile-Spiked Oil, to taste (page 268)

1. Blanch the broccoli in boiling water for 4–5 minutes. Drain and run cold water over the broccoli to cool quickly. (If you prefer, you can steam the vegetable until just crisp-tender, about 7 minutes.) To crisp further, place in an ice water bath for 5 minutes and then drain. Pat dry.

2. To make the dressing, whisk the mustard powder and vinegar until well blended. Add the remaining ingredients and let the dressing stand at least 1 hour at room temperature, or (preferably) overnight, refrigerated. This allows the flavors to mellow. Sieve to remove gingerroot and garlic. Arrange broccoli on serving platter in a single layer. Nap with the dressing. Garnish with scallions and pine nuts. Provide a cruet of Chile-Spiked Oil on the side.

SERVING SUGGESTIONS: I like to serve this with a simple grilled turkey or chicken burger or soy-basted barbecued chicken.

Flavor Flash!
Chinkiang Vinegar

Italy has its *aceto balsamico* from Modena. China venerates its Chinkiang black rice vinegar from the lower Yangtze valley in the eastern part of the continent. Throughout its centuries of regional wars and skirmishes, China's refugees are said to have fled with little more than the clothes on their backs and their precious vinegar pots. One taste of this fragrant distillate of rice will convince you why it continues to be held in such high esteem. A mere sprinkling over a long-simmered beef tendon or duck soup cuts through the richness like a warm knife through butter. Its tart, almost musty complexity is the perfect blessing on a plate of cold, gingery, fat Chinese water noodles. Use it in marinades for great grilling. Its mellow acidity provides the perfect counterpoint to the sweetness of honey, maple syrup, or palm sugar when used for a glazing sauce on grilled or broiled meats or seafood. For an interesting experiment, try exchanging Chinkiang for balsamic vinegar as your supply or whim dictates. You will be surprised at the results. And your loyalties may be shaken, as mine were.

Poblano Pepper Pilaf

STARTER or SIDE

Serves 6

Here Middle East meets Southwest, resulting in the union of two flavors—one brash (a tomato and cilantro sauce), the other subtle (a hummus sauce gently spiked with cayenne), both providing a raw but not unrefined backdrop to a mild stuffed pepper. Serve these with a fork *and* a spoon—you won't want to leave any of the addictive sauces behind.

6 poblano peppers, stems intact, if possible (also known as ancho or pasilla peppers)

THE STUFFING:

½ cup bulgur wheat

1½ cups boiling water to soak bulgur

2 medium-sized sweet onions, such as Vidalia, chopped into ½" pieces (about 2 cups)

l tbsp. olive oil or butter

2 cloves garlic, crushed and minced

1 tsp. ground cumin

2 tbsp. pine nuts

Salt to taste

2 tsp. oil for coating the baking dish

THE TOMATO-CILANTRO COULIS:

1½ cups fresh ripe, red tomatoes, peeled, seeded, excess juice removed (canned tomatoes, well drained and seeded, may be substituted)

4 tbsp. fresh cilantro leaves (reserve half for garnish)

THE HUMMUS SAUCE:

¾ cup freshly cooked chickpeas or 6 oz. canned garbanzo beans, drained

Juice of l lemon (2 tbsp.)

1 tsp. soy suce

¼ cup Root Stock (page 258) or water

¼ tsp. cayenne powder

Salt and freshly ground black pepper

1. Soak the bulgur in a bowl covered with the boiling water for 30 minutes. While soaking, cook onions in oil or butter over low heat, covered, until translucent and tender but not browned, about 7 minutes. Add garlic and cumin and cook, stirring, for an additional half minute.

2. Toast the pine nuts in a 350° oven until golden brown, about 5 minutes. Drain the cooked onions and add to the bulgur along with the nuts. Salt to taste and set aside.

3. Roast the peppers in a 450° oven for about 10 minutes, or until their skins are well browned, turning the peppers occasionally to ensure even browning. Let cool and remove skins and seeds carefully. Drain on paper toweling. Reduce oven temperature to 350°. Cut a lengthwise slit in each pepper from the stem end to within ¼" of the pointed end. Leave the stem attached for additional eye appeal. Carefully but generously stuff the bulgur mixture into the peppers. Place in a lightly oiled 2-quart baking dish and bake uncovered for about 15 minutes, or until peppers are well heated and just tender. If necessary, add a few teaspoons of water to the pan to prevent the peppers from sticking. (If you have leftover stuffing, mound beside the stuffed peppers.) While the peppers are baking, make the sauces.

4. For the tomato-cilantro coulis, whirl the tomatoes in a blender or food processor until almost completely liquefied. (A little texture adds interest to the dish.) Stir in 2 tbsp. of finely chopped cilantro leaves.

5. For the hummus sauce, whirl all the ingredients in a blender or food processor until perfectly smooth. Taste for salt and pepper.

6. To serve, nap each plate with a coating of the tomato sauce. Center a stuffed poblano on the sauce and coat each with approximately ¼ cup of the hummus sauce. Garnish with the reserved cilantro leaves and serve immediately. This dish works equally well hot or just barely lukewarm.

SERVING SUGGESTIONS: Serve this as a prelude to a dinner that stars Grilled Chicken Piccata with Lemon Times Three (page 28) or as part of a multiethnic buffet of purely vegetarian dishes, including My Fave Favas (page 87) and Roasted Rootatouille (page 125).

Flavor Flash! *Chile Peppers*

The hot chile pepper, a New World plant with its origins in South America, domesticated probably in Mexico (giving us cayenne, bell, and jalapeños) was one of the treasures Columbus (late 15th–early 16th centuries) found on his voyage of discovery and brought back to the Old World. Although he was searching for black peppercorns, what he found were hot *Capsicum* peppers, which he brought back to Spain. From there they were widely dispersed by Portuguese traders around the world and assumed a place of prominence in the native cuisines of India, Africa, the Middle East, Indonesia, and the Far East (the latter, via trade routes between China and India and China and the Middle East).

Historically, although Western Europeans provided the means for the worldwide distribution of the pungent fruits, Western European cuisines make only minimal use of them for seasoning. Central and Eastern Europeans, however, more often turned up the heat in their cooking, thanks to Turkish traders who imported hot peppers as they plied medieval trade routes through the Persian Gulf, across Asia Minor to the Black Sea and on into Hungary in the early 16th century.

It wasn't until the early 17th century that the cuisines of North America showed a fiery side with the advent of the plantation system in the American South. Working there, African slaves from the West Indies and Africa continued the well-ingrained habit of eating hot foods away from their native soil. Climatically, this region was obliging for the cultivation of many varieties of peppers, and many of the world's great cuisines are the richer for it.

Sweet and Fiery Chicken   STAR
Serves 4

How many times have you despaired of finding yet another way to prepare chicken and given in to an impulse to do the same old thing once again? Despair no more. Here is a palate awakener whose inspiration spans two continents at least. Despite some 5,000 miles separating its places of origin, this dish seamlessly melds two disparate cuisines in a stunningly colored, highly flavored, and, nicest of all, relatively low-fat entree. Northwest Pakistan contributes its tandoori barbecue technique (in a modified form) to this dish. And northwest Africa lends a few key ingredients from its pantry.

Here skinless chicken is treated to a tenderizing overnight stay in a yogurt-based marinade reddened with annatto seeds (achiote) and revved up with *harissa,* that potent peppery paste with its origins in Morocco (although other Middle Eastern cooking draws from its fire). I turn further to the Moroccan pantry for another staple, oranges, with which I temper the marinade's fire a bit using both their juice and zest for a cooling sweet accent. Don't be daunted by the long list of ingredients. Other than the time needed for marination (overnight), the active preparation time is short.

1 whole fryer chicken, about 3 lbs.

THE MARINADE:
1 quart plain nonfat yogurt
Juice of 2 oranges (about 1 cup)
2 tbsp. grated orange peel
2 tbsp. cider vinegar
2"–3" piece cinnamon stick
1 tbsp. annatto seeds (achiote)
Scant ¼ tsp. saffron threads
2 tbsp. dry white wine
4 large cloves garlic, crushed and then finely minced to a paste with 1 tsp. salt
2" piece gingerroot, peeled, finely minced
1 tsp. ground cumin
1 tsp. ground coriander
½ tsp. turmeric
1 tsp. harissa paste (available canned or in easily recloseable tubes)
Freshly ground white pepper

THE GARNISH:

½ cup red onion, sliced paper-thin

1 bunch cilantro, stems removed

2 large seedless oranges, peeled and sectioned, membrane and pith removed

1. Cut chicken into 8 parts, reserving backbone and wing tips for a stock, if desired. Remove skin.

2. To make the marinade, whisk the yogurt, orange juice, orange peel, and vinegar in a large stainless steel bowl. Grind the cinnamon stick and annatto seeds in a spice or coffee grinder until finely ground. Combine along with saffron in white wine. Add to marinade. Add garlic paste and gingerroot. Add the remaining spices, including freshly ground white pepper to taste. Add harissa. Whisk to blend. Add chicken pieces and mix to coat evenly. Cover tightly and marinate overnight in the refrigerator.

3. Next day, heat oven to 500°. Drain chicken from marinade, wiping the pieces dry with paper toweling. Lightly oil a heavy baking sheet with sides and place it in the oven for 5 minutes. Carefully place chicken pieces on the heated baking sheet and cook without turning for about 10 minutes. Continue baking, turning the chicken and basting frequently with the marinade, until fully cooked. The breast will take about 15–20 minutes. Remove from oven, cover and keep warm while the dark meat continues to cook, about 10–15 minutes longer. Do not overcook. (Note: The chicken can be cooked on an outdoor barbecue if desired, following the above recommendations for cooking times. Be sure to let the coals turn white-hot before cooking. To avoid sticking, brush the grille well with oil before placing chicken pieces on it.)

4. In a heavy saucepan, bring any remaining marinade to a boil, stirring constantly. Place red onion in a bowl of ice water to crisp for 5 minutes.

5. Make a bed of cilantro leaves for the chicken. Arrange the chicken over the leaves. Drain the red onion. Scatter the orange sections and red onion over the chicken and serve immediately with the heated marinade.

SERVING SUGGESTIONS: As side dishes, I like to serve a cone of pale yellow Moroccan couscous surmounted with Seurat's Cauliflower (page 88) to underscore the sweetness of the entree and add a bit of contrasting crunch.

Essentially Shrimp and Beans   STAR
Serves 4

This somewhat Southeast Asian blending of the essence of shrimp with the essence of green beans is tied together with a shot of high-quality bottled fish sauce. With relatively few ingredients, it's crucial that each be impeccable. And the beans are a good place to start.

It's important to know your beans before buying any. Whether you are using Chinese long beans, Kentucky Wonder or Blue Lake varieties, or French *haricots verts,* or a combination of these or others, choose beans that are firm, unblemished, and bright in color.

Purchase the fresh shrimp headless if not alive. The shells should be of uniform color. Trust your nose. They will smell fresh if they are fresh. When you purchase the tiny dried shrimp preserved in salt (most often packed in plastic bags), look for ones of good color with their shape intact. The best come from Taiwan.

It's worth the search for the Three Crabs brand of Vietnamese fish sauce, *nuoc mam.* It's the least salty-tasting and most clearly expresses the fresh briny savor of the fish— anchovies, in this case—from which it's made.

If you prepare the beans and shrimp in advance, you will find that in a matter of minutes the dish will be complete. The rest of the procedure amounts to a straightforward combining of a short list of ingredients. You can turn up the firepower here with Thai chile peppers as you wish. But if you do, be sure to provide fluffy clouds of steamed rice and well-iced beer to cool things down.

2 lbs. Chinese long beans, or other string beans as noted above

2 lbs. fresh shrimp, weighed with their shells

2 tbsp. dried shrimp (or to save time, dried shrimp powder)

1 tbsp. soybean or peanut oil

1 large clove garlic, crushed and minced

2" piece of gingerroot, peeled and minced

1 tbsp. bottled fish sauce, known as *nuoc mam* (Vietnam), *nam pla* (Thailand), or *patis* (Philippines)

Pinch granulated sugar

Thai chile peppers to taste (optional)

THE GARNISH:

> 1 cup sliced red onion, sliced paper-thin and soaked in ice water
>
> ½ cup finely chopped roasted peanuts
>
> 2 tbsp. Roasted Rice Powder (below right)

1. Trim the beans and cut into 2" lengths. Steam for approximately 3–4 minutes, just until the beans are crisp tender. When cooked, plunge immediately into a bowl of ice water to set their color and stop the cooking. Drain, dry, and set aside.

2. Peel and devein shrimp. Place in a perforated pan or colander. Cover the shrimp well with ice and set over a large pan to catch any drips from the melting ice. Store in the refrigerator

3. Soak the dried shrimp in warm water to remove excess salt. (If using dried shrimp powder, proceed to step 4 at this point.) Drain. Wash and soak shrimp two times more, draining and washing after each soaking. After the final soaking, drain and dry well on paper toweling. To dry thoroughly, place in a preheated 350° oven for about 5 minutes. Let cool and grind in a spice grinder or mince finely by hand to reduce the shrimp to a fairly fine powder.

Flavor Flash!
Roasted Rice Powder

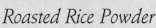

Northeastern Thai cooks have long prized the aroma and slightly gritty texture of roasted rice, *kao kua,* as a subtle enhancement in many composed salads. To prepare, use glutinous or sticky rice, also known as sweet rice. You can find this short grain variety, which cooks to a soft and sticky consistency, at any Oriental market. Place about 1 cup in a heated dry heavy sauté pan (cast-iron works best). Over high heat, sauté the rice grains until they are golden brown, shaking the pan frequently to ensure even browning. Let cool and store in a tightly covered glass jar. It's best to pulverize the roasted spice in a spice grinder or food processor just before you intend to use it. Once powdered, its toasty warmth will vanish quickly.

For adding an interesting accent to vinegared salads, soups, and stir fries of many ethnic persuasions, I keep an array of jars of pan-roasted wild, brown, and basmati rice beside the classic Thai version in my pantry. For those times when a dish needs an indefinable something to give it another layer of complexity or roundness, I reach for this perfectly simple seasoning, grind just before using, and am amply rewarded. Try it. You'll see.

4. Just before serving, preheat oven to 450°. Place a heavy roasting pan or cast-iron skillet in the oven to heat for about 15 minutes. Pour the oil into the heated pan. Add

garlic and ginger and quickly stir to coat with oil. Add fish sauce, sugar, fresh shrimp, and dried shrimp. Add blanched beans and stir to combine. Roast for about 8 minutes, or just until shrimp turn pink and are springy to the touch. Do not overcook. Add Thai chiles to taste. Cook for another minute and serve on a heated platter. Drain red onion and scatter over the beans. Sprinkle with the peanuts and the Roasted Rice Powder.

SERVING SUGGESTIONS: Besides the aforementioned rice and beer, this one could be preceded by the delicate crunch of Muncha Buncha Mungs—Crisp Bean Sprouts in a Lime-Ginger Marinade (page 162). For a follow-up I like to serve a refreshing Suite of Pears with Zingy Ginger Dunk (page 228). With dessert, a flowery jasmine tea would be pleasing.

Five-Flavor Eggplant   STARTER
Serves 4

What happens when you combine the piquancy of Chinese Szechwan peppercorns, the fruitiness of Italian olive oil, and the melting richness of ripe French Camembert—and then add the nutty aroma of lightly browned garlic to the mix? When the rallying point is chameleonic eggplant, a pantry staple common to each of these cuisines, what results is a multiethnic melange that is the perfect starter for a grilled fish or chicken dinner or a standout entry on a buffet of vividly flavored room-temperature fare.

   8 small Japanese eggplant (about 1½ lbs.total)
   Salt
   2 tbsp. fruity olive oil
   4 cloves garlic, thinly sliced
   4 slices ripe Camembert cheese, rind removed (about 6 oz. total)
   ¼ cup thinly sliced fresh basil leaves
   1 tsp. Szechwan peppercorns, freshly ground in a peppermill

1. Peel the eggplant and halve lengthwise. Salt lightly and set aside.

2. Heat the oil in a heavy sauté pan. Add the garlic and cook over medium heat until just lightly golden. Add eggplant, reduce heat, and cook for about 4 minutes, or until eggplant is just tender but not browned.

3. Remove to plates, allowing 2 slices per serving. Top each serving, while still warm, with l slice cheese. Scatter basil and ground pepper over all. Serve immediately or at room temperature.

Flavor Flash! *Pepper Mills*

For an instant boost to otherwise unfancy prepared salads, vegetable side dishes, and entrees, I like to have on hand a battery of small pepper mills, clearly labeled, each containing a different kind of peppercorn. Commercially ground pepper, of indeterminate quality and age, just cannot deliver the piquancy or aroma of ground peppercorns dispensed from a small, hand-held grinder. To release their maximum aroma, it's best to add them to a dish at the last moment whenever practical.

In addition to filling a large mill with the common black variety (whose place names of origin like Sarawak, Tellicherry, Malabar, and Ceylon often preface their names), I like to fill a smaller one with white peppercorns (usually from Muntok, off the coast of Indonesia), which have a slightly different character. Derived from the same plant as the more common variety that are picked green and simply dried in the sun, these berries are soaked or kept in moist heaps for two to three days to soften their outer coating. They are then spread out on mats in the sun for a day or two to dry, leaving a light yellowish-gray exterior. For white or pale soups and sauces, this is the pungency to choose. It's also a nice touch on apples and pears when serving a fruit and cheese plate, especially if the cheese is one of the blue-veined varieties.

Unripe green peppercorns from Madagascar are often pickled in a vinegar and salt solution (best for sauces) or freeze-dried. They provide pungency with an almost lemony undertone. The brined form takes up only a small place in my pantry; the dried ones, however, enter my parade of pepper mills for easy last-minute dispensing.

Stretching the definition some, I also keep on hand a mill filled with anise or so-called Szechwan peppercorns. These are not, strictly speaking, peppercorns at all, but rather the fruit of the prickly ash tree. I have found that a light grinding of this variety adds a complex and aromatic presence to soy-based dishes or those featuring mushrooms and cabbage. To keep things interesting, from time to time, juniper berries and whole allspice berries each take a rotation in the changing parade of pungent partners at the table. Smoked meats and fish (particularly dill-cured salmon) benefit from a delicate sprinkling of these last two just before serving.

A Coral Trio Con Brio – Salmon Stuffed with a Red Pepper Mousse, Piquant Sauce

STAR

Serves 4

When paired, two foods whose flavors and colors sing in delicious harmony are fresh salmon and red bell pepper. I never need to find an excuse to feature either or both of these. However, when running a taste and heat comparison of liquid hot pepper sauces, I reached for a bottle of Tabasco, dipped a slice of raw red bell pepper in it, and knew instantly that the two-part harmony would have to accommodate a third voice. So this special-occasion dish was born.

Thin slices of tender, melting salmon are wrapped around a red pepper mousse, centered with a slice of woodsy shiitake mushroom. The whole package, shaped to resemble pink peppers, is then baked and served atop a coral cream sauce fired with a shot of Tabasco. Even when subdued by cream, this venerable barrel-aged distillation of vinegar, hot peppers, and salt proclaims its acidic hotness loudly and clearly. Jettison the diet for this one.

2 lbs. center-cut salmon fillet, skin and any dark flesh removed
Salt and freshly ground white pepper

THE RED PEPPER MOUSSE:
2 medium-sized red bell peppers (about 1 lb. total)
1 tbsp. sweet butter
2 tbsp. flour
½ cup nonfat milk
2 eggs, separated

Pinch salt

½ oz. dried Japanese shiitake mushrooms

Butter for coating parchment and molds

THE CORAL SAUCE:

2 large shallots, chopped (about 2 tbsp.)

1 cup dry white wine

1 cup (approx.) Basic Fresh Fish Stock (page 260)

3 tbsp. tomato paste

1 cup heavy cream

1 tsp. Tabasco or other liquid hot pepper sauce

Salt and white pepper

THE GARNISH:

½ cup finely diced red bell pepper

½ cup Italian (flat leaf) parsley, leaves only

1. Inspect the salmon for any bones and remove them. Cut the fish thinly on the diagonal in slices as wide as possible. Salt and lightly pepper the fish and set aside.

2. Roast the peppers in a preheated 350° oven for about 20–25 minutes, or until skin is uniformly darkened and blistered. Turn occasionally to ensure even browning. When done, remove from oven and place in a plastic bag. When cool, the skins will peel off easily. Remove ribs and seeds. Place the peppers in a clean dish towel and squeeze out any excess juices. Puree in a food processor or blender until smooth. Set aside.

3. To make the white sauce binder for the mousse, make a roux by melting the butter in a small heavy saucepan. Add the flour to the melted butter and whisk to blend. Meanwhile, in another saucepan, heat the milk to boiling and add to the roux. Cook over low heat, stirring until smooth. Let cool. Blend in egg yolks. Add pepper puree to the white sauce. Set aside.

4. Beat the egg whites until frothy. Add a pinch of salt and continue beating until soft peaks form. Fold gently into red pepper mixture. Chill the mixture, covered.

5. Soak the shiitake mushrooms in enough cool water just to cover, about 20–30 minutes. When soft, drain and dry, reserving the soaking liquid. Cut mushrooms into ½" pieces.

6. To give support to the fish packets while they are baking, line eight 1-cup timbale molds (or 8-oz. muffin tins) with rectangles of buttered baking parchment (pan-liner paper or aluminum foil) each cut to measure 9" by 4". (If using a muffin tin, each muffin cup should have a collar of paper extending at least 1" above the top of the mold—measure paper or foil accordingly.) Preheat oven to 350°.

7. Line bottoms and sides of the prepared molds with the salmon slices. Spoon in the red pepper mousse halfway up the molds. Divide the mushrooms into eight equal portions and spoon one portion into each mold. Cover with the remaining mousse. Top off each mold with the remaining salmon slices.

8. Place molds in a pan containing boiling water that comes halfway up the sides of the molds. Cover tightly with buttered foil and bake until a knife inserted into the mousse comes out clean, about 25–35 minutes. Keep warm, covered, in a 200° oven while you make the Coral Sauce.

9. To make the sauce, in a heavy sauté pan, cook the shallots in the wine over moderate heat until the liquid is reduced to a glaze, about 5 minutes. Do not burn. Add the fish stock, tomato paste, reserved mushroom soaking liquid, and the cream and reduce over high heat until the liquid is of coating consistency, stirring occasionally. Add the Tabasco and salt and pepper to taste. Pass through a fine sieve. Discard solids. Thin the sauce, if necessary, with more fish stock.

10. Divide the sauce evenly on 4 warmed serving plates. Carefully remove the fish packets from their molds and center 2 on each plate. Scatter a confetti of red bell pepper and parsley leaves over the fish.

SERVING SUGGESTIONS: Start with Fennel-Orange Salad (page 18) and accompany the entree with a ribbon of barely steamed spinach. Toasted croutes of pumpernickel or some other rustic loaf would be especially welcome here. A good pinot noir (yes, a *red* wine) would set off the heat and richness of this dish stunningly.

Southwest by Southeast Saté

STARTER or STAR

Serves 4

This brightly flavored skewering of a Thai classic gains in complexity with borrowings from the flavor palette of the American Southwest. Cumin, fennel, and dried coriander seeds are the major players in the spice mix for the do-ahead marinade, with the Southeast (Asian, that is) connection provided by a dab of a prefabbed Thai red curry paste. A blend of ground cashews, almonds, and macadamia nuts makes up the nutty trio that stands in for the peanuts used in the original. For a stunningly varied buffet platter, I like to skewer everything from chicken, lean beef, and pork to scallops and shrimp to vegetables such as eggplant and zucchini. Be sure to marinate each of these separately for the clearest flavor.

THE MARINADE:

1 tsp. cuminseed

1 tsp. coriander seed

1 tsp. fennel seed

1 tsp. (or more, to taste) Curry Blend (page 264)

Thai red curry paste, to taste

½ cup finely ground toasted cashews

½ cup finely ground toasted almonds

½ cup finely ground toasted macadamia nuts

2 cups Thickened Yogurt (page 265)

½ tsp. coconut flavoring (optional)

Salt to taste

One recipe of marinade will suffice for any one of the following groups of ingredients:

VARIATION I (MEAT):

1 lb. boneless chicken breast, cut into strips 1" wide and pounded

or

½ lb. each boneless pork or lean beef, thinly sliced and pounded, cut into strips 1" wide

VARIATION II (SEAFOOD):

½ lb. large scallops

½ lb. large peeled and deveined shrimp (12–15 per lb. size)

VARIATION III (VEGETARIAN):

1 lb. eggplant, peeled, sliced into strips 3" long, 1" wide, ½" thick

½ lb. zucchini, sliced into strips 2–3" long, 1" wide, ½" thick

1 red pepper, sliced into strips 1" wide

1 large white potato (preferably white-skinned, waxy variety), blanched in boiling
water until barely tender

Vegetable oil for brushing cooking surface

12–16 wooden skewers soaked overnight in water to cover (to minimize burning)

1. For the marinade, toast the three varieties of seeds in a 350° oven for about 5–7 minutes, or until fragrant. Do not burn. Allow to cool. Grind in a coffee or spice grinder,
or pulverize with a mortar and pestle.

2. Combine the ground spices with the Curry Blend, curry paste, and three types of
ground nuts. Mix to combine well. Add the yogurt and coconut flavoring, and salt
to taste. Set aside.

3. Choose a Variation and place ingredients in a bowl. Coat with marinade and refrigerate, covered, for about 1 hour. Remove from marinade and thread ingredients on
skewers. Reserve marinade, refrigerated.

4. Just before serving, brush a stovetop grill or oven broiler with oil and heat until very
hot. Cook the skewered satés for about 4 minutes for chicken, beef, or seafood; 5
minutes for pork; and 5 minutes for vegetables, brushing with marinade occasionally and turning as needed to brown evenly. Serve immediately.

SERVING SUGGESTIONS: For a particularly dramatic presentation for the satés,
cut a ripe pineapple in half, keeping its tuft of leaves intact. With a sharp, slightly flexible knife, release the flesh from each half shell in one large piece. Remove the woody
core and slice the fruit into wedges ½" thick. Return the wedges to the pineapple shell
halves and place the reassembled fruit on a large, brightly colored decorative platter.
Insert the skewers into the pineapple wedges. (As you insert the skewers, you may
need to pierce through to the pineapple shell to keep the skewers upright.) You might
wish to start with Thai-Dyed Seafood Soup (page 7). Offer a Nutty Chiffonade of

Crunchy Cabbage (page 30) on the side as a kind of Asian accented slaw. Also *de rigueur* would be mountains of steamed jasmine rice, iced beer, and an exotic, cooling array of sliced tropical fruit.

Syrian Fire–Fiery Red Pepper and Walnut Spread

STARTER

Serves 6, approximately 2 cups

The first time I tasted this spicy red pepper dip amid an array of standout appetizers at a small Lebanese-owned Armenian restaurant, it was a revelation. I knew immediately that my translation of a translation of a translation would come to hold a prized place in my catalog of foods for casual entertaining. Unwilling to keep such a delicious secret for long, I feel compelled to share this garnet-colored jewel with the wide audience it deserves.

A traditional specialty of the northwestern Syrian city of Aleppo, *mouhammara,* as it is known in Arabic, combines red peppers, toasted walnuts, cumin, garlic, a hint of tart unsweetened pomegranate syrup, and just enough soft bread crumbs to yield a delicate paste. In this version the peppers, which give it its intensity of flavor, are fresh (the original commonly calls for a bottled red pepper paste as its base) and outweigh the nuts, which are often the main ingredient. Note that my version travels more than 2000 miles west from its point of origin to borrow its subtle hotness from a well-calculated dose of *harissa,* the North African chile paste, frequently the firepower in the couscous-based cuisine of Morocco.

Although the shelling process makes this more labor-intensive, this is truly an extra-special treat when prepared with the first crop of almost fruity walnuts that appears in late fall. If you need to resort to the commonplace preshelled plastic packets of walnuts of indeterminate freshness, you may boost the nutty flavor by adding a touch of walnut oil when blending the nuts into the mixture. When you serve this, have plenty of fresh Middle Eastern flatbread on hand to act as edible spoons.

For a spur-of-the-moment appetizer, I like to use the leftovers instead of tomato sauce as a base for a kind of Middle Eastern pizza using rounds of pita, topping the whole thing with a crumble of feta cheese. Just before serving, place under the broiler until the top reaches bubbling, aromatic perfection. Serve in generous wedges with a sturdy red wine, slightly chilled.

4 medium-sized red bell peppers

Olive oil to coat the peppers before roasting

1 cup shelled walnuts

1 tbsp. cuminseed

1 large clove garlic, crushed and finely chopped

1 tbsp. lemon juice

2 tbsp. pomegranate concentrate (also known as pomegranate molasses)

1 tbsp. fruity olive oil

Harissa paste, to taste

2 cups (approx.) fresh crumbs of pita bread

Salt and freshly ground black pepper

1. Rub the peppers lightly with olive oil. Place on a baking sheet and roast in a pre-heated 350° oven for about 20–25 minutes, turning once or twice to ensure even browning. When the skins are uniformly browned, remove the peppers from the oven and allow to cool. Peel and halve the peppers, remove ribs and seeds. Set peppers aside in a sieve over a bowl to save any juices that collect as they stand.

2. Toast the walnuts in the oven at 350° for about 5 minutes, stirring occasionally. Remove from oven and allow to cool. With a knife, finely chop. Set aside.

3. Toast the cuminseed in the oven at 350° for about 5 minutes, or until fragrant and slightly browned. Do not burn. When cool, grind to a fine powder in an electric spice or coffee grinder or use a mortar and pestle.

4. With a chef's knife, reduce the peppers to a rough puree. (Because the mixture can be quickly overprocessed, a food processor or blender is not recommended.) Place this puree in a mixing bowl, along with any juices that have collected from the peppers. Stir in nuts, ground cuminseed, and garlic. Mix in lemon juice, pomegranate concentrate, and 1 tbsp. olive oil. Add the harissa to taste. (Bear in mind that the hotness "opens up" upon standing; what might seem tame at first taste will seem considerably hotter after an hour.) Add just enough bread crumbs to thicken the mixture slightly (it should hold its shape when scooped with a spoon). Add salt and pepper to taste and chill for as long as an hour before serving to marry the flavors.

SERVING SUGGESTIONS: Keeping the menu geographically coherent, the richly sauced Practically Persian Turkey Fesenjan (page 82) would gamely follow this tough act of an appetizer.

Pan-Seared Bass with a Searing Melon Coulis STAR
Serves 4 generously

Relying on a trick I learned from Mexican street vendors who sprinkle dried hot chile pepper on wedges of melon or mango to make slightly underripe fruit taste sweeter, I devised a sauce for this dish that delicately balances hot, sweet, and acid flavors. With flecks of scorchingly hot *chipotle* chile, the uncooked sauce combines the musky intensity of a ripe cantaloupe with a shot of nicely acidic pineapple juice. I find that the fruity flavor of the sauce emerges most clearly at room temperature (making the sauce and spice rub in advance will allow you to fit this one into a busy schedule). Against this pale orange backdrop, a moist, firm-fleshed fillet of sea bass shows off its spice-bronzed surface to great visual advantage. (Other firm, slightly fatty varieties of fish like tuna or swordfish will work equally well here if sea bass is not a local specialty.) As with any fresh fish preparation, the key to success is to undercook the fish slightly. Let it stand for a few minutes before serving to allow it to recompose its juices.

THE SPICE RUB:
    1 tsp. annatto (achiote) seeds
    1 tsp. cuminseed
    1 tsp. coriander seeds
    ½ tsp. ground ginger
    ½ tsp. ground allspice
    ½ tsp. dried basil leaves
    ½ tsp. dried tarragon leaves
    ½ tsp. dried rosemary
    1 tsp. freshly ground white pepper
    2 lbs. skinless fillet of sea bass, cut into 4 pieces
    Salt
    Flour for dredging fish
    Olive oil to brush fish before coating with spice rub

THE SAUCE:

   ³⁄₄ medium cantaloupe, peeled and seeded, cut into chunks (about 2 cups)

   ½ cup fresh or frozen pineapple juice

   ½ tsp. (or more or less to taste) chipotle chiles in adobo sauce (usually sold canned)

THE GARNISH:

   ½ cup cilantro leaves

   1 lime, cut into 4 wedges

1. Make the spice rub by toasting the achiote, cumin, and coriander seeds in a dry skillet for about 1–2 minutes, stirring constantly. Do not burn or the mixture will become inedibly bitter. Grind seeds in a spice or coffee grinder until finely powdered. Combine with the remaining spices and herbs. (You will have some of the spice mixture left over after this recipe. Save for an instant seasoning for grilled or roasted poultry or for spicing up vegetables on the grill.)

2. Wash and dry the fish. Salt lightly. Dredge with flour and shake off excess. Brush lightly with olive oil and then dip both sides of the fillets into the spice rub. Coat with spice rub heavily and evenly. Set aside.

3. Make the sauce by pureeing the cantaloupe chunks with the pine-apple juice in a blender or food processor. Add the chipotle chile to taste and blend until combined. Store at room temperature if using later the same day, or refrigerate and bring to room temperature before using.

> # Flavor Flash!
> ## *Radish-Jícama-Apple Salad*
> For a quickly composed salad that for me defines cool and crunch, combine several thinly sliced radishes (any color will do), some julienne of crisp jícama, and slivered tart peeled apple. Lightly coat with nonfat plain yogurt spiked with ground cumin and a sprinkle of grated nutmeg. Garnish with a confetti of finely chopped scallion greens and serve on chilled plates for a startlingly refreshing opener.

4. Heat a heavy large skillet until almost white hot. (A drop of water flicked into the pan should evaporate instantly.) Carefully place the fillets in a single layer (don't overcrowd; allow enough space to turn the fish easily). Cook on each side about 2–4 minutes (depending on thickness of the fish), turning once during cooking. Remove from pan to heated plates. Pour a ring of sauce around the fish on each plate and garnish with cilantro leaves and lime wedges, as desired.

SERVING SUGGESTIONS: As an opener, I would serve a plate of Pale Perfect Poached Celery (page 6). Follow with a side dish of crusty wedges of potato studded with bits of roasted garlic. Finish on a silken note with a Lime Flan with Cajeta Sauce (page 246).

Heavenly Scented Couscous with Crisped Chapati   SIDE
Serves 4

In a delicate alternative to rice, this dish combines the fine-grained durum wheat semolina favored in North Africa and a quartet of distinct vegetables and then shades them with subtle and not-so-subtle accents from the wide-ranging Indian spice pantry.

A buffet crowd pleaser, this couscous is an inclusive catchall for whatever is good and colorful in your vegetable bin. By all means, don't feel hemmed in by the pre-scribed list of vegetables in the recipe. If your ambition doesn't run beyond preparing one dish for dinner, this one will make a memorable meal by itself. I like to double the recipe and be rewarded in the next few days with some fragrant microwaveable lunch-es or late-night snacks.

1 cinnamon stick

3 whole cloves

¼ tsp. cuminseed

⅛ tsp. black peppercorns

¼ tsp. whole hulled green cardamom

¼ tsp. coriander seed

¼ tsp. fennel seed

1½ cups Root Stock (page 258) or water

1 tsp. salt

1 tbsp. mustard oil or other light-tasting salad oil

1" piece gingerroot, peeled and finely minced

2 cloves garlic, crushed and finely minced

⅛ tsp. turmeric

1 lb. quick-cooking couscous

2 medium-sized white-skinned potatoes, peeled and cut into ½" cubes, cooked in
water until tender

1 medium leek, well washed, cut into rough ½" squares, blanched for 4 minutes or
until tender, drained, and dried

1 lb. red ripe tomatoes, peeled, seeded, cut into ½" cubes (about 2 cups)

Mustard oil for sautéing zucchini

1 large zucchini, well washed, cut into ½" cubes, about 2 cups

THE CRISPED CHAPATI:

1 tsp. black mustard seeds

Mustard oil to brush on the chapati

4 chapati (Indian whole wheat flatbread–substitute whole-wheat tortillas or pita
split in half, if chapatis are not available in your area)

1. In a heavy skillet over medium heat, toast the whole spices until aromatic, about 2
minutes. Stir occasionally to be sure that the spices are heating evenly. Do not burn.
Allow to cool and grind finely in an electric spice or coffee grinder or by hand in a
mortar and pestle.

2. Bring the stock or water and salt to a boil and keep hot.

3. Heat 1 tbsp. mustard oil in the same skillet until almost smoking hot. Add the ground
spices, ginger, garlic, and turmeric and stir until fragrant, about 30 seconds.
Immediately add the couscous and stir to coat evenly with the spices. Add the hot
stock and cover the pan with a tight-fitting lid. Place in a 200° oven to keep warm
while you prepare the vegetables.

4. Sauté zucchini in a thin film of mustard oil until tender and somewhat browned,
about 5 minutes. Remove the couscous from the warming oven and add zucchini
and the other prepared vegetables. Mound on a serving platter and return to the
oven to keep warm, covered.

5. Toast the mustard seeds in a heavy skillet for about 1 minute, or until they pop.
Crush them coarsely with a heavy rolling pin or meat pounder. Brush the chapati
lightly on both sides with mustard oil. Coat with the mustard seeds and place on a
baking sheet in a 350° oven to crisp, about 10 minutes. Cut into halves or quarters.

SERVING SUGGESTIONS: I like to pile this couscous in a conical mound or pyramid and surround it with any grilled fish or chicken entree for a dramatic one-platter supper. For a fanciful presentation, insert the wedges of chapati upright partially into the couscous to buttress the structure.

Pepper-Crusted Turkey Steak   STAR
Serves 4

Keeping fat low and flavor high is a challenge that this treatment of turkey meets handsomely. (For fullest flavor and best texture, prepare this just before serving.) Sporting a rough crust of mixed peppercorns, the lightly pounded breast meat retains its juices with a momentary flash in a searing-hot pan. A gutsy pan sauce based on Root Stock, smoky Cognac (or brandy), and a hint of sharp mustard elevates the dish into the realm of the memorable.

Preparing this often has convinced me of the utility of an arsenal of pepper mills for dispensing different varieties of peppercorns, the white and black varieties of which were employed in the kitchens of the ancient Greeks and Romans, according to Theophrastus, the 4th century B.C. founder of botany.

Armed with a battery of pepper mills, at the flick of a wrist I can easily enliven stocks, soups, sauces, and many main dishes with anything from a fine sprinkling to a coarse avalanche of the pungent pepper berries. I can't think of a more convenient way to spice up your diet (see Flavor Flash!, page 53).

1½ lbs. skinless and boneless turkey breast, sliced on the diagonal into slices ½"
    thick and then pounded lightly
Salt
Fruity olive oil for lightly coating the turkey before searing

PEPPER CRUST:
1 tsp. whole black peppercorns
1 tsp. whole white peppercorns
1 tsp. dried whole green peppercorns
1 tsp. whole Szechwan peppercorns (also known as anise pepper)

THE PAN SAUCE:

  2 cups Root Stock (page 258)

  ½ cup Cognac or brandy

  2 tsp. sharp Dijon-style mustard

  ½ cup Thickened Yogurt (page 265)

  Salt as needed

THE GARNISH:

  2 tart apples (Granny Smiths will retain their shape and best absorb the flavor of the
    stock), peeled and cored, halved, poached until just tender in 1 cup Root Stock

  ½ cup chopped fresh chives

1. Salt the turkey lightly and brush lightly with the oil. Coarsely grind the four different kinds of peppercorns in an electric spice or coffee grinder or by hand in a mortar and pestle. Coat the breasts evenly with the pepper blend. Set aside.

2. Heat a heavy skillet until almost white hot. (A sprinkling of water should evaporate
   immediately.) Carefully place the prepared turkey breast slices in the pan and cook
   for 5 minutes, turning once after the first 3 minutes. The meat should feel slightly
   springy to the touch. Do not overcook. Remove from the pan and place on a heated large serving platter and keep warm, lightly covered, in a 200° oven.

3. Deglaze the pan with the Root Stock and the Cognac. Cook, stirring, to loosen any
   browned particles clinging to the bottom of the pan. Add to the pan any juices that
   may have collected on the platter. Continue cooking over moderate heat until
   reduced by half. Swirl in the mustard and cook, stirring, for another minute. Add the
   yogurt, stir to blend thoroughly, and heat gently until hot. Do not boil or the sauce
   will separate. (If it does, you can rescue it partially by whirling in a blender briefly.)
   Taste and adjust salt as needed. Pour some of the sauce over the turkey in a thin ribbon. Sprinkle the turkey with the chopped chives. Garnish the platter with the
   poached apples. Serve the remaining sauce in a sauceboat.

SERVING SUGGESTIONS: A bracingly vinegary salad of cucumber or thinly sliced
cabbage (briefly blanched first) would serve as an appropriate warm-up for the bite of
this dish. For a contrasting side dish, any sweet, velvet-textured steamed winter squash,
such as kabocha, butternut, or acorn, enhanced with honey and a squirt of fresh lime
juice, would be ideal.

Red-Hot and Orange Halibut Harissa   STAR
Serves 4

The sunny flavors of Moroccan cooking come together in nontraditional ways here in a sizzling treatment of halibut. *Harissa,* that fiery, slightly herby chile paste often used to adorn elaborate couscous dishes, here lends fire to a fruity orange juice-based sauce for the fish. Echoing the faint presence of spice in the *harissa,* two other North African staples, cumin and coriander, are toasted whole, ground, and used as a crust for the fish, with cinnamon and caraway seed adding intrigue to the spice blend. As a final touch, dried currants, given a preliminary plumping in some of the orange juice, provide tiny bursts of sweetness amid the heat of the sauce.

Look for convenient reclosable tubes of *harissa* in Middle Eastern markets. And be sure to use fresh juice oranges that feel heavy for their size, indicating an abundance of flavorful juice, with skin that is bright-colored, smooth, and taut.

THE SPICE CRUST:

   2 tsp. coriander seeds

   1 tsp. cuminseed

   1 cinnamon stick

   1 tsp. caraway seeds

   ½ tsp. coarse salt

   1 tsp. all-purpose flour

   1½ to 2 lbs. halibut fillet, skin removed (sea bass also works well)

   1 tbsp. (approx.) fruity olive oil

   2 tbsp. finely minced shallots

THE SAUCE:

   2 tsp. harissa

   Juice of 4 small oranges, sieved, about 1 cup (reserve 2 tbsp. of juice to soak currants)

   Zest of 2 oranges, grated

   1 large ripe, red tomato, peeled, seeded, excess juice squeezed out, flesh cut into
        thin strips

   ½ cup dried currants, soaked in 2 tbsp. orange juice reserved from above

   Salt to taste

THE GARNISH:

   1 lb. steamed baby or small carrots with greens attached

1. Toast the spices in a heavy skillet over medium heat, stirring until a warm aroma wafts from the pan, about 1–2 minutes. Do not brown or the spices will taste bitter. Remove the spices to a small bowl and allow to cool. Grind until finely powdered in an electric spice or coffee grinder or by hand with a mortar and pestle. Add salt and flour.

2. Wash and dry the fish well and then coat thoroughly with the spice mixture.

3. Heat the oil in a heavy skillet until almost smoking. Add the fish and cook to brown evenly on all sides. (If using halibut, turn once after the first 2 minutes and brown the other side, cooking for another minute or so. If using sea bass, which is usually sold in long, thick chunks, turn after the first minute to the next side and continue cooking and turning until all sides are evenly browned.) It is not necessary to cook the fish thoroughly since it will finish cooking when it is returned to the sauce.

4. Wipe out any excess oil from the skillet but do not wash the skillet. Add the shallots and cook, stirring, over low heat just until softened, adding a bit of fresh oil if necessary to avoid sticking and burning. Add the harissa, orange juice, and zest and cook, stirring, until shallots are tender and the sauce is slightly thickened. Add the tomato and cook, stirring, for another minute.

5. Return the fish to the pan, cover, and cook for another 4 or 5 minutes, or until fish is opaque but still moist. Do not overcook. Remove the fish to a heated serving platter and place in a 200° oven to keep warm.

6. Reduce the sauce over high heat, stirring, until it coats a spoon. Taste for salt and add as necessary, remembering that the spice crust for the fish contains salt. Drain the currants and add to the sauce. Pour the sauce over and around the fish. Garnish by encircling the fish with the carrots, tops pointing outward over the rim of the platter, if desired.

SERVING SUGGESTIONS: Unable to resist North African tradition, I would serve a conical mound of couscous (fine grains of durum wheat semolina, properly steamed) on a separate platter. Add a side of Braised Eggplant with Pomegranate-Citrus Sauce (page 98). For festive crunch, I like to serve immense ovals of Persian flatbread or smaller rounds of toasted whole-wheat pita, accompanied by a dip of Roasted Shallot Yogurt (page 265).

Onion Crème Brûlée
STARTER or SIDE

Serves 4

Sweet Vidalia, Walla Walla, or Maui onions from Georgia, Washington, or Hawaii, respectively, provide three reasons to make this dish. Bound into an eggless "custard" thickened with a puree of tofu, softly cooked onions pay sweet homage to the creamed onions fondly remembered from Thanksgiving tables of my youth.

Here faintly scented with clove and sharpened with Tabasco sauce and Indian asafetida, this savory crème brûlée sports the thinnest crackle of burnt sugar, which serves to connect it with its once-again-fashionable dessert counterpart.

For a striking presentation, serve each portion in a hollowed-out roasted onion with its papery skin still intact. A bit of whimsy on the plate, these bear an uncanny resemblance to baked apples.

For the richer-by-design obverse of this dish, see Four-Way Bulbs, which follows.

1½ lbs. Vidalia, Walla Walla, or Maui onions

4 large cloves garlic, crushed

1 quart nonfat milk

6 whole cloves

1 lb. soft-curd tofu, well drained

½ tsp. asafetida heated in 1 tsp. flavorless salad oil until fragrant, about 30 seconds

1 cup Thickened Yogurt (page 265)

1 tsp. salt

½ tsp. freshly ground white pepper

Tabasco (or other liquid hot sauce) to taste

Salad oil or butter to lightly coat ramekins

2 tbsp. light brown sugar

FOR THE OPTIONAL PRESENTATION:

4 medium to large yellow or brown onions

Oil

THE GARNISH:

1 tbsp. finely chopped chives or fresh parsley leaves

1. Peel and roughly chop the onions. Simmer with the garlic, milk, and cloves in a heavy 2-quart saucepan over low heat until tender, about 30 minutes. By this time, most of the liquid should have been absorbed. Drain excess liquid, if any, discard the cloves, and allow the mixture to cool. Then puree with the tofu in a food processor or blender until perfectly smooth. Blend in the asafetida, yogurt, salt, pepper, and Tabasco and set aside.

2. Lightly oil or butter four 1-cup capacity ramekins or other nonaluminum molds. (If you are using the hollowed-out onions for presentation, cut a thin slice from the root end of each to enable the onions to remain upright. Brush them lightly with oil and place on an oiled baking sheet. Roast in a 350° oven just until tender but not collapsing, about 20 minutes. Remove from oven, cool slightly, and remove the top of each onion. With the point of a spoon, scoop out the centers of each, leaving a ½" wall of onion on the bottom and sides. Save the scooped-out onion pieces for another use.)

3. Fill the ramekins (or onion shells) with the onion-tofu mixture. Bake in a 350° oven for about 30 minutes, or until firm and slightly puffed. (The depth of the ramekins or the size of the onions used will affect cooking time—check frequently.) Remove from oven and lightly coat the top of each with the brown sugar. Place under a preheated broiler, about 3–4" from the flame or heating element, to melt the sugar evenly and create a golden glaze, about 2–3 minutes. Watch carefully to avoid burning. Garnish with the chives.

Flavor Flash!

Asafetida

Asafetida was a favorite flavoring of the ancient Romans. With its faint resemblance to truffles, the spice is derived from a giant fennel plant whose stems yield a milky juice. The juice solidifies into a dark yellow, resin-like mass, which is then powdered. Easiest to find in Indian markets, the powdered version, which is pale yellow, lends an oniony, garlicky pungency to vegetable and dried bean dishes, particularly favored in the cooking of Gujarat and Maharashtra in the western and southwestern parts of India.

Adding a small amount to any dish where either onion or garlic plays a leading part serves to emphasize their pungency. I also find that putting a toasted pinch of it into poultry marinades and vinegar-based dressings for smoked fish salads lends a welcome bit of bite without the aftereffects of raw onion or garlic. More is not better here, just bitter, so be parsimonious when using it.

SERVING SUGGESTIONS: Any pepper-crusted roasted meat, poultry, or fish entree would welcome such a side dish. I also like to serve this as a starter before a strongly flavored main dish such as Currying Flavor Three Ways (page 153) or Gorgeous Georgian Chicken (page 16). Finish with a Suite of Pears in a Zingy Ginger Dunk (page 228).

Four-Way Bulbs–Onion Custard   SIDE
Serves 8

This dish takes creamed onions to new heights. In a small dish with large flavor, four common varieties of the *Allium* family contribute their individual tang in an uncommon alliance. Subscribing to the school of glorious excess (diets be damned!), this dish amply demonstrates that if one is good, four are better.

The pungent white onion, the sweet red one, the gutsy leek, and the delicate shallot are pan-steamed in butter until tender. They are then pureed and amped up with a slug of prepared horseradish, bound with egg yolks and cream, and baked slowly in a water bath. What emerges is a light but firm tan-colored mousse akin in texture to the gently cooked sweet flans of Hispanic cookery. I like to serve this when adhering to a largely low-fat and low-cholesterol diet has driven me to distraction.

For its streamlined cousin, see the preceding recipe, Onion Crème Brûlée.

Butter or vegetable oil spray to coat ramekins

2 tbsp. butter

1 small white onion, roughly chopped (about 1 cup)

1 small red onion, roughly chopped (about ½ cup)

4 shallots, roughly chopped

Lower 5–6" of 1 medium leek, well washed and roughly chopped (about ¾ cup)
   (reserve the upper green leaves for the garnish)

1 tsp. salt

1 tbsp. sugar

6 egg yolks (egg whites may be substituted here for a lower fat and cholesterol
   count)

1 cup heavy cream

1 tsp. prepared horseradish or fresh grated, if available (use more if mild)

⅛ tsp. ground nutmeg

THE GARNISH:

½ cup thinly sliced green part of leek

Oil

1. Lightly butter or oil four 1-cup or eight ½-cup ramekins or nonaluminum molds. Melt the 2 tbsp. butter in a heavy skillet. Add the onions, shallots, and leek, and cook over low heat until tender, about 20–25 minutes (this process is often called "sweating"). Stir occasionally to avoid browning.

2. Puree onions in a blender or food processor until perfectly smooth. Add the salt, sugar, egg yolks, cream, horseradish, and nutmeg and process just until well combined.

3. Fill the prepared ramekins two-thirds of the way up to the top. Place in a roasting pan and fill it with enough boiling water to come halfway up the sides of the ramekins. Bake in a preheated 350° oven for approximately 50 minutes, or until the custards are firm and puffed. Allow to cool slightly, then unmold on individual heated plates. (If you are dividing 4 molds into eight portions, slice each custard horizontally and carefully plate them.) Keep plates warm in a 200° oven.

4. Fry the leek greens in oil until crisp and browned. Drain on absorbent paper toweling and scatter over each portion.

SERVING SUGGESTIONS: Choose a plain entree to pair with this, such as poached salmon fillet or a boneless chicken breast wrapped in spinach leaves and steamed on a bed of thinly sliced lemon. A plate of chilled sliced pineapple or peeled and sectioned honey tangerines would be an invigorating finale.

Ovenroast of Jumbled Grains with Tomato-Chile Coulis

SIDE

Serves 4

Modern Persians (Iranians) and some Caribbeans say that the best part of a pilaf is the crisp layer of rice that has stuck to the bottom of the pan after most of the cooking liquid has been absorbed. With this dish, although we go against the "grain" and eschew rice entirely, no one has to fight over who gets the honor of enjoying the *tah diq* or *bunbun,* as it is respectively called in Iran and Trinidad. After an initial cooking or steeping in vegetable stock, all of the constituents that make up this quintet are united for a long and leisurely roasting in the oven, which ensures that each kernel remains deliciously separate (a legacy of classic pilaf procedure) but equally crisp (my own interjection). Strictly speaking, one of the members of the group, buckwheat, is a fruit, not a grain, but it's flavor, not botanical precision, that I'm after.

Here, as in many pilafs, fruits and nuts play a part. Cubes of tart apple enter the mix during the last few minutes of oven time. As truly last-minute additions, raisins lend sweetness and deeply toasted almonds bring their own special crunch to the assemblage. With or without its piquant salsa of sorts on the side, this dish proves that there's a whole grainy world of tastes and textures out there beyond rice, corn, and oats.

THE SAUCE:

> 2 lbs. ripe red tomatoes, blanched in boiling water to facilitate peeling, peeled and seeded
>
> 2 (more or less to taste) hot red chiles, seeded (Thai bird peppers work nicely here, but any hot, fresh red variety will do)
>
> 2 tsp. fruity olive oil
>
> Pinch sugar
>
> Pinch salt

THE GRAINS:

> 1/2 cup quick-cooking barley
>
> 1/2 cup quinoa
>
> 1/2 cup kasha (roasted whole buckwheat kernels)
>
> 1/2 cup quick-cooking couscous
>
> 1 cup bulgur wheat

7 cups (approx.) Root Stock (page 258) or water

Pinch salt

1 tbsp. fruity olive oil

1 tsp. Shallot-Infused Oil (page 269)

1 medium-sized onion, cut into ½" cubes (about 1 cup)

4 cloves garlic, crushed and finely minced

1 large tart apple, peeled, cored, and cut into ½" cubes (about ½ cup)

½ cup dark or golden raisins, soaked in hot water for 5 minutes and then drained

¼ cup slivered almonds, toasted in 350° oven until golden brown, about
    8–10 minutes

Salt and freshly ground black pepper

THE GARNISH:

2 mild red or green chiles (or 1 of each), finely chopped

¼ cup finely chopped fresh parsley leaves

1. Make the sauce by pureeing tomatoes, chiles, oil, sugar, and salt in a food processor or blender just until smooth. Pass through a fine sieve to remove any visible seeds or skin. Cook in a small heavy saucepan, stirring occasionally, until somewhat thickened and bright reddish orange. Set aside.

2. In separate small heavy saucepans, covered, over low heat, cook the barley and quinoa each in approximately 1½ cups stock until tender and all the liquid has been absorbed, about 12–15 minutes. Fluff each with a fork and set aside.

3. Over low heat, cook the kasha in a small heavy saucepan, covered, with about 1 cup stock until tender. When done, separate the kernels with a fork and set aside. To retain their separateness, the kasha kernels should remain somewhat resistant to the bite.

4. In a small heavy saucepan, bring 1 cup stock to the boil with a pinch of salt. While stirring, pour in the couscous in a thin stream. Cover the pot and let stand until all of the liquid has been absorbed and the couscous is well puffed. Stir with a fork to ensure that the individual grains are separate. Set aside.

5. In a heavy 1-quart saucepan, bring remaining 2 cups of stock to a boil and stir in bulgur. Reduce heat to a simmer and cook, uncovered, for 10 minutes. Remove from heat, cover, and let stand for about 15 minutes. Drain any excess liquid and set bulgur aside.

6. In a heavy skillet, heat the oils until hot. Add the onions and cook over low heat, stirring occasionally, until translucent and tender. Do not brown. Add the garlic and cook for another minute, stirring constantly.

7. Gently combine all the grains in a large bowl. Blend in the onion and garlic mixture. Place the mixture on a lightly oiled baking sheet and roast in a 350° oven for about 30 minutes, or until the grains are nicely crisp but not burned. (If they are browning too quickly, adjust oven temperature and cover lightly with foil.) Mix in the apples and roast for approximately another 5–10 minutes. Remove from the oven, combine with the raisins and almonds, and season to taste with salt and pepper. Place on a heated decorative platter, surrounded by a thin circle of the sauce. Garnish with the chiles and parsley.

SERVING SUGGESTIONS: Turning up the heat a notch, I like to serve Pepper-Crusted Turkey Steak (page 65) with this, followed by a Warm "Salad" of Watercress, Arugula, and Roasted Red Pepper (page 174).

CHAPTER 3

Attractive Opposites and Joyous Juxtapositions

**MINGLING THE BITTER WITH THE SWEET,
THE SWEET WITH THE SOUR, AND THE HOT
WITH THE SWEET**

The dishes in this chapter celebrate the pleasures of complexity—not in their method of preparation but in their flavor. Here two opposite flavors are combined in a single dish for a richly layered taste impression, an old idea that has prevailed in classical cooking through much of the Middle East, and all of Asia. In dishes such as Hot Shrimp and Sweet Plantains with an Indonesian Tinge (page 102) and Warm Compote of Sweet Potato and Tart Apple in a Tamarind Sauce (page 107) you will experience richly complex taste sensations that bombard the palate not once, but twice with each bite. The first flavor perceived may be one of hotness, followed by a surprisingly sweet aftertaste. Or you may be beguiled by a predominantly sweet first impression, only to be given a pleasant jolt of bittersweetness with the next bite. Here are cross-cultural recipes that highlight foods with one predominant flavor note and deepen their overall taste by introducing another layer of flavor for contrast. Here the whole is greater than the sum of its parts.

Juxtapose two main ingredients in a dish—say, one bitter and the other mellow and sweet—and hold them in a delicate balance, and *voila,* something special and complex is achieved. Each characteristic plays against the other, leaving the palate excited, continually refreshed, ready for more even after three bites.

Take, for example, Witloof with Love (page 96) where the natural bitterness of braised endive is contrasted winningly with a sauce of naturally sweet roasted carrot. Or, Rice-Crusted Whitefish with Dates and Lime (page 104) in which dry vermouth sets up a delicious contrast to the sweet and sour fruits in the sauce. Here a flavor blend altogether unique and complex is placed before the palate.

These are only a few of the taste sensations ahead where perceptions of bitter, sweet, hot, and sour are redefined when combined as if for the first time.

Key Ingredients

For creating dishes that mingle the bitter with the sweet, the sweet with the sour, and the hot with the sweet.

ANGOSTURA BITTERS—a bottled liquid derived from gentian root; its name is derived from the town in Bolivia, Angostura, where it was first made; lends a pleasant bitterness to beverages, both alcoholic and non-, and may be used instead of Campari, or other bitters-based aperitifs in mixed drinks

BITTER GREENS—dandelion, mustard greens, chard

BITTER ORANGE MARMALADE—English or Scottish quality and tradition reign supreme

CAMPARI—*sui generis* among aperitifs, developed in Milan, Italy, about 1890, bitters-based, a neon scarlet in color

CHICORY—both a salad green and an adulterant for coffee

CHOCOLATE, BITTERSWEET—the best is Swiss; other than the obvious confectionery and pastry use, it's often used in highly spiced Mexican sauces

CRANBERRIES—fresh or dried, sauced or whole

CYNAR—a wonderfully bittersweet Italian apertif based on artichoke extract

ENDIVE, BELGIAN—also known as witloof or *barbe-de-bouc,* at its peak in winter and fall; actually a form of escarole grown in total darkness to avoid the light-dependent green chlorophyll from coloring the leaves; other varieties of leaf endive which don't require blanching are easy to grow even by the unconscientious gardener, and like the Belgian variety, are a refreshing punctuation to a salad of crisp sweet lettuces

ESCAROLE—a milder variant of chicory, particularly wonderful in Italian-style chicken soup

GINGER IN SYRUP—also known as stem ginger in syrup, where the youngest shoots of gingerroot are repeatedly cooked in a sugar syrup until tender; available in Chinese and Japanese versions; in a pinch, I rely on this to turn a scoop of vanilla ice cream into a special dessert

KAFFIR LIMES, FRESH—looks like a smaller, rounder lime with acne; fragrant without the citrus tang, its aroma and flavor are somewhat more floral and more intense than the so-called Persian limes widely available in supermarkets. Dried, these often appear as a last-minute flavoring (*limoo*) in the long-cooked stews of Persian cuisine

LIME JUICE, FRESH—Ranjipur or Rangpur are wonderfully fragrant, thin skinned, and yield a lot of flavorful juice

MANGO, FRESH

PAPAYA—fresh ripe (used as a fruit) or green (used as a crunchy vegetable in some Southeast Asian salads)

RADICCHIO—pleasantly bittersweet salad greens; the round Verona variety and the Treviso with its long, tapered leaves are the most commonly found

SAKANJABIIN—a Middle Eastern bottled syrup made of mint, vinegar, sugar, and water (see Flavor Flash!, page 86)

THAI SQUID SAUCE—sweet and hot chili sauce (*num chim kai* in Thai; *nuoc cham ga* in Vietnamese, also known as "sauce for chicken")

VERMOUTH—a white wine whose herbal complexity stands it in good stead as a base for sauces and marinades

VINEGARS—balsamic, sherry wine vinegar, Chinese Chinkiang (a black vinegar made from rice), seasoned Japanese rice, and Southeast Asian palm (mild, and often a milky white)

Charbroiled Chicken with Afghan Aubergines

STAR

Serves 4

With its roots in Near Eastern and Indian cookery, this Afghan-inspired dish defines for me the perfect balance between sweet and tart—with the sweetness of perfectly cooked eggplant and freshly chopped mint, the tartness of ripe tomato and yogurt. Using naturally mellow Japanese eggplant eliminates the need to salt and weigh the vegetable to remove bitterness before cooking. The smoky char of the grill adds yet another dimension to this satisfying dish. This is food that is as pleasing to the eye as it is to the palate—black, orange, white, and green in striking contrast. Easy to assemble at the last minute, it makes the perfect hot or room-temperature star on any multi-ethnic buffet. Great for summertime entertaining when the vegetable garden is in full swing and the barbecue is the cooking tool of choice. If you'd prefer less protein in your meal, the vegetarian portion of this dish can stand alone as a vibrant Starter or Side on a warm summer evening.

4 boneless chicken breasts (8–10 oz. each), skin and all visible fat removed

THE SPICE RUB:

1 tsp. ground cinnamon

1 tsp. coriander

1 tsp. cuminseed

½ tsp. dried ginger

⅓ tsp. black peppercorns

½ tsp. annatto (achiote) seed

½ tsp. salt

Grated rind of 2 fresh lemons

THE AFGHAN AUBERGINES:

4 large Japanese eggplant (approx. 2 lbs. total)

2 tbsp. olive oil for brushing and frying eggplant, plus additional oil as needed for coating grill surface

Salt and freshly ground black pepper

3 cloves garlic

1 lb. fresh roma or plum tomatoes (if unavailable, substitute 1 can [2 lbs. 3 oz.] imported Italian tomatoes, well drained)

1 tsp. turmeric

1 cup nonfat plain yogurt

THE GARNISH:

½ bunch fresh mint, leaves only

1. For the spice rub, grind all spices together in a spice mill or coffee grinder. Add salt and grated lemon rind and mix to blend. Wash and dry boneless chicken breasts and rub well with the spice rub. Let stand for about 30 minutes in the refrigerator, covered, to allow the spices to flavor the chicken.

2. For the Afghan Aubergines, halve the eggplants lengthwise. Brush lightly with olive oil and salt and pepper to taste. Smash the garlic cloves with the flat edge of a heavy knife. Slip the skins off and set aside.

3. If using fresh tomatoes, place them into a pot of boiling water and boil just until the skins crack. Remove from the water, plunge into cold water, and peel. For both fresh or canned tomatoes, squeeze out the excess juice and seeds and chop roughly. Set aside. Discard the juice or reserve for another use.

4. Using a thin coating of olive oil per batch, cook the eggplant in a single layer in a heavy 8" sauté pan over medium heat for about 5 minutes until lightly browned, turning once during cooking. Continue cooking eggplant using the remaining oil until done. As they are browned, transfer to a large stovetop casserole dish. Add crushed garlic, tomatoes, and turmeric. Cover and cook the casserole over low heat for about 10 minutes, or until eggplant is tender but still intact.

5. Carefully remove eggplant to a serving dish and array it skin side up in a single layer. Cook the remaining tomato sauce mixture until it is of coating consistency. Reserve.

6. Over a medium-hot grill that has been brushed lightly with olive oil, cook the chicken breasts until just done. This should take about 5 minutes; turn the breasts once during cooking. Do not overcook. Arrange the chicken attractively on top of the eggplant. Nap the chicken breasts with the tomato sauce. Spoon a dollop of yogurt evenly over each serving. Scatter chopped mint leaves over the dish and serve.

SERVING SUGGESTIONS: This dish needs nothing more than some grilled pita brushed with a hint of garlic oil. I like to end the meal on a light fruity note with Broiled Oranges with Brown Sugar-Lime Glaze (page 255).

Practically Persian Turkey Fesenjan

STAR

Serves 4

Here is a seductive and complex combination of sweet and sour. Thanks to the Persians we can enjoy this recipe, which draws its inspiration from two plentiful crops in northern Iran: pomegranates and walnuts. I am updating the recipe by using low-fat turkey breast instead of the traditional chicken or duck of the classical version. The fat content of the ground walnuts serves as the perfect enrichment for the lean white meat of the bird. (Try Gosh Garnet It's Turkey, page 84, if you prefer dark meat.) Be sure to use pomegranate concentrate (also known as pomegranate molasses), not the sweetened bottled juice, to achieve a sauce with the rich fruity tartness that is the hallmark of this dish.

As accompaniment, it's worth the effort to seek out the long, slender-grained basmati rice (now widely available in better supermarket chains around the country) which is the rice of choice in most Indian, Pakistani, Afghan, and Iranian kitchens. Grown in the foothills of the Himalayas, its prized toasty aroma lends a subtly smoky backdrop to the finished dish. In preparing the rice, I ignore the custom of soaking, washing, and then draining the rice to remove excess starch before cooking. Omitting these steps, I find that a bit of residual starchiness in the rice adds to its appeal without affecting its clean, separate-kernel integrity. I have found the Dehraduni variety (any brand) from India to be reliably good and well cleaned.

Flavor Flash!
Turmeric

A member of the potent ginger family, turmeric is perhaps most familiar as the ingredient that imparts the bright yellow color to curry powder and prepared mustard. Like paprika, which is often relegated to the position of a mere visual embellishment for foods, turmeric, too, undeservingly gets a bum rap. More than just a color, turmeric has a flavor and aroma reminiscent of ginger but distinctively its own. Use it "gingerly" in a yogurt dressing over sweet slices of jicama for a crunchy one-ingredient salad.

THE SAUCE:

    2 tbsp. vegetable oil

    1 large onion, finely grated

    2 cups ground walnuts

    3 cups defatted chicken or turkey stock

    1 cup bottled pomegranate concentrate (unsweetened)

1 tsp. ground cinnamon

2 tbsp. tomato paste

Granulated sugar to taste

Lemon juice to taste

THE TURKEY:

2 lbs. boneless turkey breast, sliced into cutlets and slightly pounded

2 quarts water

1 cup finely grated onion

½ tsp. turmeric

Salt and pepper to taste

THE RICE:

1 cup basmati rice

1½ cups water

½ tsp. salt

1 bay leaf

Peel of 1 lemon, removed in long strips

THE GARNISH:

4 rounds of pita bread, cut into 6 triangles each, toasted until crisp

1 fresh pomegranate, quartered (optional)

1. To prepare the sauce, heat the oil in a heavy saucepan and cook the onion until tender but not browned, stirring frequently. Add the ground walnuts and sauté just until they darken slightly, stirring constantly to avoid burning. Add the chicken or turkey stock and bring to a boil. Add pomegranate syrup and cinnamon. Bring to a boil again and add tomato paste. Reduce heat and cook until sauce is thick but pourable. Add sugar and lemon juice to taste (the sauce should be tart, not sweet—taste as you go when you are adding the sugar. I like the final flavor to be quite tart, so I use the juice of one large lemon here). Simmer covered until flavors blend, about a half hour.

2. To prepare the turkey, bring water, onion, and turmeric to a boil in a skillet large enough to hold the cutlets in a single layer. Add cutlets, cover, lower heat to a simmer and cook for about 6–8 minutes, or until done. Do not overcook. Set aside. Add salt and pepper to taste and keep covered and warm in a 200° oven.

3. Cook the rice in a covered 2-quart saucepan over medium heat with the water, salt, bay leaf, and lemon peel for about 20–25 minutes, or until tender and all the liquid is absorbed. Keep warm until serving. Remove bay leaf and lemon peel and fluff rice with a fork before serving.

4. To serve, place a mound of rice on each plate, top with a warm turkey cutlet, and sauce generously. Garnish with toasted pita triangles, and fresh pomegranate wedges if desired.

SERVING SUGGESTIONS: I like to serve a guilt-free nonfat starter as a lead-in to the rich complexity of this dish. I find that either a simple and soothing bowl of cubed cucumber in a cumin-scented yogurt sauce or a composed salad of radish, jícama, and tart apple in a similar sauce works perfectly to fit the bill.

Gosh Garnet It's Turkey

STAR

Serves 4 generously

As a variation on the preceding Practically Persian Turkey Fesenjan, this dish will appeal to those with somewhat sophisticated palates who are tempted by tartness rather than seduced by sweetness. Furthermore, this dish proves that tart and hot can be a potent team. Drawing some of its inspiration from classical Persian cuisine, it's yet another perfect reason to serve dark-meat turkey as a main dish at any season. Here the emphasis is on fruits, not nuts—in fact, three fruits—pomegranates, prunes, and grapes. Leaving the nuts out entirely and yet wishing to retain an artful balance between fat and lean components in the dish, I have chosen to use exclusively dark-meat turkey with its higher fat content.

Here, too, bottled unsweetened pomegranate juice is the key ingredient, which produces a richly crimson and fragrant pan sauce. But in this case it's thickened with tart, dried Bukhara prunes, an Afghan specialty (dried apricots can be substituted if need be). A staple in the pantry of Iranian cooks for centuries, and widely available in Middle Eastern as well as Indian markets, pomegranate juice in its concentrated form is the basis of the braising liquid and lends its deep dark color to the already dark meat. As in the Practically Persian Turkey Fesenjan, the garnet-colored juice is combined with defatted chicken stock, but here it gets some added amperage from long, skinny, yellow Hungarian wax peppers. The resulting sauce is an intense foil for the somewhat gamy leg meat. If pomegranate juice is unavailable, use cranberry juice concentrate, which has the same tartness but lacks the depth and color of the juice of choice. Thighs can be substituted for legs to similar effect.

4 slender leeks, finely chopped

2 tbsp. olive oil

4 turkey legs, skin removed (about 2 to 2¼ lbs. total)

1½ cups pomegranate concentrate

1½ cups defatted chicken stock

3" piece of lemon peel, removed from the lemon with a vegetable peeler

1 or 2 Hungarian wax peppers, or other medium-hot chiles (depending on degree of hotness desired)

2 cloves garlic, finely chopped

1 bay leaf

½ tsp. freshly ground black pepper

½ cup Bukhara prunes, pitted (substitute dried apricots if necessary)

Salt to taste

THE GARNISH:

4 small bunches of red seedless grapes (about ½ lb. total)

1. In a heavy pan large enough to accommodate the turkey legs in a single layer, sauté the leeks in the olive oil over medium heat. Cook, stirring, until softened. Do not brown.

2. Add turkey legs and the remaining ingredients except prunes, salt and the grapes. (I like to salt this to taste at the end of the cooking process.) Cook covered in a pre-heated 350° oven for approximately 30–35 minutes or until meat is tender. Remove turkey from pan and keep warm, covered.

3. Remove lemon peel and bay leaf from the sauce. Defat the sauce as needed by skimming any visible fat from the surface. Add the prunes and cook over high heat until sauce is reduced to coating consistency. (The prunes will have disintegrated into the sauce.) Add salt to taste.

4. Place one turkey leg per serving on a plate, nap with the sauce, and garnish each with a bunch of grapes.

SERVING SUGGESTIONS: This dish cries out for a bay-scented kasha or pilaf of basmati rice and kasha. Store-bought quince preserves transformed by some toasted chopped walnuts and a spritz of fresh lime juice would also be a nice touch. In keeping with the Middle Eastern flavor, Sharply Minted Cucumber Salad (next) would provide just the right crunch.

Flavor Flash! *Sakanjabiin, Afghan Mint Syrup*

In the Middle East, mint, both fresh and dried, occupies an important place as a culinary herb in everything from breakfasts to salads and beverages. The simple morning meal centers around cheese and flatbread with fragrant mint the intriguing go-between.

Scouring the shelves of my local modern souk, I happened upon a bottle of mint syrup that must be one of the clearest translations of mint's true flavor. Called sakanjabiin, it may be found on the shelves of most Arab markets somewhere near the bottled rose and orange-flower waters. This liquid, a year-round mainstay in my multiethnic pantry, is a golden distillation of fresh mint, vinegar, sugar and water. In Afghanistan, street peddlers use it as a dipping sauce for crisp wedges of romaine, served garnished with a few fresh mint leaves. A hefty spoonful stirred into a tall glass of ice water or sparkling mineral water makes a drink that's sure to beat the desert (or any other) summer heat.

Sharply Minted Cucumber Salad

STARTER or SIDE

Serves 4

I use the syrup here as a ready-made dressing for a cucumber salad that is best made no sooner than one hour before serving. To serve 4, choose 8 small Persian cucumbers (you'll recognize them by their often bulbous shape and smooth dark green skin, which need not be removed before slicing; English hothouse cucumbers may be used instead). Slice them on the diagonal. Salt lightly. There should be about 6 cups. Place in a decorative bowl. Grind a generous dusting of fresh black pepper over the cucumbers. Pour ½ cup of *sakanjabiin* over the cucumbers. Dust with hot red pepper flakes to taste. Garnish with a garland of fresh mint leaves, if you wish. Refrigerate. To give the dish a refreshing, authentic look, cover the salad with a layer of ice cubes, broken into shards, about 15 minutes before serving. Place at room temperature to allow the ice to melt somewhat. By serving time, the dressing will be properly diluted.

My Fave Favas
Serves 4

STARTER or SIDE

Also known as broad beans, fava beans mean spring is here in many parts of the world, from Italy and France to the Middle East. Although the shelling is time-consuming, there is a certain sensuous pleasure in the ritual of removing the meaty, tart beans from their shells. More fun is in store when you slip the tender cooked inner beans from their tough outer casings. But the real pleasure awaits you when you sit down to a plate of these subtly flavored beans in my take on a Middle Eastern classic. Here the pleasantly bitter edge of the beans is offset by the smoky sweetness of charred red peppers. Lemon, garlic, and yogurt each play an equal role in a highly versatile dressing. (Try it on cold grilled swordfish or shark.) Cayenne throws some heat into the mix to keep the palate in a state of surprise and anticipation. Here sweet, tart, bitter, and hot all converge in a dish of perfectly satisfying simplicity.

2 lbs. unshelled fresh fava beans (or substitute 1 lb. frozen Fordhook lima beans)
1 large sweet red pepper

THE DRESSING:
2 large cloves garlic
½ tsp. salt
Juice and grated zest of 1 medium-sized lemon
1 cup nonfat plain yogurt
2 tbsp. fine-quality fruity olive oil
Freshly ground black pepper
4 large Boston or butter lettuce leaves
2 medium-sized green onions, white part only, finely minced
Cayenne pepper

1. Remove the beans from their pods. Steam for approximately 5 minutes. Their outer casings will have split, which makes for easy removal of the beans themselves. (If using frozen limas, prepare according to the package directions.)

2. Blacken the skin of the red pepper directly over an open flame (or place under broiler). When completely black, plunge into ice water and quickly slip off the skin. Cut in half, remove the ribs and seeds, and dice into ½" cubes.

3. To prepare the dressing, mince the garlic and mix with the salt. Mash the garlic into a paste and transfer to a small mixing bowl. Add the lemon juice and grated lemon zest. Whisk in yogurt and then olive oil until smooth.

4. Carefully fold the dressing into the beans. Season to taste with black pepper. Divide among 4 plates lined with the lettuce leaves. Sprinkle the favas with chopped green onions and dust with cayenne pepper to taste.

SERVING SUGGESTIONS: As a crisp accompaniment, serve some fresh whole-wheat pita bread, grilled and brushed with Freshly Minted Oil (page 270).

Seurat's Cauliflower

SIDE

Serves 4

This dish is as much about texture as it is about taste. Back in my formative years, had I been served cauliflower with some crunch left in it I would have emptied my plate more often. Back then, overcooking vegetables was considered standard operating procedure, vitamins and texture be damned. Thankfully, most of us have learned the value of a little more texture with our fiber, and vegetable cookery is the finer for it.

Here a whole head of cauliflower is thrice cooked but amazingly emerges with both its texture and taste intact. First it's given a brief steaming just long enough to lose its raw edge. Then it's roasted and basted with a mellow vinegar sauce touched with honey. Finally, it gets its surface glow from a short stay under the broiler and its cooking is complete. It arrives at the table in a crust of toasted white poppy seeds stippled with chives, a bit of pointillist perfection.

    1 medium-sized head of cauliflower (about 1½ lbs.)
    1 tbsp. fruity olive oil
    1 cup Tropical Vinegar (page 271)
    ¼ cup fragrant honey (lavender, lime blossom, or raspberry are my favorites)
    Salt and freshly ground white pepper

1 cup white poppy seeds (available at Indian markets; if unavailable use black poppy
   seeds but skip step 2)
1 small bunch chives, finely chopped

1. In a small heavy saucepan, boil the vinegar until it is reduced by half. Remove from
   the heat and add the honey. Stir to combine. Let cool. Preheat the oven to 375°.

2. In the oven, toast the poppy seeds on a cookie sheet with sides for about 4–5 minutes. Watch carefully to avoid burning. Let cool and set aside.

3. Cut the tough core from the center of the cauliflower, leaving the florets intact. Place
   in a steamer rack over boiling water and steam for about 4 minutes. (It should be
   barely cooked at this point.)

4. Brush the steamed cauliflower with oil and place on a baking sheet. Roast at 375° for
   about 15 minutes, basting frequently with the honey-vinegar glaze. Reserve a bit of
   glaze for a final coat before serving. When barely tender, place under the broiler and
   brown slightly. Brush the cauliflower with the remaining glaze, press the poppy
   seeds into its surface and sprinkle the chopped chives liberally over all.

SERVING SUGGESTIONS: I like to feature this as the centerpiece of a varied constellation of vegetable dishes including Slightly Smoked Eggplant and Company with
Roasted Shallot Yogurt Sauce (page 204) and Roasted Rootatouille (page 125). It's also
a perfect complement to Sweet and Fiery Chicken (page 48).

Philippine Scallop Rolls   STARTER
Serves 4 generously

With a homemade wrapper that is a cross between a thin noodle and a crêpe, these
Philippine style eggrolls, somewhat like *lumpia,* are a gossamer introduction to
any meal. A chop of sweet scallops and a crunch of pale Napa cabbage and jícama are barely held together with a whisper of chicken mousse. In place of the more traditional but prosaic carrot, an unorthodox shred of sweet potato adds color to a mostly alabaster filling. Those old standbys, soy sauce, ginger, and garlic, make room for a
couple of upstarts, lemongrass and fresh mint, in a slightly sweet Dip with Zip, which

is as versatile as it is delicious. It makes an especially splendid dunk for a plain steamed chicken breast.

VARIATION: *Smoked Salmon Rolls*

For a neat variation on the theme, I like to replace the scallops with an equal amount of smoked salmon. (Note: Reduce the fish sauce and soy sauce in the filling by as much as half of the amounts given below if the smoked salmon is particularly salty.) Garnish these additionally with a scattering of garlic chives or yellow chives, and instead of the Dip with Zip, accompany them with a Rosemary-Orange Dipping Sauce (see step 9 below).

Both the scallop and smoked salmon versions work particularly well when poached gently in Root Stock (page 258) or a Gingery Chicken Stock (page 259) for an altogether different, but equally delightful, lower-fat starter.

If convenient, you can make the crepes and filling in advance and assemble just before serving. Then fry or poach the assembled rolls, as desired.

THE CRÊPE WRAPPERS:
3 whole eggs
1¼ cups water
½ cup cornstarch
Peanut oil for frying

THE FILLING:
1 tsp. peanut or safflower oil
2 cloves garlic, finely minced
1 tbsp. finely minced shallots
½ cup finely shredded sweet potato
1 cup finely shredded Napa cabbage
½ cup cubed jícama (¼" cubes)
½ lb. boneless chicken breast, skin removed
2 egg whites
½ lb. fresh scallops, chopped into ½" pieces
1 tbsp. fish sauce
2 tsp. soy sauce
Peanut or safflower oil for frying; or
3 quarts Root Stock (page 258) or Gingery Chicken Stock (page 259), for poaching

THE DIP WITH ZIP:

   2 cloves garlic, crushed and finely minced

   2" piece of gingerroot, finely minced

   2 fat stalks of fresh lemongrass, crushed to release aroma, finely chopped

   4 tbsp. Tropical Vinegar (page 271) or white wine vinegar

   2 cups ketjap manis (Indonesian sweetened soy sauce or substitute $1\frac{1}{2}$ cups dark
       soy sauce combined with $\frac{1}{2}$ cup dark molasses)

   $\frac{1}{4}$ cup chopped fresh mint leaves

   Dried hot chili peppers, crushed, to taste (optional)

THE ROSEMARY-ORANGE DIPPING SAUCE:

   1 large sprig fresh rosemary, crushed and finely minced

   2 cloves garlic, crushed and finely minced

   Juice of 4 large oranges, sieved (about 2 cups)

   1 tbsp. fruity olive oil

   Soy sauce to taste

THE GARNISH:

   1 head soft-leaf lettuce, such as butter or limestone, sliced into long shreds

   8 long fresh lemongrass leaves

   $\frac{1}{2}$ bunch fresh mint

OPTIONAL GARNISH FOR THE SMOKED SALMON VARIATION:

   Garlic chives or yellow chives, chopped

1. To make the crêpe wrappers, beat the eggs in a bowl just until frothy. In another
    bowl, gradually add water to cornstarch with a whisk to make a smooth liquid.
    Add to eggs and whisk to combine. Brush an 8" nonstick skillet with some oil and
    heat until a drop of water sizzles when added to the pan. Ladle or spoon $\frac{1}{4}$ cup of
    the batter into the pan, swirling the pan to coat the bottom evenly. Cook for about
    2 minutes, or until the crepe is dry and slightly golden brown in color. (No need to
    brown both sides of the wrapper.) Invert the pan over a plate and stack finished
    crepes with wax paper or parchment layered in between. You should have approx-
    imately 20 thin crêpes. Set aside and make the filling.

2. To make the filling, in a heavy sauté pan, cook the garlic and shallots in the oil over
    medium heat. Cook, stirring, for about 2 minutes, until tender but not browned.

Add the sweet potato and cook, stirring lightly, for about 30 seconds. Add the cabbage and cook for 2 minutes more, until the cabbage is crisp tender. Add the jícama and cook, stirring, for 1 minute.

3. In a food processor or blender, make a chicken mousse by pureeing the chicken with the egg whites until smooth. Set aside.

4. Lightly mix the chicken mousse into the vegetable mixture. Fold in the scallops. Blend in fish sauce and soy sauce and set aside, refrigerated, until ready to fill the wrappers.

5. When ready to assemble the rolls, spoon a mound of the filling down the center of each wrapper, placed unbrowned side down, leaving a ½" margin at each end. Fold one side firmly over the filling. Then fold in each end tightly against the filling. Keeping the filling well contained within the wrapper, continue rolling until seam side is down. Remove to a platter and refrigerate until ready to cook.

6. To fry, coat a heavy sauté pan with a light film of oil and heat. Cook as many scallop rolls as the pan can easily accommodate. Cook until the filling is firm and the wrapper is well browned. Drain on absorbent paper, if necessary. Serve as soon after frying as possible.

7. Alternately, to poach, bring 3 quarts of Root Stock or Gingery Chicken Stock to a boil in a large stock pot. Reduce the heat to a simmer and add half of the rolls. Cook until the filling is firm. Remove from the liquid with a slotted spoon and drain on absorbent paper. Poach the other half and set aside at room temperature until up to a half hour before serving. If you wish to poach these earlier in the day, refrigerate, well wrapped, and bring to room temperature before serving.

8. To make the Dip with Zip, combine the garlic, gingerroot, and lemongrass in a small stainless steel or crockery bowl. Add the vinegar and let stand for 10 minutes until fragrant. Put through a fine sieve, pressing hard on the solids. Reserve the liquid, discarding the solids. Add the ketjap manis, mint leaves, and chile to taste.

9. To make the Rosemary-Orange Dipping Sauce, combine all the ingredients in the container of a blender or food processor. Process for 30 seconds. Pass through a fine sieve.

10. If possible, use large plates for this dish to show it off to best advantage. For each serving, arrange 5 rolls in a circle on top of the lettuce. Crisscross 2 of the lemongrass leaves on each plate. Garnish with a generous sprig of mint (and for the salmon rolls, a scattering of garlic or yellow chives). Provide each person with a small bowl of dipping sauce on the side.

SERVING SUGGESTIONS: With a protein-rich starter such as this one, I would opt for a Toss-Up of Red and Yellow Peppers with Crisp Water Chestnuts (page 175) and a ring of steamed sweet squash (either acorn or butternut would be my choice). End with some Grilled Pineapple and Banana in Sugarcane Juice Glaze, with Coconut Crunch Topping (page 230). Serve with cups of flowery jasmine tea.

Malaysian Melange   STARTER or STAR
Serves 4 as main dish; 6 as appetizer

Inspired by *rojak*, the intriguing Southeast Asian salad traditionally composed of tropical fruits and vegetables, with seafood my own elaboration, this dish is one that you can build around whatever produce looks best in your refrigerator. Rough versions can be found from Thailand south to Indonesia and at many points in between, with each cuisine adding its own subtle slant. In its native land, this is street-vendors' fare, born simple and served without fuss.

There are no hard-and-fast rules to be observed here. Simply purchase some raw shrimp in their shells as the starting point and then let your sense about color, texture, and taste take over from there. Just be sure to represent the citrus family with at least one member of what's seasonally best. Use the recipe only as a point of departure en route to a flight of fancy you can truly call your own. Without pretense of authenticity, there's no need to be rigorous in your specific selection of ingredients. Merely choose what's best and best priced in your market. Feel free to experiment with different combinations as new exotic fruits or vegetables catch your eye.

I like to serve this dish family-style for two reasons: first, to lighten the load of the cook, and second, to give each person the opportunity to design their own free-form confederation from the array of ingredients offered.

The unifying thread that ties this miscellany together is an addictive, somewhat sweet/sour, hot/mild dressing, touched with the barest hint of shrimp paste, which underlines the flavor of the fresh shrimp in the salad. I always like extra sauce on hand to enliven a host of other ethnically diverse dishes whose origins stray far from the Malaysian archipelago. (It will keep well, refrigerated, about a week.) Make it a day in advance to allow its exotic flavors to harmonize. Then adjust the balance of sweet to sour and hot to mild according to your mood. Serving this at room temperature allows the flavors of lushly ripe fruits to emerge clearly against the cooler, quieter backdrop of the vegetable components.

THE DRESSING:

    2" piece fresh galangal (see page 42), peeled, crushed slightly, and sliced into coins ½" thick

    2 tbsp. Tropical Vinegar (page 271) or white wine vinegar

    ¼ cup tamarind concentrate

    ½ cup ketjap manis (or substitute 6 tbsp. dark soy sauce combined with 2 tbsp. dark molasses)

    ½ tsp. shrimp paste (blacan from the Philippines or trasi from Malaysia and Indonesia)

    ½ tsp. sambal oelek (Indonesian chile paste)

    Salt and granulated sugar to taste

    2" piece gingerroot, peeled and sliced into coins ½" thick

    Zest of 1 medium lemon

THE SALAD:

    1½ lbs. medium shrimp, in their shells

    1 bunch bok choy, or 1 small head white cabbage, chopped (about 5 cups)

    1 large red bell pepper, sliced into long thin strips about ¼" wide

    1 large cucumber, peeled, seeded, and cut into ½" cubes

    1 cup cubed jícama (peeled and cut into ½" cubes)

    1 large pink grapefruit, peeled and sectioned, free of membrane or seeds

    1 large navel orange, peeled and sectioned, free of membrane or seeds

    1 cup fresh pineapple wedges (½" thick wedges)

    1 cup cubed fresh mango or papaya (peeled and cut into ½" cubes)

THE GARNISH:

   1 bunch fresh cilantro, leaves only

   Zest of 1 brightly colored lime, grated

   1 cup ground roasted peanuts

1. One day in advance of serving, make the dressing. Place galangal in a stainless steel or crockery bowl and mix with vinegar. Add tamarind, ketjap, shrimp paste, and sambal oelek, whisking to combine. Add just enough water to thin slightly. Add salt and sugar to taste. (The resulting dressing should leave a tart but not sour aftertaste; when combined with the intense sweetness of the fruits, sweet and tart should be in perfect balance.) Remove the galangal from the dressing before using.

2. Using a 2-quart pot, place the gingerroot and lemon zest in enough water to cover. Bring to a boil, reduce to a simmer, and add the shrimp. Cook just until the shells turn bright pink or red and the shrimp feel spongy to the touch, about 4–5 minutes. Do not overcook. Allow to cool in the liquid. Remove from liquid, peel and devein, and set aside.

3. Bring 2 quarts of water to a boil. Pour over the bok choy or cabbage and let stand until cool. Drain, refresh with cold water, and drain again. Dry and place on large decorative serving platter.

4. In concentric circles, arrange the prepared vegetables and fruits. Place the shrimp in the center. Decorate the border with cilantro leaves. Sprinkle grated lime zest and chopped peanuts over all. Serve the dressing separately in a sauceboat.

SERVING SUGGESTIONS: In small portions, this is a light but satisfying palate awakener before a meal of Village Baked Chicken with Pan-Crisped Noodles (page 150) or You Don't Have to Chiu This Chow (page 21), a spicy beef soup, Chinese immigrants' style. If neither poultry nor beef appeals to you, keep the palate in a perpetual state of excitement with small servings of Birds in the Bush (page 207), smoked pasta nests, piquantly sauced, preceding entree-sized portions of this room-temperature salad.

Witloof with Love–Braised Endive with Roasted Carrot Sauce

STARTER

Serves 4

Lettuces of many kinds have their place outside the salad bowl. Even after it's cooked, romaine, for instance, lends some of its sweet bite as a delicate wrapper for a velvety fish mousse, or as the main ingredient in a creamy pureed soup. Here endive, also known as witloof (from the Flemish for "white leaf"), with its sometimes overwhelming bitterness tamed by an aromatic braising, provides a contrasting sharpness to an almost candy-sweet sauce based merely on oven-roasted carrots and leeks. I like to double the recipe for the sauce, freeze the excess and then reap the dividends in a spin-off soup. Merely thin the extra sauce with a ladleful of Root Stock, add a handful of leftover cooked rice if you like, and with little effort, you'll have an any-season soup that nourishes the body as well as the soul.

1 large leek (about ½ lb.), split, well washed

4 medium carrots (about 1 lb. total), peeled

1 tbsp. fruity olive oil

2 cloves garlic, crushed and minced

4 large (or 8 small) Belgian endive, bottoms trimmed slightly

1 quart Root Stock (page 258)

1 cinnamon stick

2 whole cloves

1 bay leaf

Salt and freshly ground black pepper

1 bunch fresh thyme leaves, about ½ cup (discard stems)

1. Place the leek in a pot of boiling water, reduce the water to a simmer, and cook until just tender, about 7–10 minutes. Drain and refresh under cold running water; dry. Set aside one piece of leek measuring about ½" wide by 3" long cup to be used as a garnish.

2. Lightly coat the carrots with a teaspoon of the olive oil. Roast them along with the remaining leeks in a preheated 350° oven for about 20–25 minutes, turning to avoid

overbrowning. The leeks should be evenly golden brown and the carrots should be tender when tested with the point of a sharp knife.

3. Heat the remaining oil in a heavy skillet just until fragrant. On low heat, cook the garlic, stirring to coat evenly with the oil. Cook until aromatic but do not brown. Pour off any excess oil (reserve for another use) and add the endive. Turn to coat in the oil and then add the stock, cinnamon, cloves, bay leaf, salt, and pepper. Continue to cook until the endive is tender but still retains its shape. Remove the endive to an ovenproof plate and keep warm, covered. Sieve out solids from the skillet, reserving the liquid.

4. In a food processor or blender, puree the roasted carrots and leeks, adding the reserved braising liquid. Taste and adjust salt and pepper, if necessary.

5. Slice the reserved blanched leek into thin juliennes and set aside.

6. Mask 4 heated serving plates with a pool of the sauce. Arrange the endive on top of the sauce, spoon some of the remaining sauce over it, and garnish with the leek julienne. Scatter fresh thyme leaves over all.

SERVING SUGGESTIONS: Grilled swordfish on a skewer would be a strong follow-up to this forthright appetizer. As a side dish, half servings of Pasta Agrodolce (page 111) would keep the flavors bright but not too busy. End with a Grilled Fruit Salad (page 254) sauced with cranberries or raspberries, or lacking either, jarred lingonberries from Sweden.

Flavor Flash! *Tamarind*

An inimitable flavoring in foods from Mexico to India, and from Thailand and Indonesia to England, tamarind is sometimes known as the date of India. Other than the consistency and color that they share, dates and tamarind are at opposite flavor poles. The latter is as tart as the former is sweet.

The large tropical tamarind tree produces unlovely brownish pods that contain hard seeds coated with a fibrous fruity pulp. Shelf stable, it can be found in the more comprehensive Asian and Hispanic markets. It is sold in three main forms: dried in its original pods; in still-soft dehydrated bricks (both of which require a hot water bath and sieving to separate fiber and seeds from usable pulp), or in a thick concentrate that makes up for its somewhat duller flavor with its unsurpassed ease of use.

Despite a deep-seated resistance to most shortcut foods, I must admit that I am more apt to be inspired to find uses for tamarind when I can merely spoon it out of a jar. Whatever form you choose, use it to lend a pleasant tartness to everything from chutneys and sauces (Worcestershire sauce is the British connection) to soups and drinks. A little goes a long way, so buy it in small amounts.

Braised Eggplant with Pomegranate-Citrus Sauce

STARTER or SIDE

Serves 4

Keeping an open mind when shopping the ethnic groceries can often lead to some sparkling discoveries and stellar improvisatory cuisine. The quarry that I cornered one day in a large Middle Eastern market included a bag of dried Kaffir limes (*limoo*, in Persian) which certainly don't *look* promising but lend a complex, elusive fragrance to many braised dishes from traditional Persian cookery. (In their fresh form, the leaves and the peel from the Kaffir limes appear in the often tart, hot cooking of Thailand.) As luck would have it, just down the aisle stood row upon row of bottled pomegranate concentrate. I put a bottle in my shopping cart and then the wheels of creative cooking-in-the-mind started to turn. With a quick glance down the produce aisle, I spotted a beautiful array of glossy, fat eggplant (at a special price, no less), and I knew then that the dish was taking shape, long before it was cooked. When I finally got down to the actual cooking, the dish practically made itself.

The result of such a stroll is this uncommon treatment of a common vegetable in a dish that owes its appealing tartness to my wild pairing of ingredients, one bagged, the other bottled.

After a preliminary searing, the meaty, almost sweet slabs of eggplant become fork-tender courtesy of a slow braising in a vegetable stock-based sauce. For a final touch, this memorable interplay of contrasting tastes and textures is topped with caramelized walnuts and a chop of parsley. Whoever said that vegetables had to be boring could not have tasted this bit of delicious whimsy.

THE GARNISH:

    1 cup walnut halves (or large pieces)
    ½ cup sugar
    ¼ cup water
    Tasteless salad oil to coat surface for caramelized walnuts

    1½ lbs. eggplant, peeled
    Salt and freshly ground black pepper
    Fruity olive oil for searing the eggplant
    4 cloves garlic, crushed and thinly slivered
    2 cups (approx.) Root Stock (page 258)
    1 cup pomegranate concentrate
    2 dried Kaffir limes (*limoo*), soaked in boiling water for 10 minutes to soften, quartered
    Juice and zest, finely grated, of 1 lemon
    2 large firm ripe tomatoes, peeled, seeded, and cut into ½" cubes
    ½ cup finely chopped parsley leaves

1. To make the caramelized walnuts, toast the walnuts in a heavy skillet until evenly golden brown. In a heavy small saucepan, bring the sugar and water to a boil without stirring. When the syrup has turned a rich golden brown, immediately add the walnuts and swirl to coat evenly. Pour out onto a lightly oiled surface (preferably metal or marble) and let cool. When cool, break up the nut brittle into large bite-sized pieces (roughly ½" square). Set aside.

2. Cut the eggplant into thick slices ½" wide, then lightly salt and pepper them. Heat the oil in a heavy skillet and sear just to give the eggplant a well-browned surface on both sides. Remove to absorbent paper toweling and discard excess oil, if any, from the pan.

3. Add the garlic to the pan and cook over low heat, stirring, just to release its fragrance. Do not brown. Add the stock and pomegranate concentrate and bring to a boil. Add the eggplant and reduce the heat to low. Simmer covered for 15 minutes. (The liquid should cover the eggplant; if not, add more stock as needed.) Add the dried limes, lemon juice and zest, tomatoes, and salt and pepper to taste. Simmer for another 5 minutes, covered.

4. Remove and discard the limes. Transfer the eggplant and tomato to a serving platter and keep warm, covered, in a 200° oven. Reduce the pan juices to coating consistency.

5. Pour the reduced pan juices over the eggplant and garnish with caramelized walnuts and parsley.

SERVING SUGGESTIONS: Serve in generous portions with Ovenroast of Jumbled Grains with Tomato-Chile Coulis (page 73), or Mixed-Grain Pilaf with a Hint of Smoke (page 215) (no entree needed), or accompanying Rice-Crusted Whitefish with Dates and Lime (page 104). Follow with Suite of Pears in a Zingy Ginger Dunk (page 228) for a just-tart-enough finale.

Swordfish Yin Yang   STAR
Serves 4

Food and philosophy come together on the dinner plate in a dish where an artful balance of opposing elements is inspired by an Oriental duality as old as time: yin, the dark accepting element, and yang, the bright generating element. Here two sauces for grilled fish are the contrasting elements that interact, reinforcing each other to create a harmonious whole.

Sauced with a dark, highly concentrated, almost winey reduction of roasted root vegetable stock (the yin, if you will), thick slabs of quickly broiled fish are set atop a bright puree of uncooked yellow and orange tomatoes accented with red pepper (the yang). With each bite of the twice-sauced fish, flashes of flavor from bright and tart to sweet and intense mingle and explode in a kind of cinematic progression on the tongue.

If yellow and orange tomatoes are unavailable in your market, use a combination of canned tomato sauce brightened with an uncooked puree of the best red tomatoes you can find. The visuals won't be as riveting, but the overall taste contrasts should hold true. Insist on fish with as little darkened flesh (indicating bruising) as possible.

YIN, THE ROOT STOCK GLAZE:
  3 cups Root Stock (page 258; when making stock, roast vegetables first until evenly browned, for approximately 35 minutes in a 350° oven before adding remaining ingredients)
  Feathery tops from 1 bulb fennel
  1 tbsp. balsamic vinegar

YANG, THE TOMATO COULIS:
$1\frac{1}{2}$ lbs. yellow tomatoes
$1\frac{1}{2}$ lbs. orange tomatoes
1 large red pepper, roasted in 350° oven for 25 minutes, or until skin is evenly
    browned; then remove skin, seeds, and ribs
Salt and freshly ground white or black pepper

THE ACCOMPANYING ROASTED VEGETABLE MEDLEY:
Fruity olive oil for lightly coating the following before roasting:
    4 cloves garlic, crushed and finely chopped
    1 lb. eggplant, peeled, sliced into slabs $\frac{1}{2}$" thick
    1 fennel bulb, quartered

THE SWORDFISH:
$1\frac{1}{2}$ lbs. swordfish fillet, cut $\frac{1}{2}$" to $\frac{3}{4}$" thick, skin removed, cut into 4 equal pieces
Salt and freshly ground white or black pepper
Fruity olive oil to brush the broiling pan and the fish steaks lightly before broiling

TO LINE THE EDGES OF THE SERVING PLATTER:
1 lb. fresh spinach leaves, well washed

1. Prepare the Root Stock glaze by bringing the stock to a boil with the fennel tops and cooking over high heat for 5 minutes. Remove the fennel tops and continue cooking over moderate to high heat until the liquid is reduced to a coating consistency. Add the vinegar and set the glaze aside. Keep it warm over a pot of hot water.

2. Prepare the tomato coulis by dropping the yellow and orange tomatoes in a large pot of boiling water. Cook only until the skins have cracked. Drain and plunge into ice water to stop the cooking. Peel the tomatoes. Halve and then squeeze out excess juices and the seeds. Puree with the prepared red pepper in a blender or food processor until smooth. Adjust seasoning with salt and pepper as needed. Set aside and keep warm over a pot of hot water.

3. Lightly coat the garlic, eggplant, and fennel with the oil. Roast the fennel in a heavy skillet in a 350° oven for about 30 minutes. Add the eggplant and continue roasting for about 15 minutes more. Turn off oven, add the garlic to the skillet, cover it well, and keep it warm.

4. Line a broiler pan with aluminum foil brushed lightly with oil. Preheat broiler. Salt and pepper the fish and brush lightly with oil. Place the fish steaks on the broiler pan and cook for about 15 minutes, turning once after the first 10 minutes.

5. While the fish is cooking, blanch the spinach in a pot of boiling water. Drain, refresh in cold water, and dry. Arrange around the edge of a decorative platter. Pour the tomato coulis in the center of the platter. Carefully place the fish on the coulis. Drizzle with the Root Stock glaze. Garnish with the roasted vegetables.

SERVING SUGGESTIONS: I like to serve this with a pilaf of fragrant basmati rice lightly tinged with turmeric and topped with some thin slivers of fried leek or shallot. Conclude the meal on an especially intense note with thin slices of Ah! Sweet Mystery Torte (page 226) and strong coffee.

Hot Shrimp and Sweet Plantains with an Indonesian Tinge

STARTER or STAR

Serves 8 as an appetizer; 4 as an entree

Alone, the heat of *sambal oelek*, Indonesian chile paste, does a fast burn on the tongue and lips, whereupon your face lights up, sinuses clear, and you're ready to brave another bite. Although used sparingly here, it dominates a bright marinade-cum-sauce for shrimp, accented with a liberal dose of crushed garlic and pineapple juice and edged with a splash of dark soy and fresh lime juice.

Nestled in a bed of caramelized plantains for sweet contrast, grilled, lacquered shrimp almost glow with the slightly vinegary firepower of the sauce. Cooled by the creamy tropical fruit, the palate remains in a continual state of anticipation for the next heatwave.

Plan ahead here by allowing an overnight marination for the shrimp to absorb the full effect of the marinade and achieve the best melding of flavors. Be sure to use plump plantains with skins that are fully blackened, indicating perfect ripeness.

If you choose to confer star status on this dish, provide generous amounts of pan-crusted sticky rice to absorb the heat. In smaller portions, it's a perfect appetite-sparker on its own.

1 lb. large shrimp (about 16–20), peeled, deveined, well washed, and dried

THE MARINADE:

2 tbsp. sambal oelek

2 cups unsweetened pineapple juice

2 tbsp. dark soy sauce

6 cloves garlic, crushed and finely minced

1 tbsp. fresh lime juice

1 tsp. lemon juice

1 tsp. fruity olive oil to brush shrimp before grilling

Vegetable oil spray to coat grill lightly

THE CARAMELIZED PLANTAINS:

3 large plantains (about 2 lbs. total), peeled

1 tbsp. butter

½ cup brown sugar

¼ cup pure maple syrup

Freshly ground black pepper

THE GARNISH:

Few perfect leaves of cilantro

1. Butterfly the shrimp by making a shallow cut along the outside ridge of each one. Press to flatten slightly.

2. Combine the sambal oelek, pineapple juice, soy sauce, garlic, and citrus juices in a stainless steel or crockery bowl. Place shrimp in the marinade and refrigerate, covered, overnight.

3. Preheat the oven to 350°. Slice the plantains lengthwise and cut into 2" lengths. Coat a heavy 10" skillet with the butter. Place the plantains in a single layer in the pan. Combine the brown sugar with the maple syrup and pour over the plantains. Bake at 350° for approximately 20–25 minutes, or until the plantains are tender. Briefly place the pan under a preheated broiler to caramelize the surface of the fruit. Watch carefully to avoid burning. Season to taste with freshly ground black pepper. Keep warm, covered lightly with foil, in a 200° oven.

4. Remove shrimp from marinade and pat dry. Sieve the marinade and reduce over high heat in a small heavy saucepan until it lightly coats a spoon. This should take about 10 minutes. Reserve and keep warm.

5. Brush shrimp lightly with the olive oil. Spray grill or stovetop grill pan with vegetable oil and heat until a drop of water evaporates almost instantly when dropped on the surface. Cook the shrimp 1–2 minutes on each side, or until just opaque and slightly springy to the touch. Do not overcook or they will toughen.

6. To serve as an entree, center the plantains in a low pyramidal shape on each of 4 heated serving plates. Arrange 4 shrimp like the spokes of a wheel on top of the plantains and spoon the sauce evenly over the shrimp. To serve as an appetizer, arrange the shrimp and plantains similarly in 8 equal portions. Pour sauce evenly over the shrimp. Accent the center of each arrangement with a cilantro leaf.

SERVING SUGGESTIONS: Precede this entree with a Warm "Salad" of Watercress, Arugula, and Roasted Red Pepper (page 174). Finish with a refreshing frozen persimmon or mango "sorbet," made by simply freezing perfectly ripe fruit first cut into halves (skin on) and then letting them thaw enough in the refrigerator to allow a spoon to easily scrape this nonfat treat.

Rice-Crusted Whitefish with Dates and Lime   STAR
Serves 4

The Persian pantry ranges from the basic to the sublime. On one shelf sits a large bag of basmati or jasmine rice. Other shelves hold treasures like fat Medjool dates (particularly in winter), dried limes, and bottles of pomegranate syrup and quince preserves.

Enchanted by this colorful array and the Persian partiality for the freshwater lake fish resembling whitefish, I devised this recipe to celebrate several of these standout ingredients at once. Dates fill a sweet pocket cut into the fillets, rice becomes the crisp surface, and lime (in three forms) combines with dry herbal vermouth and tomato to flavor a tart sauce that balances the rich flesh of the fish perfectly. Ginger, garlic, and cinnamon each adds its own fragrant dimension to the dish.

Shop a reliable source and select fish with firm flesh, sparkly skin, and a pristinely fresh smell. If possible, prepare this with some of the fresh crop of gargantuan Medjool dates that appear in late fall or early winter. Date-lovers already know this pleasure; others, new to the fresh date experience, are bound to be converted. Buy some extras to eat out of hand. (I always freeze a generous bunch for off-season delectation.)

THE STUFFING:

4 oz. Medjool dates (or other moist whole variety), pitted and roughly chopped
3" long cinnamon stick, freshly ground (about ½ tsp.)

1½– 2 lbs. whitefish fillets, skin removed, cut into 4 equal portions
Salt and freshly ground white pepper
Flour for dredging fish

THE RICE CRUST:

1½ cups water
1 cup basmati or jasmine rice
½ tsp. salt
2 egg whites

Olive oil to sauté the fish

THE SAUCE:

1 tbsp. finely minced gingerroot
3 medium cloves garlic, crushed, and finely minced
Juice of ½ lemon (about 2 tbsp.)
Juice of 1 lime (about 1 tbsp.)
Zest of 1 lime, grated
1 dried Kaffir lime (*limoo*), soaked in hot water for 10 minutes, drained and then
    halved
¼ cup extra-dry vermouth
1 tbsp. sugarcane vinegar or Date-Lime Vinegar (page 273)
1 large fresh tomato, skinned, seeded, roughly chopped (about 1 cup)

THE GARNISH:

4 large dates, pitted
2 tsp. finely chopped fresh parsley

1. Gently mix the 4 oz. dates and cinnamon in a small bowl. Wash the fish under cold running water and dry well on absorbent paper toweling. Lightly salt and pepper the fish. Cut a wide pocket in the thickest part of each fillet. Stuff with the date mixture. (If you have more stuffing than can fit into the fish, place in the dish along with the fish before placing in the warming oven.) Dredge fish lightly on both sides with flour. Set aside, refrigerated.

2. Bring the water to a boil and add the rice and ½ tsp. salt. Cook over medium heat in a covered heavy saucepan for about 12–15 minutes, or until the rice is tender and all the cooking liquid has been absorbed. When done, let sit covered until cool, about 15–20 minutes.

3. Combine the cooked rice with the egg whites. Coat the side of each fish fillet where the skin has been removed with the rice mixture, pressing the rice into the fish to make sure that it adheres. Set aside.

4. Heat oil in a large heavy skillet. When hot, place the fish fillets, rice-coated side down. Cook uncovered for about 7 minutes, or until the rice coating is set and golden brown. Carefully turn the fillets over and continue cooking for an additional 5–8 minutes, or until fish is firm and opaque throughout. Remove to an ovenproof dish and keep warm in a 200° oven.

5. Using the skillet in which you cooked the fish (wiped of excess oil, but not washed), first cook the gingerroot and garlic over low heat, stirring constantly to avoid browning. Add the lemon juice, lime juice and zest, Kaffir lime, vermouth, and vinegar and cook for 5 minutes over medium heat, stirring to loosen any browned particles that cling to the skillet. Remove the kaffir lime halves and discard. Add the tomato and cook for 5 minutes or until the liquid is reduced by half but the tomatoes are still visible as rough chunks.

6. Pour some of the sauce on each of 4 heated serving plates. Center the fish on the sauce. Garnish with a whole pitted date, dipped in the finely chopped parsley.

SERVING SUGGESTIONS: My Fave Favas (page 87), with their well-balanced tartness, would be a suitable introduction to this entree. Some sweet steamed acorn or butternut squash would be a welcome side dish. Finish the meal with Broiled Oranges with Brown Sugar-Lime Glaze (page 255), or fresh seedless grapes drizzled with orange-flower water or ice-cold eau-de-vie (pear or raspberry are breathtaking here).

Warm Compote of Sweet Potato and Tart Apple in a Tamarind Sauce

SIDE

Serves 4

The alternating rounds of deep-orange sweet potato and rings of poached apple used here perfectly define for me the embodiment of fall—a worthy, if somewhat untraditional, entrant on the Thanksgiving table, hearty and profoundly satisfying. In this version of a dish that does not betray its simple casserole origins as the *tzimmes* found in Jewish cookery, tartness comes in two forms: plump prunes, a traditional tzimmes ingredient, here lending texture, too; and prepared tamarind concentrate, an escapee from the Mexican and Southeast Asian pantries, which adds its characteristic tang and dark tone to a shiny sepia-colored sauce. All this tartness is nicely offset by a touch of honey and aromatic whole spices. The dish emerges capped off with a layer of toasty hazelnut crunch for good measure. Whatever the season, this is fare to give thanks for.

2 lbs. sweet potatoes, preferably with deep orange flesh

1 tbsp. honey

½ cup water

8 whole cloves

1 cinnamon stick

2 medium-sized tart apples, cored and cut into rounds (Greenings or Granny Smiths work best)

6 large pitted prunes, halved

1½ tsp. tamarind concentrate

Salt and freshly ground black pepper

THE GARNISH:

½ cup hazelnuts, toasted in a 350° oven until the skins are loosened, about 10 minutes, then skinned and roughly chopped

1. Steam the sweet potatoes, in a tightly covered steamer, until tender, about 25–35 minutes.

2. Bring the honey, water, cloves, and cinnamon stick to a boil in a small saucepan. Reduce the heat to a simmer and add the rings of apple, poaching until just tender,

about 5 minutes. Do not overcook or the fruit will be mushy. Remove the apples to a plate to cool. Place the prune halves in the hot poaching liquid and allow them to plump for about 8–10 minutes. Remove the prunes and set side. Sieve the poaching liquid, discarding the solids, and add the tamarind concentrate, cooking in a heavy saucepan over medium heat until slightly thickened. Add salt and pepper to taste. Set the sauce aside and keep it warm, covered.

3. Peel the sweet potatoes and slice them into ½" thick rounds. On a decorative heated round or oval serving platter, arrange them in concentric circles alternating with the apple slices. Scatter the prune halves as you wish over the potatoes and apples. Drizzle the sauce over all and liberally shower the dish with hazelnuts. Serve hot or warm.

SERVING SUGGESTIONS: Other than the obvious, large avian centerpiece for which this would be an apt accompaniment, this dish would complement Smoky Chicken Packets Steamed in Banana Leaves (page 190); or, lightly sauced, it could play Jack Sprat to Madame Sprat's Pan-Grilled Foie Gras with Cassis-Vinegar Sauce (page 177).

Petti di Pollo Semiamaro   STAR
Serves 4

With their slightly bittersweet personality (*semiamaro*, in Italian), fresh artichokes lend flavor and zing to many Mediterranean dishes. (Make this in late spring when fresh artichokes are plentiful and cheap.) Here, caramelized roasted onions combine with Campari, that bright-red, bitter Italian aperitif, to power the sauce for a vibrant chicken dish that's both bitter and sweet and features a generous handful of small fresh artichoke hearts.

   If you can find baby chickens or guinea hens, use them here. They may be found at kosher meat markets or upscale health food stores (two will serve four). Small artichokes will cook at the same rate as the smaller, more tender chickens, producing an elegant entree with a cooking time of less than 45 minutes from start to finish. If you can rely on a frozen cache of Root Stock, the preparation time will be slashed even more. If not, a quick brown stock from the backs, necks, and wing tips of the chicken will yield a sauce of rich color and flavor.

If you can find it, Cynar, another Italian aperitif, based on the essence of artichokes, would be an ideal substitute for the Campari.

1 quart Root Stock (page 258); or brown chicken stock (see steps 1 and 2 below)
2 small chickens or guinea hens (or one 3–4 lb. whole frying chicken or 2 Cornish
    hens)

THE BROWN CHICKEN STOCK:
Reserved backs, necks, and wing tips from above
Water
½ tsp. dried oregano
½ tsp. dried thyme
1 cup roughly chopped carrot
1 cup roughly chopped celery
1 cup roughly chopped onion

THE DREDGE:
Flour
Salt and freshly ground black pepper
Pinch cayenne

4 small fresh artichokes
Juice of 1 lemon
Fruity olive oil
4 large cloves garlic, finely minced
2 medium onions, peeled, brushed lightly with olive oil, and roasted in 350° oven
    until tender and browned, about 30 minutes, and then pureed in a blender or
    food processor until smooth
½ cup Campari (or Cynar)
Salt and freshly ground black pepper
Granulated sugar, to taste, if needed

THE GARNISH:
½ bunch fresh parsley leaves, washed well and dried, finely chopped

1. Cut the chickens in half. Remove the wing tips, legs, and thighs. (Reserve the legs and thighs for another use, or simply roast for another use while the breasts complete their cooking in the oven.)

2. To make the chicken stock, brown the reserved backs, necks, and wing tips in a heavy ovenproof saucepan in a 400° oven for about 25 minutes. Remove from the oven and add water to cover, along with seasonings. Cook at a simmer for about 30 minutes. Sieve out and discard the solids and set aside the liquid to be used later for the sauce. (Do not add salt or pepper to the stock at this point.)

3. Dredge the chicken breasts with the first joint of the wing attached in the flour mixed with salt, pepper, and cayenne. Set aside.

4. Cut off the top inch of the artichokes and discard. Remove the fuzzy choke from the artichoke halves and then trim the leaves surrounding the heart, leaving only the heart with the artichoke stem attached. Drop into a bowl of water to which lemon juice has been added. Set aside.

5. In a heavy skillet, heat a thin coating of olive oil. When hot, brown the chicken over moderately high heat, turning once after the first 8 minutes. Brown on the other side and remove from the pan.

6. Pour any excess fat from the skillet, add the garlic and cook, stirring, for about 1 minute. Do not brown. Add the stock and the onion puree and deglaze the pan to loosen any browned bits that adhere to it. Add the Campari, and over medium heat, carefully flame it to cook out the alcohol (stand well back from the pan at this point). When the flames subside, add the browned chicken and artichoke hearts, drained and dried. Place the skillet, covered, in a 350° oven for about 20–25 minutes, or until the chicken tests done and the artichokes are tender. Remove the chicken and the artichokes to a heated serving platter, keeping it warm and covered in a 200° oven, and reduce the sauce, as necessary, on the stovetop over medium heat to a coating consistency. Taste the sauce and adjust salt and pepper, adding sugar if the sauce tastes too tart for your liking. Pour over the chicken and garnish with the chopped parsley.

SERVING SUGGESTIONS: I like to build up to this dish with a warm starter of Golden Melting Moments (page 144), medallions of goat cheese in a bright and perky gazpacho sauce, and then present crusty triangles of grilled or broiled polenta, a firm cornmeal porridge, to accompany it. A Merlot would be liquid velvet with this.

Pasta Agrodolce

STAR, STARTER, or SIDE

Serves 6 as an appetizer or side dish; 4 as an entree

T he only thing thin here is the pasta. Long strands of spaghettini are the delicate foil for a contrastingly robust sauce where roughly chopped tomatoes help to define the *agro* or bitter dimension and a shot of balsamic vinegar adds a darkly tart tinge. On the *dolce* side, roasted garlic and caramelized red onion sweetly announce their presence. The whole, under a blizzard of fine Parmesan cheese, adds up to a balanced, richly flavored dish whose main ingredients first formed the basis for an improvisatory salad I chanced to devise when, aside from fresh garden-picked Roma tomatoes, neither the refrigerator nor the pantry held much that seemed promising.

10 large cloves garlic

1 lb. red onions, unpeeled

Fruity olive oil

2 lbs. ripe Roma (or plum) tomatoes, peeled, seeded, excess juice squeezed out

2 tbsp. balsamic vinegar

Salt and freshly ground black pepper

1½ lbs. fresh spaghettini, capellini, or fedelini pasta (dried imported varieties from Italy are usually reliable)

THE GARNISH:

Freshly grated Parmesan, to taste

1. Brush the garlic and red onions lightly with the oil. Place in a 350° oven and roast until golden brown and just tender. (The garlic should take about 20 minutes; the onions should be nicely caramelized and soft after about 35 minutes.) As they are done, remove from the oven and set aside.

2. Peel the garlic and mash into a rough paste. Peel and chop the onion into rough ½" pieces. Chop the tomato roughly. Place the garlic, onion, and tomato in a heavy 2-quart saucepan and cook over high heat just until most of the liquids evaporate. Add the vinegar and cook over medium heat for about 2 minutes more. Add salt and pepper to taste. Set aside and keep warm, covered.

3. Bring a large pot of lightly salted water to a boil. Add the pasta, stirring, and cook until just tender. When properly cooked, the pasta should retain a bit of its firmness. Do not overcook. Drain and serve mounded on heated serving plates or serve fami-

ly style on a large, decorative heated serving platter. Spoon a generous portion of sauce over the pasta and pass the grated cheese for use at the discretion of each diner.

SERVING SUGGESTIONS: Born simple, perhaps, but as a side or starter, this dish gets along fine with more complex mates such as Poblano Pepper Pilaf (page 45) or Pepper-Crusted Turkey Steak (page 65). As the main event, I like to start with a Fennel-Orange Salad (page 18) or Warm "Salad" of Watercress, Arugula, and Roasted Red Pepper (page 174). For a fine ending, something citrus like Lime Flan with Cajeta Sauce (page 246) or Broiled Oranges with Brown Sugar-Lime Glaze (page 255) ensures a smooth transition from bittersweet to sweet.

Flavor Flash!
Herbal Thirst Quencher

When you crave a hot-weather cooler with a kick, try mixing some fresh lemon juice sweetened with a touch of sugar and a handful of crushed fresh herbs of your choice (basil and rosemary are on the top of my list). Add water and ice cubes to fill the glass. Then top it off with a splash of balsamic vinegar. Stir, sit back, and relax. For me the pleasantly bittersweet tang imparted by the vinegar quenches like no other summer beverage.

Sweet-and-Sour Braised Fennel with Roasted Tomato Sauce

STARTER or SIDE

Serves 4

Two sauces, one edged with the mellow sweetness of carrots and caramelized onion, and the other rough-and-ready, play equally supporting roles in this celebration of a versatile though underused vegetable. Presented like an almost fully opened large cabbage rose, afloat in some of its braising stock that has been reduced, fennel here takes on two personalities, presenting a bit of each in every mouthful.

Whether served hot, warm, or at room temperature (all the components may be made in advance for a last-minute assembly, each served at a different temperature if you'd like), this dish accords a place of honor to a vegetable that deserves an audience wider than that created by those Mediterranean cooks of endless invention who already understand its virtues. I hope you'll be converted.

Even in a small garden, Florentine fennel is particularly rewarding to grow from seed; its ease of cultivation places it on the top of my list for spring planting. Its wispy presence poking through the soil almost seems to say, "You must believe in spring."

Here is one vegetable that rewards at every stage of its growth; when the feathery tops reach about 3"–4", I snip some to add last-minute flavor to a broth or salad; picking the immature bulbs when they are about the thickness of scallions is one time when I'm not conflicted about that often painful but necessary process of thinning out the rows of emerging plants. I like to poach these briefly in an herbal vegetable stock, and then serve them cold with a sharp, mustardy vinaigrette for a sparkling spring appetizer. (See Superb Sources, pages 289–292, for seeds to get you started.)

> 1 large fennel bulb (about 1 lb.), top stalk removed and reserved
> Juice of 1 lemon

THE BRAISING BROTH:

> 1 large yellow or brown onion, unpeeled
> 2 quarts water
> 4 medium carrots, roughly chopped (about 2 cups)
> 2 stalks celery, roughly chopped (about 1 cup)
> Fennel stalks from above tops (reserve the feathery part for garnish)
> 4 cloves garlic, crushed
> 2 bay leaves
> 1 tbsp. whole black peppercorns, crushed
> 2" piece gingerroot
> 6 whole allspice
> 1 tsp. cuminseed
> 1 tsp. dill seeds
> 1 tsp. fennel seeds
> ½ cup white wine vinegar
> Salt to taste

THE ROASTED TOMATO SAUCE:

> 1 lb. highly flavored, ripe, red tomatoes, cored
> 1 medium leek, both white and green parts, well washed, roughly chopped
>   (about 2 cups)
> ¼ cup roughly chopped red bell pepper
> 2 tbsp. fruity olive oil
> ½ tsp. salt

THE GARNISH:

Feathery part of fennel stalk, chopped

1. With a small sharp knife, carefully remove the cone-shaped core from the bottom of the fennel bulb and discard. Place the bulb in water to cover (to which the lemon juice has been added).

2. Make the braising stock by first roasting the onion, halved, in a 400° oven until well browned, about 35 minutes. The skin should be darkened and the onion very soft. Roughly chop it and place along with the water, vegetables, herbs, aromatics, and vinegar in a large heavy saucepan with a cover. Bring to a boil, reduce the heat to a simmer, cover, and cook for about 35–40 minutes, or until vegetables are tender. Place the whole fennel bulb in the stock and simmer until tender, about 30 minutes. Allow to cool. Remove the fennel to a plate. (If you are making this in advance of serving and wish to serve the dish hot or warm, the fennel may be reheated in a 200° oven.) Pour the stock through a fine sieve and return it to a clean saucepan. Cook over high heat until reduced to a light coating consistency, about the viscosity of maple syrup. Set aside.

3. Make the roasted tomato sauce by placing the tomatoes, leek, and red pepper all coated lightly with the olive oil on a heavy baking sheet. Roast in a preheated 350° oven for about 50 minutes. The tomato and leeks should be browned and tender. When done, puree in a food processor or blender until almost smooth, adding salt. A bit of texture adds personality to the sauce.

4. Pour the reduced braising liquid into a decorative shallow bowl, to a depth of about 1 inch. Arrange the fennel like an open flower, starting with the outer "petals," over-lapping each layer of petals slightly and working toward the center until all the leaves are used. Drizzle some of the tomato sauce over the tips of each "petal," serving the remainder in a sauceboat. Garnish with the feathery part of the fennel stalk.

SERVING SUGGESTIONS: I like to offer this in a smorgasbord of small dishes that includes (but is not limited to) the following: Smoked Seafood Spring Rolls (page 211), My Fave Favas (page 87), Wild Rice Pancakes (page 187), and A Caper of Oven-Roasted Beets (page 158). A less international but more orthodox approach might pair this with an entree such as Broiled Trout Aegean (page 4) or Gilded Chicken with Lemon Confiture (page 13).

Hot, Sweet, and Tart Sea Bass with Coconut Jasmine Rice

STAR

Serves 4

Here's an eclectic fish dish that takes the most accessible flavors of Thai and Vietnamese cuisine and applies a French cooking technique, sauce reduction, to concentrate these flavors down to their essence. At the base of the sauce is a native of Southeast Asia, fresh pineapple, with all its lush sweet-sour intensity, used here as a kind of untraditional crucible that unites and ultimately transforms an array of signature ingredients into a cohesive whole from these twin cuisines. Relying on a lavish use of lemongrass, basil, mint, cilantro, and chile (in two forms, fresh and bottled in a sweet sauce), the exuberant sauce for the fish spells, for me, tropical with a capital T. Fragrant jasmine rice from Thailand, cooked with some unsweetened coconut milk, offers a snowy white canvas against which the bold flavors of the entree can be experienced.

Don't feel limited to sea bass if striped bass, halibut, or some other moist, firm-fleshed fish looks and smells good. When buying the pineapple, check for ripeness by consulting your nose. Even overripe fruit is preferable to green, rock-hard specimens that are sure to be tasteless.

1¼ lbs. sea bass fillet, preferably in one piece

Salt and freshly ground white pepper

½ cup Roasted Rice Powder (page 51)

1 tsp. Kaffir lime powder

Oil

THE SAUCE:

1½ cups fresh pineapple puree (from 1 large peeled and cored pineapple), passed
   through a fine sieve to remove any solid fiber

1 large bunch lemongrass, thick root ends crushed to release flavor

1 bunch fresh basil, roughly chopped (reserve a few sprigs)

1 bunch fresh mint, roughly chopped (reserve a few sprigs)

1 bunch fresh cilantro, roughly chopped (reserve a few sprigs)

2 tbsp. Tropical Vinegar (page 271) or rice vinegar

2 tsp. fish sauce

1 tsp. (or more, to taste) Thai sweet chile sauce (*num chim kai* in Thai or *nuoc cham ga* in Vietnamese)

1 fresh red Thai chile, ribs and seeds removed, finely chopped

1 fresh green chile (jalapeño or serrano), ribs and seeds removed, finely chopped

THE RICE:

2 cups jasmine rice

2 cups water

1 cup unsweetened coconut milk (or substitute Mock Coconut Milk, page 267, if desired)

½ tsp. salt

THE GARNISH:

A few sprigs of basil, mint, and cilantro reserved from above

1. Wash and dry the fish. Salt and pepper it. Mix the rice powder and the Kaffir lime powder and coat the fish evenly with the mixture. Set aside.

2. In a heavy 2-quart saucepan, bring the pineapple puree to a boil. Add all of the lemongrass, and half each of the basil, mint, and cilantro. Cook at a simmer for about 20 minutes to infuse flavors. Sieve to remove the solids and set aside.

3. Heat enough oil to coat the bottom of a heavy skillet until almost smoking. Carefully place the fish in the pan and cook for 3 minutes on each side. The surface of the fish should be golden brown. Place pan in a 350° oven to finish the cooking, about 15 minutes, or until the fish is opaque but still moist. While the fish is in the oven, cook the rice.

4. Over low heat, cook the jasmine rice in a covered, heavy 3-quart saucepan with the water, coconut milk, and salt for about 18 minutes, or until all the liquid has been absorbed. Let stand, covered, for 5 minutes more. Leaving a 1" margin all around, spoon the rice evenly on a heated serving platter. Center the fish on the rice and keep warm, covered, in a 200° oven while the sauce is being finished.

5. Add the sieved pineapple-herb liquid, the vinegar, and the fish sauce to the pan in which the fish was cooked and deglaze over high heat, scraping with a wooden spoon to dislodge any browned particles that cling to the pan. Continue to cook until the sauce is of light coating consistency. Add the remaining basil, mint, and

cilantro, the chile sauce, and the fresh chiles and cook for 30 seconds more. Pour the sauce over the fish. Garnish with the reserved herbs.

SERVING SUGGESTIONS: For a menu that is purely oriented to the East, start with a salad of Chilled Chinese Crunch (page 43) and end with Tropical Times Two (page 232), a cross-cultural coupe of intensely caffeinated Vietnamese coffee ice cream, served with lush mango sauce. A plate of crisp sesame biscotti would finish things off in high style.

Indian Potato Salad, Street-Food Style   STARTER or SIDE

Serves 4

Cubes of boiled potato are a tender, cooling foil here for three distinct sauces, one hot, one somewhat sweet, and one truly tart. This version veers somewhat from its irresistible Indian model, *papri chat,* in its rather unorthodox second and third sauces.

The first sauce, a pourable, heat-adjustable herbal chutney of sorts, hews basically to Indian tradition and combines cilantro with green chiles; the second, edged with mint, pairs ripe sweet pear with tart tamarind and vinegar; the third sauce is merely Thickened Yogurt (page 265), diluted yet enriched slightly with buttermilk and spiked with roasted cumin and coriander seeds.

With its components easily made-in-advance, here's a dish that is a cinch to assemble at the last minute as part of an international picnic with or without a kitchen close at hand.

2 lbs. russet or Idaho potatoes, peeled and cut into ½"–¾" cubes

THE CILANTRO SAUCE:

1½ bunches fresh cilantro, about 2 cups when tightly compacted

Green chiles to taste (seeded for less heat, if you prefer)

1" piece gingerroot, peeled

2 whole cloves garlic, peeled

Water

Salt to taste

THE PEAR CHUTNEY:

1½ cups cubed ripe but firm pears, peeled, cored, and cut into ½" cubes (fragrant Comice or Bartletts work best)

1 tbsp. tamarind concentrate

1" piece gingerroot, peeled, minced

2 tbsp. white vinegar

½ cup sugar

¼ cup chopped fresh mint leaves

Salt

THE YOGURT SAUCE:

1 cup Thickened Yogurt (page 265)

½ cup (approx.) buttermilk

½ cup cucumber, cubed, peeled, seeded (cut into ½" cubes)

1½ tsp. cuminseed

2 tsp. coriander seeds

Salt to taste

FOR THE PRESENTATION:

Large romaine lettuce leaves, washed and dried

Whole leaves of radicchio or red chard, washed and dried

THE GARNISH:

Mixture of fresh coriander and mint leaves

Mixed roasted cumin and coriander seeds, reserved from above

1. Cook the cubes of potato in a pot of boiling water for about 10 minutes, or until just tender. Drain and refresh under cold running water. Drain and set aside. (If you wish, the potatoes can be steamed instead.)

2. For the cilantro sauce, in a food processor or blender puree the cilantro, chiles, gingerroot, and garlic until smooth, adding just enough water to make a sauce of pourable consistency. Add salt to taste.

3. For the pear chutney, in a small heavy saucepan over medium heat, cook the pears, tamarind, gingerroot, vinegar, and sugar until slightly thickened, about 15 minutes.

Sieve out the pears and reserve. Cook the liquid further until it is reduced to a thick syrup, about 5 minutes more, being careful not to burn the mixture. Combine with the reserved pears. Add the mint and salt to taste. Set aside.

4. In a heavy skillet, toast the cumin and coriander seeds just until fragrant and lightly browned. Do not burn or they will taste bitter. Allow to cool slightly and grind in a coffee or spice grinder. Reserve half of the spices for garnish. For the yogurt sauce, dilute the yogurt with enough buttermilk to achieve an almost pourable mixture. Blend in the cucumbers and the remaining spices. Add salt to taste.

5. To assemble, mound the potatoes on a platter lined with alternating leaves of romaine and radicchio or red chard. Drizzle a ribbon of the cilantro sauce around the potatoes. Spoon the pear chutney evenly over the potatoes. Accent with ribbons of the yogurt sauce. Scatter the coriander and mint leaves over the salad. Sprinkle the spices evenly over all.

SERVING SUGGESTIONS: I like to serve this as a provocative lead-in to Sumatran Salmon with Honey Glaze (page 41) or make it the room-temperature entry on a meatless hot buffet including your choice of the following: Bitter Greens in a Honey-Lemon Drizzle (page 25), Seurat's Cauliflower (page 88), or Carrots Slow and Sweet (page 127).

Flavor Flash!
Impromptu Chutney

Who says chutneys have to be laborious, long-cooking sauces with precise combinations of ingredients? All you need are 6 basic ingredients: fresh fruits (check the fruit bin in your refrigerator for odd bits and pieces of apple, banana, cut-up melon, or pineapple), some aromatic spices (like ground cinnamon, cloves, allspice, and mace, often available in a jar labeled "Indian milk spice"), onion, garlic, sugar, and vinegar. If you're really pressed you can forget the onion and garlic and merely combine 1 lb. fruit and 1 tbsp. spices with enough sugar and vinegar to achieve the desired balance of sweet and tart. Cook in a heavy saucepan for about 7 minutes over medium heat. There you have it—a wonderfully simple enhancement for the simplest cold chicken or roast or humble turkey burger or meatloaf, great just out of the pot or chilled.

For another chutney choice from the seemingly limitless possibilities, see the recipe for Date-Tomato Chutney (next).

Date-Tomato Chutney
Makes approximately 1 pint

Inspired by the chance union of choice dates and lime zest in an infusion that became Date-Lime Vinegar, I devised another fruity, mellow version of chutney that combines arguably the sweetest fruit, the date, with the sourest, the lime, with some tomato mediating. In this one, the dates take the place of refined sugar. I find that using the Date-Lime Vinegar amplifies the fruity flavor of the resulting chutney.

1 lb. red ripe tomatoes (cherry tomatoes work well)

6 oz. soft pitted dates

¼ cup Date-Lime Vinegar (page 273), or white wine vinegar

2" piece gingerroot, peeled and minced

2 cloves garlic, crushed and minced

Juice of ½ lime (about 1½–2 tbsp.)

Freshly ground chile powder

In a heavy 2-quart saucepan, bring the tomatoes, dates, and vinegar to a boil. Pass through a sieve, pressing hard on the solids, and return the sieved mixture to the saucepan, discarding the solids. Add the gingerroot and garlic and simmer the mixture over low heat for about 20 minutes or until thickened, stirring occasionally to avoid burning. Add the lime juice and chile powder to taste. Allow to cool. Store in the refrigerator in a glass jar with a tight-fitting lid. This will keep well for at least a month if refrigerated.

CHAPTER 4

Intentionally Intense

FLAVORS FRONT AND CENTER

In describing one nonpareil meal she had enjoyed in Marseilles, M. F. K. Fisher rhapsodized in *A Considerable Town* about foods that define the modus operandi of this chapter. "There was one place on the Rive Neuve . . . an oasis of elegance. . . . The food was among the best of my life, and best served. It seemed to leap from the sea to the plate, with one quick pause in midair over the chef's enchanted kitchen." Using that mythical meal as a touchstone, I've created these recipes for foods that arrive on the plate almost spontaneously with seemingly little intervention from the cook.

With a strong palette of Key Ingredients that includes highly perfumed tropical fruits, ripened cheeses in their prime, fresh herbs, and luxury foods like caviar and foie gras lending their own special magic, the time-pressed cook can create dishes of stunning flavor with relatively little effort. In fact, the best approach when using these ingredients is the most straightforward approach. The goal here is to allow foods to taste like themselves, sensitively enhancing rather than masking their inherent flavors and personalities.

Here you will find recipes for some hauntingly memorable and diverse dishes like Deep, Dark, and Ducky (page 156), which pairs braised duck with grapes and peppercorns, and, in an updated version of a classic, Arugula "Caesar" with Polenta Croutons (page 146). These represent just one shake of the kaleidoscope of intentionally intense flavors that lie ahead in this chapter. I invite you to indulge.

Key Ingredients

Creating flavors that are haunting and memorable, not quick to fade from your taste memory, these ingredients star in the recipes where they appear. They are front and center and pleasantly so.

ANCHOVIES

ARUGULA—*roquette* in French; *rucola* in Italian; a salad green easy to grow from seed; plant every few weeks for a continuous crop from spring to summer, and pick young for a pleasantly peppery bite; I don't let them go beyond 5" or 6" before harvesting; older and taller, they bite back

BASIL, FRESH

BERRIES, FRESH—summer blackberries, raspberries, and strawberries usually are the most highly perfumed

CAVIAR—the real thing, Iranian or Russian sturgeon roe, in varying grades at varying prices, from pearl gray to almost black

CARDAMOM—the seed pod of a cousin to ginger, available as seeds or in powdered form (often used in Scandinavian pastries); seed-containing green or black pods are available in Indian and Asian groceries

CHEESES—including goat and blue varieties

CHOCOLATE, DARK—Swiss is most intense

CINNAMON (AND ITS RELATED CASSIA)—whole sticks and ground

COCONUT, FRESH, and **COCONUT MILK** (fresh or canned)—the canned or flat plastic pouch variety is often found in freezer cases of ethnic markets, not to be confused with sweetened coconut milk

CORIANDER, FRESH—also known as cilantro or Chinese parsley

CORIANDER SEEDS

CUMIN—ubiquitous in curry spice mixes and a staple in Mexican cooking; particularly fragrant when its seeds are freshly roasted and then ground

DATES—the new harvest appears on the market early fall to late winter; look for giant Medjools and round Barhis (honey dates)

DILL, FRESH

FIGS, fresh or dried

FISH SAUCE—found in Asian groceries labeled variously as *nuoc mam, nam pla,* or *patis*

FOIE GRAS (duck or goose liver)—French, American, Israeli; see Superb Sources, page 290)

FRUITS, TROPICAL—in the form of frozen purees; available at Latin American and Southeast Asian markets

GARLIC, FRESH—who can do without it?

KETJAP MANIS—Indonesian sweetened soy sauce

LAVENDER HONEY—the French variety from Provence is worth the search

MAPLE SYRUP, pure

MINT, FRESH

MOLASSES

NUTMEG, freshly grated

OYSTER SAUCE—thick, soy sauce-based liquid flavored with oyster essence

PASSION FRUIT—juice, puree, or concentrate; fresh, frozen, or bottled

PEPPERS, YELLOW BELL

PINEAPPLE, fresh or dried

SAKANJABIIN—a Middle Eastern bottled syrup made of mint, vinegar, sugar, and water (see Flavor Flash!, page 86)

SALMON ROE—large pink pearls; a more economical substitute for pricier sturgeon roe

SESAME PASTE—rich brown, made from well-toasted sesame seeds

SESAME TAHINI—a Middle Eastern staple, made from unroasted hulled sesame

SHAD ROE—fresh or smoked

SHRIMP PASTE—*kapi* in Thailand, *trasi* in Indonesia

SOY SAUCE, DARK

STAR ANISE

TARAMA—bottled carp roe from Greece

THAI TEA (see Flavor Flash!, Serendipi-Tea Sauce, page 214)

TOMATOES, YELLOW (low-acid varieties)

VANILLA (see Flavor Flash!, page 237)

Roasted Rootatouille

STARTER or SIDE

Serves 6–8

For an earthy starter or side dish on a chilly autumn-becoming-winter night, this fresh variation on a traditional Provençal specialty makes the simplest herbed grilled chicken breast seem special. Here an initial steaming of the roots, combined with a leisurely oven roasting, seems to intensify the natural sweetness of the vegetables. I sometimes double the recipe to have this keeper on hand to use as an impromptu pasta topper.

Note that parsley root, a relative of the parsnip, is a member of the umbelliferous family, grown expressly for the root with its pleasantly aggressive flavor, perhaps best described as a cross between celery root and carrot. (Its green leaves however, can be eaten, and have a taste reminiscent of a slightly bland Italian, flat-leaf parsley.)

An Old World vegetable whose use was traditionally confined to Germany, Holland, and Poland, most of what is now available practically year round in the United States is grown in New Jersey. Low in calories but high in sodium, the creamy beige root teams up particularly well with other root vegetables, including onion, parsnip, rutabaga, and turnip. As with other root vegetables, slow roasting softens its slight pungency.

1 large celery root bulb (about 1 lb.)
1 bunch parsley root (about 1 lb.)
1 bunch parsnips (about 1 lb.)
2 medium-sized carrots (about ½ lb. total)
2 medium-sized red onions (about ½ lb. total)
Juice of 1 lemon, sieved
4 tbsp. olive oil
Salt and freshly ground black pepper
4 large tomatoes (about 2 lbs. total)
8 cloves of garlic
1 bunch fresh basil, leaves only
⅓ cup balsamic vinegar

1. Wash the celery root, parsley root, and parsnips well with warm water and peel with a vegetable peeler. Cut into pieces roughly 1" square. Peel the carrots and cut into rounds 1" thick. Peel and halve the red onions.

2. In a vegetable steamer, cook the celery root, parsley root, and parsnips for about 10 minutes, or until crisp-tender. Do not overcook. They should be somewhat crunchy but not raw. Place in a bowl with the raw carrots and red onions.

3. In a small bowl, mix the lemon juice and olive oil. Add salt and freshly ground black pepper to taste. Blend well and pour over the prepared vegetables.

4. Preheat oven to 325°. Place the vegetables on a heavy baking sheet lined with foil. Arrange the whole tomatoes and the unpeeled garlic cloves among the other vegetables and roast at 325° for about 1 hour, stirring occasionally to avoid sticking. The vegetables should be well browned and the carrots and onion will have begun to look caramelized. Remove all vegetables, except tomatoes and garlic, from baking sheet and place in a mixing bowl. Then peel the roasted tomatoes and squeeze out excess juice and seeds. Squeeze the roasted garlic out of its skin. Place tomatoes and garlic in a small bowl and mash until well combined.

5. Reserve a few sprigs of the basil for a garnish. Mix the remaining basil, roughly chopped, into the roasted vegetables. If using dried thyme, simply blend into vegetables. Gently blend in the tomato-garlic sauce and place the mixture in a serving bowl. Splash evenly with the balsamic vinegar and garnish with the reserved basil. Serve warm or at room temperature.

Flavor Flash!
Balsamic Vinegar

As complex as fine wine, balsamic vinegar, a specialty from Modena, a city in Italy's gastronomic center, is a staunch ally in the kitchen. Whether starring alone as a splash over mixed baby greens, drizzled over out-of-season strawberries to make them taste sweeter, or stirred into fresh lemonade, this wine-dark elixir is an essential on my multiethnic pantry shelf. Give me a perfectly ripe avocado with nothing more than a benediction of Modena's finest and I'm happy.

SERVING SUGGESTION: When served over pasta, this dish can be followed perfectly by a small salad of bitter greens like endive, radicchio, and arugula spritzed with fresh lemon juice and a soupçon of olive oil. Serve some bread with a crisply crackling crust and the meal's complete.

Carrots Slow and Sweet

Serves 4

A long leisurely roasting in a moderate oven does wonders for the overused, often abused carrot. When treated to a scant coating of fruity olive oil, a spritz of fresh lemon juice, and a bit of loving care that leaves them tender and sweet, carrots become something new and special. Underscoring their caramelized sweetness is a rough sauce made from barely steamed Swiss chard leaves (leaves from the ruby-veined variety are prettier if you can find them) and fresh basil bound together lightly with Roasted Shallot Yogurt. For a rustic variation on the theme, I often use beet greens to stand in for the red chard—a nice bonus when you buy or grow fresh beets. With this dish, the enlightened eater can enjoy a suavity of texture and richness without resorting to guilt-inducing fats. Whack the carrots into generous oblique cuts; their larger surface area results in the most intensely sweet earthiness. Be sure to shake the skillet frequently during roasting to ensure even browning. Serving these warm, not hot, seems to show off their concentrated natural sugars to best effect.

> 2 lbs. carrots, peeled, cut on the diagonal into pieces 2–3" long
> 1 tbsp. fruity olive oil
> Juice of 1 lemon
> Salt and white pepper
> Pinch of sugar (optional, depending on natural sweetness of the carrots)
> 1 bunch Swiss chard leaves, white or ruby variety (or substitute beet greens)
> 1 cup Roasted Shallot Yogurt (page 265)
> 6 large fresh basil leaves, sliced into long thin strips

1. Place the cut carrots in a mixing bowl and toss with olive oil, lemon juice, and salt, and white pepper to taste. Add the pinch of sugar, if using.

2. Place the carrots on a heavy baking sheet. Roast in a preheated 325° oven, turning the carrots frequently, for approximately 40 minutes, or until the carrots feel tender when a sharp knife is inserted into their thickest part. Do not overcook; they should have some bite to them.

3. Place the chard leaves (or beet greens) in the basket of a steamer set over boiling water. Reduce the heat to just under a boil and steam for approximately 2 minutes.

Chop the leaves finely, retaining any juices that accumulate. Add leaves and juices to the Roasted Shallot Yogurt. Mix in half of the basil shreds, reserving the remainder to be used as a garnish. Taste for salt and pepper.

4. Nap the serving platter with the chard and mound the carrots on top. Keep warm, covered, in a low oven. Just before serving, garnish with remaining basil shreds.

SERVING SUGGESTIONS: I like to serve these with an uncomplicated broiled salmon steak or pan-seared scallops and a Mixed-Grain Pilaf with a Hint of Smoke (page 215). For a bit of savory symmetry, end with a Warm "Salad" of Watercress, Arugula, and Roasted Red Pepper (page 174) to echo the sweet/tart elements of the carrots.

Dark and Dusky Chicken–Boneless Chicken Stuffed with Chard, with Shiitake Sauce   STAR

Serves 4

Why not a chicken dish featuring dark meat for a change? When you hanker for something a bit more assertive than a boneless chicken breast, try these stuffed *jambonettes* ("mini hams," from the French) with a lingering woodsy sauce based on dried shiitake mushrooms and chicken stock. Early in the day simply bone the chicken thighs, make the stock, and prepare the stuffing and the sauce. Refrigerate all, and when you're ready to complete the process, dinner will be on the table in a matter of minutes.

8 chicken legs (about 2½ lbs. total)
Salt and freshly ground pepper

THE STOCK:
Chicken leg bones, reserved from above
2 ribs celery
1 large carrot, roughly chopped
1 medium whole onion, stuck with a few cloves
1 bay leaf

½ tsp. dried thyme

Pinch salt

Water

THE STUFFING:

2 oz. dried imported shiitake mushrooms (Japanese are best)

1 bunch fresh Swiss chard, well washed

1 tbsp. olive oil

1 medium yellow onion, peeled and finely chopped

2 cloves garlic, crushed

½ cup fresh bread crumbs

Salt and freshly ground black pepper

¼ cup pine nuts

Flour for dredging the chicken (approx. ½ cup)

1 tbsp. olive oil for cooking the jambonettes

1. Remove the skin from the chicken and discard. With a small sharp knife, remove the thigh bone: Keeping the knife parallel and close to the bone, free the meat from the bone along one side. Turn the leg over and repeat the procedure along the other side. Free the meat from the ball joint at the thick end of the leg and remove any thick tendons by holding their ends in place with a damp dish towel while bearing down and away from you with the blunt end of a knife. Salt and pepper the boned chicken legs lightly. Reserve the bones.

2. To make the stock, place the bones in a 2-quart saucepan. Add celery, carrot, onion, bay leaf, thyme, salt, and water to cover and bring to a boil over medium heat. Skim any scum that rises to the surface. Cook at a simmer for about 30 minutes. Let cool. Skim the fat from the surface, or if the stock has been chilled, remove the congealed fat from its surface. While the stock is simmering, soak the dried mushrooms for approximately 15 minutes in hot water to cover. Set aside.

3. Put the stock through a sieve, pressing hard on the solids. Reserve the liquid. You should have 2 cups of finished stock. Add water to the stock, if necessary, to measure 2 cups.

4. To make the stuffing, remove the chard leaves from their woody stems (reserve stems for a vegetable stock, if desired) and steam the leaves until just tender, about

3–4 minutes. Refresh under cold water and chop finely. Reserve. Heat the olive oil in a small sauté pan and cook the chopped onion and crushed garlic over low heat until tender but not browned. Add the cooked chard to the pan, and combine with bread crumbs. Pack the chard mixture firmly in the chicken leg cavity where the bone was. Refrigerate until ready to sauté.

5. Toast the pine nuts in a 350° oven for about 5 minutes, or until golden brown, stirring occasionally to avoid burning. Set aside.

6. Drain mushrooms and reserve the soaking liquid. Strain the soaking liquid through a cheesecloth-lined sieve. Remove the tough mushroom stems (discarding them or reserving for a vegetable stock, if desired) and slice the caps into strips $\frac{1}{2}$" wide. Salt and pepper lightly. In a medium-sized sauté pan, cook the mushrooms until tender, about 8 minutes, in the reserved mushroom soaking liquid mixed with 1 cup of the defatted reserved chicken stock. Remove the mushrooms from the pan, set aside, and cook the resulting liquid over medium heat until it coats a spoon lightly.

7. Lightly dredge the stuffed chicken legs with flour. Heat the olive oil in a heavy sauté pan large enough to fit the chicken legs in a single layer. Brown the chicken legs on all sides over medium heat, about 8 minutes. Remove chicken from pan and set aside on a plate, covered. Wipe out fat remaining in pan and deglaze with the remaining chicken stock (use a wooden spoon to loosen any browned bits that cling to the pan). Reserve covered. NOTE: The dish can be prepared up to this point and refrigerated until ready to complete just before serving.

8. Return the chicken to the pan and cook covered over low heat for about 12 minutes or until the meat tests done. Remove the chicken to a heated serving platter in a 200° oven to keep warm. Combine the mushrooms, the reduced mushroom liquid, and the pan juices from deglazing the sauté pan and cook briefly until the sauce almost coats a spoon. (If the sauce reduces too much, simply thin as necessary with a bit of chicken stock or water.) Nap the chicken with the sauce, and garnish with the pine nuts.

SERVING SUGGESTIONS: Start the meal with the acidic crunch of Pale Perfect Poached Celery (page 6), then complete the entree plate with a bed of pastina or brown rice pilaf and Carrots Slow and Sweet (page 127). Try a Grilled Fruit Salad with Berry Coulis (page 254) for just the right light finishing touch.

Can't Be Beet Borscht

Serves 6

Here's a soup that's pure gold when served hot in winter or icy cold in summer. Suave and earthy at the same time, it's a make-ahead dish that will mystify even seasoned vegetarians who, without a clue based on color, may wonder just what its main component is. (If golden beets are unavailable, the garden-variety crimson globes can pinch-hit, although to somewhat less dramatic effect.) A swirl of fresh cilantro and basil fired up with a bit of Hungarian yellow wax or jalapeño pepper contrasts with the sweetness of the beets. A dollop of tart yogurt paired with rings of sweet broiled onion provides the finishing touch.

3 golden beets, tops removed, about 1½ lbs. total (if unavailable, red beets will do)

2 leeks, white parts only, finely chopped (about 1 cup)

1 medium potato, peeled and cubed (about 1 cup)

1 cup Fresh Tomato Puree (page 263)

2½ quarts Root Stock (page 258)

1 tbsp. red wine vinegar (or more to taste, depending on the sweetness of the beets)

Pinch of sugar

Salt and freshly ground white pepper

THE HERBAL SWIRL:

1 cup fresh cilantro leaves, well packed into measuring cup

¼ cup fresh basil leaves

1 Hungarian yellow wax pepper or 1 jalapeño pepper, seeds and ribs removed

1 clove garlic

1 tsp. balsamic vinegar

THE GARNISH:

1 large sweet onion (Vidalia or Walla Walla, if available), sliced into rings ¼" thick (about 1 cup)

1 tbsp. oil for coating foil used to line broiler pan (vegetable oil spray works well too)

¾ cup Thickened Yogurt (page 265)

1. Wash the beets well and trim off stems. Steam until tender, about 35 minutes. Slip off skins and cut into ½" cubes. Place in a 3-quart (or larger) saucepan with the leeks, potato, and Fresh Tomato Puree. Add the Root Stock and cook over medium heat about 45 minutes, or until all vegetables are tender. Add the vinegar, pinch of sugar, and salt and white pepper to taste. Puree in food processor or blender until smooth. (The soup can be cooled and then chilled for use later in the day or refrigerated for up to 3 days.)

2. To make the Herbal Swirl, puree herbs, pepper, garlic, and vinegar until almost smooth but not completely liquefied. Set aside until serving.

3. For the garnish: Slice the onion into rounds 1/4" thick. Line broiler with lightly oiled foil. Grill onion about 4" from heat source, turning once to brown evenly, about 5 minutes.

4. Serve the borscht cold or reheat slowly over low heat until just below the boiling point. Divide evenly into wide shallow bowls. Center approximately 2 tbsp. of the Herbal Swirl on each serving. Place 2 broiled onion rings over the swirl and spoon 2 tbsp. of yogurt over all. Serve immediately.

SERVING SUGGESTIONS: This soup works well as a prelude to a pasta dinner of Orecchiette Vegetale (next) or as a lead-in to a simply grilled fish with a spritz of lime juice.

Orecchiette Vegetale

STAR

Serves 4

This is one of those dishes inspired by a rare moment when the weather, the soil, and the gods who rule the vegetable garden cooperated. From that happy coincidence sprang a diverse and bountiful bouquet of vegetables that provided brilliant color, crunch, heat, and sweetness in delicate balance to a dish of perfectly cooked pasta. Here I feature orecchiette, those small but sturdy saucer-shaped rounds of pasta from the heel of the Italian boot, that hold their own in the highly flavored, earthy Root Stock that unites the dish. This pasta seems to absorb the flavors of the vegetable broth better than other extruded pastas or even hand-cut ribbon varieties.

If the season does not allow exactly the same combination of vegetables as suggested, be guided by what looks freshest to comprise your own medley. Begin with perhaps two greens, a brightly flavored hot pepper or two, and a seasonal squash for the basics and then fill in as your whim dictates. The Root Stock can be made in advance and frozen (I recommend always having a supply on hand, well covered, in the freezer). If you lack Root Stock and the time to make one, you can create a short-cut version of this dish by simply starting with water. The resulting dish will have a less robust flavor but will be special nonetheless.

Some raw garlic and a final fillip of dill, cilantro, and grated goat cheese elevate what could be just another pasta primavera to a dish for all seasons.

> 1 quart Root Stock (page 258) or water
> 1 bunch baby bok choy (about ½ lb.) sliced lengthwise into strips ½" wide
> 2–3 hot Hungarian wax peppers, sliced into ¼ inch-wide strips
> 1 bunch spinach, well washed, leaves only
> 12 whole cherry tomatoes (halved, if large)
> 1 small zucchini, sliced into ½" diagonals (about ½ cup)
> ½ cup sugar snap peas, left whole
> 12 oz. orecchiette pasta
> 2 cloves garlic, crushed and finely minced
> Salt and freshly ground black pepper

THE GARNISH:
> 2 tbsp. chopped fresh dill
> 2 tsp. chopped fresh cilantro
> Grated well-aged goat cheese (or fine Parmigiano Reggiano) to taste
> ¼ cup sliced French or Italian green olives

1. Bring Root Stock (or water) to a boil. Reduce to a simmer and add bok choy and peppers. Cook for about 2 minutes, or until vegetables are crisp-tender. Remove to a ovenproof bowl to keep warm. Add spinach and cook, stirring, until just wilted. Remove to the bowl. Add cherry tomatoes, zucchini, and snap peas and cook, stirring carefully, for 2 minutes. Remove to the bowl. Keep warm, covered, in a 200° oven.

2. Over high heat, reduce the vegetable cooking liquid by half. Meanwhile, cook pasta in a large pot of boiling water for about 10 minutes, or just until tender but slightly resistant to the bite. Test it frequently to avoid overcooking.

3. Just before assembling the dish, remove vegetables from the warming oven and add the garlic and salt and pepper to taste.

4. Divide the cooked drained pasta among 4 deep plates. Ladle some of the reduced cooking liquid into each bowl. Top with an array of the vegetables, some dill and cilantro, and sprinkle to taste with the grated cheese. Strew a few sliced olives over all and serve immediately.

SERVING SUGGESTIONS: Follow this with a lightly dressed salad of sweet and bitter greens in which you might include some romaine and escarole. For a dessert, I suggest a plate of room-temperature semisoft or hard cheeses served with iced grapes of every available color. Don't forget the hearth-baked bread.

Sham Spaghetti Anti-Pesto   SIDE
Serves 4–6

When is spaghetti not spaghetti? When that devilishly delicious impostor, spaghetti squash, fairly convincingly stands in for the real thing. This vegetarian dish is like money in the bank at the end of a blistering summer day. Make it before you or your kitchen has lost its cool, refrigerate it, and let it come back to room temperature an hour before serving.

Boasting a brash twist on pesto, this dish features the verdant refreshment of fresh mint leaves in place of basil, and nutty brown toasted almonds instead of the often-used pine nuts. And it's cheeseless too. A ladleful of Freshly Minted Oil, which embodies the essence of mint and a bit of lemon zest, rounds out a short list of ingredients to produce a perfect topping for steamed strands of spaghetti squash. A shred of lightly cooked cucumber provides the finishing touch. After tasting this dish, you'll see why the Mexicans call mint *yerba buena*.

1 spaghetti squash (about 2 lbs.)
½ cup blanched almonds (or hulled sunflower seeds for a gutsier sauce)

THE FRESH MINT ANTI-PESTO:

    1 bunch fresh mint (to yield approximately 2 cups of leaves)

    1 large clove garlic

    Zest and juice of 1 lemon

    ½ cup Freshly Minted Oil (page 270)

    Salt and freshly ground black pepper

THE GARNISH:

    1 cucumber, peeled, seeded, and cut lengthwise into strips ¼" by 2"

1. Bake the squash on a baking sheet in a preheated 350° oven for approximately 35 minutes, or until the squash yields easily to gentle pressure. Let cool and cut in half lengthwise. Gently scrape out the spaghetti-like strands and arrange in a ½" layer on a wide platter.

2. Toast the almonds (or sunflower seeds) on a baking sheet in a preheated 350° oven for about 5–7 minutes, stirring occasionally to ensure even browning.

3. To make the Fresh Mint Anti-Pesto, wash and dry the mint leaves and place in a food processor or blender (hand chopping results in a rougher but no less effective sauce). Add the garlic, toasted almonds (or sunflower seeds), lemon zest, and oil. Process until almost completely smooth, about 1 minute. Add lemon juice and salt and pepper to taste. Set aside.

4. Steam the julienned cucumber for about a minute, or until it tests just crisp-tender. Drizzle the pesto over the squash (thin to drizzling consistency with some Root Stock, if available, or water) and strew the cucumber julienne over all. For the fullest flavor, serve at room temperature.

SERVING SUGGESTIONS: For a winning vegetarian trio, I would suggest Slightly Smoked Eggplant and Company with Roasted Shallot Yogurt Sauce (page 204) and Sizzled Shiitakes (page 200), both of which would ably support this dish without competing with its bold yet delicate flavor. If you wish to pair it with some protein, Grilled Chicken Piccata with Lemon Times Three (page 28) would be my choice.

Soothing Salmagundi Soup

Serves 4

STARTER

Although salmagundi has come to mean any miscellany or mixture, traditionally it connotes a salad-like dish from France or perhaps Italy comprised of chopped meat, anchovies, eggs, onions, and oil. Although this version takes a bit wilder approach to combining ingredients, its mellifluous name seems a perfect match for its tastes and textures.

Leaving aside matters of etymologic and culinary origins, this adventurous grouping of flavors looks beyond Europe for inspiration. Here is a sensuous soup that features dried mushrooms from Eastern Europe and the Far East underpinned by the smoky edge of charred silken eggplant borrowed from the cuisines of the Middle East. Wild rice in all its nutty, chewy glory ties the whole together in a surprisingly harmonious package. What on paper might seem an unlikely combination of ingredients, in the bowl becomes a provocative melding of flavors that for me approaches the ultimate comfort food. For best results, start with a robust Root Stock and don't stint on the dried mushrooms. If you're short of shiitakes, double up on the so-called Polish varieties imported nowadays from Chile (often found in the kosher foods aisle of your local supermarket). Although they lack the subtlety of their Japanese counterparts, they are a reasonably full-flavored substitute here.

1 oz. dried shiitake mushrooms

1 oz. dried Polish mushrooms

2 medium-sized red bell peppers (about ½ lb. total)

1 tbsp. sweet butter

1 cup finely chopped onion

4 large cloves garlic, crushed and then minced

2 quarts Root Stock (page 258)

4 large Japanese or other Asian eggplant (about 1½ lbs. total)

2" piece gingerroot, peeled and sliced in rounds ½" thick

4 star anise

2" piece cinnamon stick

½ cup uncooked wild rice

Salt and freshly ground black pepper

THE GARNISH:

2 tbsp. Forest Fragrance (see below)

½ cup finely chopped scallion greens or garlic chives

1. Soak the dried mushrooms in boiling water to cover for 15 minutes. Strain, reserving the soaking liquid. Sieve the liquid through a fine sieve lined with dampened cheesecloth. Carefully pick over the mushrooms and discard any tough stems. Cut the remaining mushrooms into ½" pieces. Set aside.

2. Roast the red peppers on a baking sheet in a 350° oven for about 20 minutes, or until the skins are uniformly charred. Turn occasionally during roasting. Let cool slightly and then remove the skins. Slit open to remove the seeds and ribs. Puree in a food processor or blender until smooth. Set aside.

3. Melt the butter in a 4-quart soup pot. Add the onions and garlic and cook over low heat, stirring occasionally, until the mixture softens but does not brown. Add the dried mushrooms, mushroom soaking liquid, and Root Stock.

4. Place the eggplant in a preheated 400° oven and roast until the skin is blistered and the flesh is tender, about 10 minutes. Remove from oven, peel, and chop into fine dice. Add to pot.

Flavor Flash!
Forest Fragrance

Every time I open my jar of Forest Fragrance, I am put in mind of the dark mystery of damp forests primeval. Here's how to capture that essence in a simple-to-make yet complexly flavored powder that works wonders in everything from clear soups and pasta dishes to salad dressings and marinades for grilled poultry and sturdy, meaty fish such as shark, tuna, or swordfish.

In a spice or coffee grinder, process to a fine powder 2 tbsp. of dried mushrooms (shiitakes are best), 1 tbsp. sun-dried tomatoes, 2 whole star anise, and ½ tsp. whole black peppercorns. (If the capacity of your blender cannot accommodate the whole mixture at once, merely blend what you can in batches and combine the batches upon completion.) This keeps for several months if tightly closed in a glass jar. As you would all spices, store in a cool, dark, dry place. Have at the ready when your culinary ambitions at dinner won't allow more than a simple bowl of pasta. After a hard day, dust some on a butter-gilded mound of *al dente* noodles and you're sure to experience a lift to your sagging spirits.

5. Add gingerroot, star anise, and cinnamon. Cook over low heat, covered, for about 30 minutes, or until mushrooms are very tender.

6. Add wild rice and cook over medium heat for about 30 minutes longer, or until rice is well softened. Remove gingerroot, star anise, and cinnamon stick. In a food processor or blender, puree the soup until smooth. (Note that the rice will not disintegrate entirely.) Add salt and freshly ground black pepper to taste.

7. If the soup was made in advance, gently reheat over medium heat just until hot. Pour into wide shallow serving bowls. Spoon a wide swath of the red pepper puree on the surface of each portion and dust with some Forest Fragrance and finely chopped scallion greens or garlic chives.

SERVING SUGGESTIONS: This stick-to-the-ribs starter could precede Pepper-Crusted Turkey Steak (page 65), or Village Baked Chicken (page 150) (minus its noodle accompaniment). If appetites are smaller, I would suggest a lightly dressed seasonal salad of whatever greens and vegetables lurk in your refrigerator and call it a meal.

A Whole Different Kettle of Fish   STARTER or STAR
Serves 6 as first course; 4 as main dish

This dish is a kind of family reunion in which common and not-so-common members of the umbelliferous clan show how well they can get along in a pot. Here carrots and their less-used cousins, bulbous fennel and feathery fresh dill, stand out, reinforcing and echoing each other's flavors in a lightly potato-thickened fish stew. Make this from fall through spring when the most highly flavored fennel appears on produce shelves.

Be sure to save some of the feathery tops of the fennel to combine with the dill for the Herbal Swirl that tops the soup at serving time. A subtle undertone of now-you-taste-it, now-you-don't curry lends an unexpected counterpoint to the Mediterranean herbal notes of fresh rosemary and thyme. I like to use a diverse array of fish, from mild sea bass and halibut to stronger varieties including salmon (for color contrast) and swordfish. Use whatever kinds are reliably freshest from your source.

Make the stock base for the soup a day or so ahead of serving, and with only a few quick steps, this can be on your table within minutes.

1 tbsp. fruity olive oil

3 medium carrots, cut into ½" cubes (about 2 cups)

1 large onion, cut into ½" cubes (about 1 cup)

½ bulb fennel, cut into ½" cubes (about ½ cup)

2 large cloves garlic, crushed and finely minced

1 cup dry white wine

⅛ tsp. saffron threads

3 cups Fresh Fish Stock with Fennel (pages 260–262)

½ bunch dill, finely chopped

½ cup finely chopped feathery fennel tops

1 whole sprig of fresh thyme (or 1 tsp. dried thyme)

1 bay leaf

2 cloves

1 large white-skinned potato, peeled and cut into ½" cubes (about 2 cups)

1 lb. assorted filleted fish, skin removed, cut into 1" cubes (see introductory note
above)

2 tsp. Curry Blend (page 264)

THE HERBAL SWIRL:

½ bunch fresh dill

½ cup feathery fennel tops

1 cup hot liquid from soup to facilitate pureeing

1 tsp. mild vinegar

1. Heat the oil in a stockpot until it releases its aroma. Add the carrots, onion, fennel, and garlic and cook until softened but not brown. Stir frequently to avoid browning.

2. Soak the saffron in the white wine until a reddish-orange color is apparent. Add to the vegetables in the pot.

3. Add the fish stock. Add the dill and fennel tops. Using a 4" square cheesecloth, make a bouquet garni containing the thyme, bay leaf, and cloves. Tie securely with kitchen string. Add to the pot. Simmer for 30 minutes, or until vegetables are tender. (The soup can be prepared ahead to this point and refrigerated, covered. Before proceeding, reheat to a simmer.)

4. While the soup is simmering, make the Herbal Swirl. Reserving ¼ cup of the chopped dill and fennel tops for the garnish, puree the remaining dill and fennel with 1 cup soup liquid until smooth. Add the vinegar and blend. Finely chop the reserved dill and fennel tops and reserve.

5. Twenty minutes before serving, add the potatoes to the soup. Cook over moderate heat for 10 minutes and then add the fish and the Curry Blend. Cook at a simmer for 10 minutes more. At this point the fish should be just cooked. Avoid overcooking.

6. To create a verdant frame for the soup, pour a ring of the Herbal Swirl around the bottom edge of heated serving bowls. Then carefully ladle the soup into the center of each bowl. Garnish with the chopped dill and fennel tops.

SERVING SUGGESTIONS: I find this filling enough to serve as the centerpiece for a dinner on a cool fall night. Provide ample wedges of oven-crisped sourdough bread and sweet butter. Follow with a salad of tender butter or limestone lettuce, lightly dressed with a few drops of olive oil and lemon juice. For a simple finale, you might end with a plate of chilled crisp pears and, for the licorice lovers, some Almond-Aniseed Crisps (page 242) or store-bought anise biscotti.

Brazilian Onion Salad   SIDE
Serves 4

A bit of culinary alchemy is at work here in a dish that draws its inspiration from a northeastern Brazilian side dish called *molho a champanha*, the South American answer to Mexico's *salsa cruda*. When combined, the humble onion and a short list of other ordinary ingredients are transmuted into minimalist splendor.

The great German architect Mies van der Rohe might as well have been referring to this shiningly simple dish when he said "Less is more." Here a few well-chosen herbs and the right proportions of sharp mustard, oil, and vinegar are all that are needed to spark a sweet firestorm on the palate and set off any smoky grilled food superbly.

Make this about an hour before serving to allow the flavors to meld and soften. Omit the tomato if the current local supply is insipid.

Boiling water to blanch the onion

1 large white onion, peeled and sliced paper-thin (about 2 cups)

3" sprig of fresh rosemary, finely chopped (about 1 tbsp.)

¼ cup roughly chopped cilantro leaves

2 bay leaves

¼ cup finely chopped fresh parsley leaves

1 small clove garlic, crushed and finely minced

1 ripe medium-sized tomato, peeled, seeded, and chopped into ¼" cubes (optional)

1 tbsp. strong French-style mustard

Scant 1 tbsp. white wine vinegar

3 tbsp. fruity olive oil

Pinch sugar

Salt and freshly ground black pepper

THE GARNISH:

4–8 leaves of brightly colored red-leaf lettuce, radicchio, or red cabbage (amount depends on size of leaves and size of plates)

1. Bring the water to a boil. Place onion slices in a crockery or stainless steel bowl and pour the boiling water over them. Let stand about 10 minutes. Drain the onions and soak in ice water for 10 minutes to crisp. Drain and dry and place in a serving bowl. Cover the chopped rosemary with boiling water and let stand for 5 minutes. Drain through a fine sieve.

2. Add rosemary, cilantro, bay leaves, parsley, garlic, and the optional tomato to the onion. Combine lightly.

3. In a small bowl, whisk the mustard with the vinegar until smooth. Add oil in a thin stream, whisking until smoothly incorporated. Add sugar and salt and pepper to taste. Pour the dressing over onions and let stand at room temperature for about 1 hour before serving. Serve at room temperature, on deep plates, lined with your choice of red leaf lettuce, radicchio, or red cabbage.

   For an alternate presentation, mound the salad on a strikingly bright green bed of stir-fried collard greens kissed softly with garlic. (Wash and dry the greens well before a quick sauté.) Refrigerate the salad for extended storage. (Beyond 2 days, it will lose much of its crispness, however.)

SERVING SUGGESTIONS: This is a fine lead-in to strong-flavored dishes such as Southwest by Southeast Saté (page 57), or Pan-Seared Bass (page 61). Be sure to provide plenty of delicate toasted brioche (or other egg bread) to make the most of the sublime dressing. Hewing to the South American tradition where enormous amounts of red meat are consumed, serve it in small amounts as a kind of condiment with grilled steaks or skewered beef.

Leek-Wrapped Grilled Shrimp with Tarama Sauce

STAR

Serves 4

A bit of pastel perfection on the plate, this dish, inspired by the sunny, uncomplicated flavors of Greek cooking, features a lemony sauce based on coral-colored carp roe (tarama). Tender, blanched leek leaves seal in the moisture of large whole shrimp, which, in turn, gain in flavor when grilled quickly after a brush with fruity olive oil. A touch of fresh thyme or oregano and a fine scattering of chopped black olives punctuate the ensemble. If you can find them, the long but more slender baby leeks will provide a less fibrous (but equally subtle) envelope for the shrimp.

1½ lbs. large shrimp (12 or fewer to a pound), peeled and deveined

1–2 leeks, of medium thickness, leaves separated from the root, well washed, kept intact, top 2" of green part removed (be sure to choose long leeks to enable easy wrapping of the shrimp)

2 tbsp. fruity olive oil

THE SAUCE:

1 cup white part of leeks, from above

1 small red pepper, roasted, peeled, and seeded (about 1 cup)

1 small clove garlic, grated

Juice of 1 large lemon (about ⅓ cup)

Zest of 1 medium lemon, grated (about 2 tbsp.)

¼ cup tarama (carp roe)

1 cup Thickened Yogurt (page 415)

THE GARNISH:

2 small sprigs fresh thyme or oregano

½ cup finely chopped pitted oil-cured olives

1 large lemon, cut into wedges

1. Butterfly the shrimp by making a shallow slit from the head end three-quarters of the way down toward the tail. Open up the shrimp and flatten slightly. Refrigerate.

2. Bring 2 quarts of water to a boil. Reserving the white part of the leeks, cook the green leaves in the water just until tender, about 5–7 minutes. Drain and refresh under cold water. Dry thoroughly.

3. Trim the blanched leek leaves to approximately 5" lengths and brush lightly with the oil. Wrap each shrimp with a leaf, allowing some of the shrimp to show through. Brush the packets again lightly with the oil. Set aside.

4. For the sauce, chop 1 cup of the reserved white part of the leeks (save any additional for another use). Cook in boiling water just until tender. Drain, refresh under cold water and dry. In a blender or food processor, puree with the red pepper and garlic. Incorporate this mixture along with the lemon juice and zest into the tarama, whisking until smooth. Blend in yogurt. Set aside.

5. Heat a ridged cast-iron stovetop griddle or oven broiler until very hot. Grill the shrimp just until pink and slightly spongy to the touch, about 4 minutes, turning once. Do not overcook. Reserve any pan juices that accumulate and blend into the sauce.

6. Nap each of four warmed serving plate with some of the sauce. Place 4 or 5 shrimp on each plate. Garnish with the herb sprigs, olives, and lemon wedges.

SERVING SUGGESTIONS: Serve these with some whole wheat pita and a side of My Fave Favas (page 87) or oven-crisped sliced potatoes. You might offer a cruet of your pantry's best olive oil as a do-it-yourself drizzle for the shrimp. This one calls for a not-too-tannic red like pinot noir or a fresh fruity nouveau Beaujolais if just released.

Golden Melting Moments–A Late Summer Soup of Yellow Tomato and Yellow Pepper

STARTER

Serves 4

This suave soup grew out of a search for a less-acidic yet full-flavored version of gazpacho. A bumper crop of homegrown low-acid yellow tomatoes and an irresistible display of deep-yellow bell peppers at a local farmer's market provided just the inspiration needed for this bit of culinary alchemy. When golden tomatoes are unavailable, ripe red specimens will do, but expect the resulting soup to be less mellow and, of course, more orange than golden.

Although the peppers are roasted to deepen their flavor and facilitate removing their skins, the tomatoes, once blanched and peeled, enter the soup raw with all of their sundrenched splendor intact. Topped with a coin of unaged goat cheese melted on a croute of peasant bread, this soup arrives in the bowl with no more than a hint of its rough beginnings. Serve it at room temperature or lukewarm, when the bright flavor and delicate aroma are at their peak.

2 medium-sized yellow bell peppers (about 1 lb. total)

2 tbsp. olive oil

6 medium-sized yellow tomatoes (about 2 lbs. total)

2 shallots, peeled and minced (about 4 tbsp.)

1 medium cucumber, peeled, seeded, and chopped (about 1 cup)

1 clove garlic, crushed and minced

1 tsp. salt

½ tsp. freshly ground white pepper

¼ tsp. ground turmeric

2 tbsp. uncooked white raw rice

¼ cup dry vermouth

2 cups Root Stock (page 258) or water

4 slices (¼" thick) rustic French or Italian bread, crust removed, toasted

2 oz. fresh goat cheese, sliced into rounds ½" thick

THE GARNISH:

2 tbsp. freshly snipped chives or chopped fresh dill (feathery part)

Fruity olive oil to drizzle on top of soup (optional)

1. Preheat the oven to 350°. Halve the peppers and remove the ribs and seeds. Lightly brush with some of the olive oil. Place on baking sheet and roast at 350° for approximately 20 minutes, or until the skin is evenly browned. Remove from oven and allow to cool. Carefully peel off skins. In food processor or blender, puree peppers until smooth. Set aside.

2. With a sharp paring knife, cut a shallow X into the end of the tomato opposite the stem end. Place in a large pot of boiling water and blanch for about 1 minute (do not cook). Remove from pot and plunge in a bowl of ice water to cool rapidly. Carefully remove the skin of each tomato. Halve them and pass through a food mill. Pass the puree through a fine sieve to remove any lingering seeds. There should be about 2 cups of sieved puree. Set aside.

3. In a 1-quart saucepan, heat the remaining olive oil until hot. Over moderate heat, cook the shallots, stirring constantly, until tender but not browned. Stir in the cucumber. Add the garlic and cook for 30 seconds. Add the salt, pepper, and turmeric. Add the rice and stir to coat the grains with the oil. Cook over low heat for 5 minutes, stirring occasionally to prevent sticking. Add the vermouth and stock or water and cook until the cucumber and rice are tender and most of the liquid has been absorbed. Watch carefully to avoid burning.

4. Puree this mixture in a food processor or blender until smooth. Blend in the pepper and tomato purees. Allow to cool to lukewarm or room temperature. Adjust salt and pepper, if necessary.

5. Float a croute of bread topped with a round of slightly melted goat cheese on each serving and shower with chopped herbs. Provide olive oil at the table for a last-minute enhancement.

SERVING SUGGESTIONS: In summer with the barbecue in full swing, I like to serve this as an alfresco appetizer before a grill-it-yourself entree of turkey or chicken burgers. Follow up with a mass of mixed greens and everyone will be satisfied but not stuffed. Close with a platter of sliced fresh melons or pineapple and a bowl of sugared walnuts.

Arugula "Caesar" with Polenta Croutons   STARTER
Serves 6

With its fleshy leaves and sometimes startlingly hot peppery bite, arugula (or ruco-la, rocket salad, roquette, et al.) is a salad green whose flavor, like fine wine, is hard to convey in words. Perhaps "earthy" and "gutsy" come closest. However you describe it, once addicted, always addicted. Thankfully no longer the preserve of swank American Italian restaurants, this perky green has become available year round in most of the better supermarkets nationwide.

When the nontaste of ordinary salad greens begins to pall, try *eruca sativa*. Here I turn the old continental restaurant workhorse upside down. This favorite Mediter-ranean green, whose leaves could act as a body double for radish tops, puts romaine to shame in a salad that's anything but a cliché. Crunchy squares of fried cornmeal mush (sublime in everything but name) outshine the standard bread croutons hands down. One more twist on the original brings an unlikely hint of Thai shrimp paste to the fore (instead of anchovies) in an eggless dressing.

1 large bunch arugula

THE DRESSING:

1 tbsp. balsamic vinegar

1 tsp. fresh lemon juice (or more to taste)

2 tbsp. Dijon mustard

2 tsp. Thai shrimp paste

1 small clove garlic, crushed and finely minced

1 cup Thickened Yogurt (page 265)

2 tsp. fruity olive oil

Freshly ground black pepper

THE POLENTA CROUTONS:

½ cup fine-grained cornmeal

1½ cups water

¼ tsp. salt

½ cup flour mixed with ¼ cup fine cornmeal to coat the croutons

Peanut, canola, soy, or safflower oil for coating the baking sheet on which the
  polenta cools and for frying the croutons
¼ cup grated Parmesan (Parmigiano Reggiano makes a real difference here), plus
  additional to serve with the salad

1. Wash the arugula well in slightly warm water. Drain, spin-dry, and wrap in a damp
   paper or cloth towel. Refrigerate until serving time.

2. Make the dressing by whisking vinegar, lemon juice, mustard, and shrimp paste
   together in a small bowl until smooth. Add the garlic and stir until evenly distributed. Whisk in the yogurt and the oil. Taste for salt. Add a healthy dose of freshly
   ground black pepper. If the dressing is too thick, dilute it by whisking in more lemon
   juice, vinegar, or water as needed to achieve a light coating consistency.

3. Make the polenta by dissolving the cornmeal in ½ cup of the water until smooth. In
   a heavy 1-quart saucepan, bring the remaining water and salt to a boil and stir in the
   dissolved cornmeal, whisking constantly to keep the mixture smooth. Cook, stirring
   frequently, for about 20 minutes, or until the polenta leaves the sides of the pot. Turn
   mixture out onto a lightly oiled baking sheet and smooth to an even rectangle, about
   ½" thick. Allow to cool. Cut into ½" cubes. There should be about 24 cubes. Freeze
   until firm, about 15 minutes. Lightly coat cubes with flour and cornmeal mixture.

4. Just before serving the salad, heat ¾" to 1" of oil in a small heavy saucepan. Fry the
   polenta cubes without crowding for about 3–5 minutes, or until golden brown. Turn
   once during cooking. Drain on absorbent paper toweling and dust with grated
   Parmesan.

5. Assemble the salad by tearing the arugula into bite-size pieces, stems and all. Coat
   lightly with the dressing, serving the remaining dressing in a sauceboat at the table.
   Top each salad with some of the croutons and serve with additional grated cheese
   if desired.

SERVING SUGGESTIONS: This is a hard act to follow, but robust dishes such as
Broiled Trout Aegean (page 4) or Petti di Pollo Semiamaro (page 108) can hold their own
nicely after such a full-flavored intro. At meal's end, a plate of fresh tropical fruit (mango,
papaya, pineapple) would cut beautifully through the richness of the foregoing.

Risotto Island in an Herbal Broth

STARTER

Serves 4

Northern Italians know that it takes two things to make the perfect plate of cooked rice: high-quality rice and an impeccable stock in which to cook it gently. For this dish, the rice variety of choice is either Arborio or Vialone, the first long-grained, the second-medium grained (both available widely), and the cooking liquid is Root Stock accented with cabbage, ginger, and vermouth.

This is a quiet but richly aromatic dish where flavors are reduced to their essence— first, in the clear, almost sweet vegetal notes of a tremulous "island" of molded rice, scented with the stock in which it cooked, and then in the green herbal sea that surrounds it (composed of that same richly flavored stock zinged at the last moment with a puree of fresh herbs).

Diverging from the classical risotto tradition of freely using butter and cheese to act as enrichment and binder, this vegetarian version relies on nonfat yogurt to hold things together and a mere sprinkling of highly flavored aged goat cheese to complete the dish. (See Superb Sources page 292, for a mail-order source for the cheese.)

Be sure to use the freshest herbs you can find—they should smell fresh. Although supermarkets increasingly stock a supply of fresh hothouse herbs all year round, there are none fresher than those plucked from a kitchen garden. A few sprouted seedlings from a local nursery and a small amount of space (even an urban windowsill with lots of sun) are all you need. I hope this dish inspires you to become even the slightest bit horticultural.

THE COOKING LIQUID FOR THE RICE:

4 cups Root Stock (page 258)

½ lb. Napa cabbage, roughly chopped (about 2 cups)

½ lb. celery root, peeled, roughly chopped (about 1 cup)

2" piece gingerroot, peeled, sliced into thin rounds

½ cup dry vermouth

2 tbsp. dark ruby port

THE RISOTTO:

1 tbsp. fruity olive oil or unsalted butter

2 tbsp. finely chopped shallots

1½ cups Vialone or Arborio rice

The cooking liquid from above
Salt and freshly ground black pepper
1 cup Thickened Yogurt (page 265)

THE HERBAL BROTH:
4 cups Root Stock (page 258)
½ bunch fresh dill, feathery tops only (about 1½ cups)
1 bunch fresh cilantro, leaves only (about 2 cups)
½ bunch fresh basil, leaves only (about 1½ cups)
4 cloves garlic, crushed and finely minced
Salt and freshly ground black pepper
½ lb. celery root, peeled, sliced into thin julienne (about 1 cup)

THE GARNISH:
½ cup shredded aged goat cheese, or Parmigiano Reggiano

1. Make the cooking liquid by placing the stock in a 2-quart saucepan. Bring to a boil. Add the cabbage, celery root, gingerroot, vermouth, and port and simmer uncovered for 30 minutes. Reduce by one-third to concentrate flavors. Keep warm over low heat.

2. To make the risotto, heat oil or butter in a 10" skillet. Add the shallots and cook over moderate heat, stirring constantly, until tender but not browned, about 3–5 minutes. Add the rice, stirring to coat the grains evenly. Add the stock in ½-cup increments, allowing each addition to become absorbed before adding the next. This process takes about 15–20 minutes in all. Stir the rice gently to be sure it is not sticking to the bottom of the pan. Take care not to mash the delicate grains while stirring.

3. When all the stock has been added, allow the rice to cook over low heat uncovered just until the liquid is absorbed. Season with salt and pepper to taste. Mix in yogurt and form into 4 equal cakes by packing the rice into shallow round molds 4" in diameter. Remove the rice cakes by freeing the sides with a small sharp knife, then rapping sharply on the bottom of the molds. Keep cakes warm, covered, in a 200° oven.

4. Just before serving, make the herbal broth by heating 4 cups stock to just under the boiling point. Remove 1 cup of the stock to a food processor or blender. Add the herbs and puree until smooth. Season to taste with salt and pepper.

5. Cook the julienned celery root in the remaining stock. Add the herbal puree. Reheat briefly just until hot, if necessary.

6. Center one rice cake in the bottom of each of 4 wide, shallow bowls. Carefully pour the heated herbal broth around it, distributing the celery root julienne evenly in a circle around the rice. Garnish with the cheese.

SERVING SUGGESTIONS: The delicacy of this dish seems to call for a policy of vegetables-only in the follow-up dishes. For a well-rooted meal, my palate would be stimulated by some Roasted Rootatouille (page 125) paired with a Bittersweet Bouquet (page 27) of greens and some steamed seasonal squash.

Village Baked Chicken with Pan-Crisped Noodles
STAR

Serves 4

D on't be misled by the homey simplicity of the name. This dish's flavor is anything but simple. The village in this case is in rural China, with all that implies about the gamut of seasonings that come into play—some of the usuals like garlic, gingerroot, and scallions, plus a few not-so-usual such as sweetened soy sauce (from Indonesia), lemon rind, and palm sugar.

After an overnight marination, the chicken is stuffed under the skin, French style, with a fine chop of scallion, gingerroot, and garlic for additional zest. Enclosed in an ovenproof bag, the chicken is suffused with the flavor of its marinade during baking. When reduced over high heat, the marinade becomes a deep mahogany glaze for the chicken during the final few minutes of its oven stay. The noodles that serve as a bed for the bird catch any glaze that threatens to stray. Transcending its humble beginnings, this dish defines lacquered luxury.

1 3–4 lb. frying chicken

THE MARINADE:
   ¼ cup palm sugar or brown sugar
   ¼ cup Chinkiang black rice vinegar

¼ cup liquid from Pickled Ginger (page 273)

1 cup ketjap manis (Indonesian sweetened soy sauce)

4 large cloves garlic, crushed and finely minced

2" piece gingerroot, peeled and sliced into thin rounds

Zest from 1 large lemon, removed in strips with a vegetable peeler

Salt and freshly ground white pepper

THE UNDERSKIN STUFFING:

1 bunch scallions, white and green parts, finely chopped (about 2 cups)

4" piece gingerroot, peeled and finely minced

4 cloves garlic, finely minced

Salt and freshly ground black pepper

1 lb. wide egg noodles (or Asian rice noodles)

Oil for coating the cooked noodles and for pan-frying

THE GARNISH:

Candied peel of 1 lemon (page 275)

½ cup julienned scallion

1. Wash and dry the chicken. Cut through the backbone and flatten chicken to facilitate even absorption of flavors from the marinade. Place in ovenproof roasting bag and set aside.

2. To make the marinade, in a small bowl, whisk the vinegar and ginger liquid into the palm sugar (or brown sugar) to dissolve. Stir in ketjap manis. Add the garlic, gingerroot, and lemon zest. Stir to blend. Pour over the chicken and secure the roasting bag tightly. Place in a large bowl and refrigerate overnight, turning occasionally.

3. Combine the scallions, gingerroot, and garlic. Remove chicken from marinade and wipe dry. Loosen the skin covering the breast, thighs, and legs of the chicken. Carefully spoon the stuffing evenly under the skin. Salt and pepper the chicken.

4. Preheat oven to 375°. Place the chicken in its bag on a roasting pan. Cut a few small slits in the top of the bag and bake at 375° for about 1 to 1¼ hours. The juices should run yellowish or clear when a knife is inserted between the thigh and the body of the chicken. Remove chicken from the oven, allowing the juices to redistribute through the chicken. Remove from the bag, pour the cooking liquid into a bowl, and place the chicken on a poultry rack or icing grate set over a sheet pan.

5. Defat the cooking liquid by spooning off any visible fat. Remove solids by sieving into a heavy skillet. Cook over high heat to reduce to a glaze. When thick enough to coat a spoon, brush glaze evenly on surface of the chicken. Return to the oven and continue basting every few minutes until the chicken is well glazed. Turn off oven. Cut the chicken into 8 pieces. Keep warm, covered in the oven.

6. Bring a large pot of lightly salted water to a boil. Add the noodles and cook until just tender but not mushy. Drain but do not wash, and coat lightly with oil. Coil the noodles into round nests approximately 3" in diameter. Fry in approximately ¼" of oil until crisped and well-browned on the bottom. Drain on absorbent paper if necessary.

7. Place the noodle nests, browned side up, on a heated serving platter. Arrange the chicken pieces over this. Garnish with the candied lemon peel and julienned scallion.

Flavor Flash!
Palm Sugar

Beets and sugarcane aren't the only sources for sugar. A number of varieties of palm, including the wild date, palmyra, and coconut, are tapped, like the maple, for their sap, which is then boiled down into a crystallized mass. Often found wrapped in leaves, or sold canned, palm sugar (called jaggery in Asian stores) is very dark brown and pleasantly strong-flavored. Because it contains a high proportion of non-sucrose sugars, it tends to remain permanently sticky. I like to use it to sweeten my bowl of nine-grain cereal as a slightly wicked alternative to maple syrup.

   This, incidentally, is not to be confused with date sugar, made from dried dates that have been pulverized.

SERVING SUGGESTIONS: This works well with the clean and direct flavors of a Warm "Salad" of Watercress, Arugula, and Roasted Red Pepper (page 174). Clear the palate with some chilled seasonal citrus.

Currying Flavor Three Ways—A Southeast Asian Lasagna

STARTER or STAR

Serves 6 generously

If, as the story goes, Marco Polo brought back to Italy the pasta that he found in the Orient, then this Southeast Asian-flavored "lasagna" comes by its origins rightfully. Only here the noodles are based on rice rather than wheat flour and the dish is cheeseless. Replacing the traditional *tricolore* of red tomato, green basil, and white cream sauces are green, yellow, and red curry sauces, which provide a sinfonietta of resounding flavors that with each bite echo each other, harmonize, and ultimately resolve themselves into a friendly assault on the palate.

If you can't find uncut sheets of fresh rice noodles (most often available in Asian groceries near the produce array), use the dried Thai version and soak them in hot water to soften before simmering in water until tender.

Don't be daunted by the long list of ingredients. Once they are gathered, the actual preparation is quick and foolproof. Before assembling the dish, however, allow each of the curry sauces to breathe at room temperature and then sample them to check and correct the balance of hot, mellow, and fragrant seasonings to suit your palate. Freshness and quality of spices vary widely, as does personal taste, so it's best to confirm that the spicing is right for you. If necessary, gradually add more aromatics like lemongrass, cilantro, parsley, cumin, and cinnamon to cool them down and, conversely, more gingerroot, chiles, black pepper, or chile sauce to heat them up. With its eclectic array of seasonings, this dish will give you a good reason to build (or refresh) your stock of fresh spices.

Any leftovers can be reheated to crisp perfection in a heavy skillet in a bit of oil and served with the curry sauce of your choice.

2 lbs. (approx.) fresh rice noodle sheets, unfolded and soaked in hot water for
    15 minutes (known as *gwaytio lod* in Thai)

Salt for the boiling water in which the noodles are plunged

Sesame oil to coat the noodles and baking dish lightly

6 Japanese eggplant (about 1¾ lbs. total), peeled and sliced into long strips, brushed
    lightly with oil on both sides and broiled until tender

GREEN CURRY SAUCE:

1 tsp. cuminseed

1 tsp. coriander seeds

1 tbsp. salad oil

1 fresh jalapeño pepper, seeded

2" piece gingerroot, peeled and finely minced

2" piece of the base of lemongrass, crushed to release aroma

½ cup water

½ cup finely chopped cilantro leaves

½ cup finely chopped parsley leaves

½ cup finely chopped cooked fresh spinach leaves, well washed

1 tsp. Southeast Asian shrimp paste

1 cup Mock Coconut Milk (page 267)

Juice of ½ lime

YELLOW CURRY SAUCE:

1 tbsp. cuminseed

½ tsp. fenugreek seeds

½ tsp. achiote (annatto) seeds

6 whole cloves

2 tbsp. salad oil

1 jalapeño pepper, seeded

½ cup finely chopped onion

2 large cloves garlic, crushed and finely minced

¼ cup water

½ tsp. turmeric

½ tsp. freshly ground black pepper

Salt

4 tbsp. Thickened Yogurt (page 265)

Fresh lemon juice to taste

RED CURRY SAUCE:

1 tsp. cuminseed

2 cinnamon sticks, each about 2" long

1 tbsp. Curry Blend (page 264)

1 tbsp. salad oil

2 cloves garlic, crushed and finely minced

1" piece gingerroot, peeled and finely minced

1 medium-sized red bell pepper, oven-roasted, peeled and seeded, and pureed (about 1 cup after processing)

1 cup Fresh Tomato Puree (page 263)

Sambal oelek (Indonesian chile paste) or Thai *sriracha* sauce to taste (any bottled thick, full-flavored chile sauce will do)

THE GARNISH:

2 cups very thinly sliced leek greens and whites, deep-fried in oil just until golden brown, drained on absorbent paper

Light soy sauce to taste

1. For the green curry sauce, toast the cuminseed and coriander seeds in a small heavy skillet until fragrant, about 2 minutes, stirring to heat evenly. Do not burn. Grind finely in an electric spice or coffee grinder or use a mortar and pestle.

2. In a heavy 8" skillet, heat the oil. Add the ground spices from above and stir for about 30 seconds to release their fragrance. Add the jalapeño pepper, gingerroot, and lemongrass, stirring for another minute. Add water and stir to blend all ingredients. Add the cilantro, parsley, and spinach and cook for 30 seconds. Remove from heat and place contents in a blender or food processor. Blend until smooth. Pass through fine sieve and then add the shrimp paste, Mock Coconut Milk, and lime juice. Set aside in a covered bowl.

3. For the yellow curry sauce, toast cuminseed, fenugreek seeds, achiote seeds, and cloves in a heavy skillet just until fragrant but not burnt, about 45 seconds. Allow to cool and grind as in step 1 above.

4. Heat the oil until hot in a heavy skillet and add the ground seeds, stirring for about 30 seconds. Add the jalapeño, onion, and garlic and cook for about 3 minutes over moderate heat, stirring frequently. Add water, turmeric, black pepper, and salt, cooking over low heat for about 8–10 minutes, until onions are tender. Blend, add yogurt and lemon juice, and place in a separate covered bowl.

5. For the red curry sauce, toast the cuminseed and cinnamon sticks in a heavy skillet until fragrant. Allow to cool and grind as in step 1 above.

6. Heat the oil in a skillet. When hot, add the garlic and gingerroot. Reduce heat to low and add the Curry Blend and the ground spices. Cook, stirring, for about 30 seconds, or until fragrant. Add red pepper and tomato purees and cook over moderate heat for about 5 minutes. Add chile paste to taste and cook for another minute.

7. Plunge the rice noodles in a large pot of salted boiling water and remove immediately. Drain well. Coat lightly with the sesame oil and arrange in a single layer to avoid sticking, then divide noodles into three roughly equal amounts.

8. Preheat the oven to 350°. Lightly oil a 2-quart baking dish with sesame oil. Overlapping slightly, layer enough of the first amount of noodles to cover the bottom of the dish. Spread a thin amount of the green curry on this layer of noodles. Alternate eggplant and more of the green curry between each layer of the remaining first third of the noodles. Proceed with the next third of the noodles and layer in the yellow curry sauce. Finish with the last third of the noodles and the red curry sauce, ending with at least two layers of noodles for the top of the dish. (Reserve any leftover curry sauces for another use.) Brush top lightly with sesame oil and bake until heated through, about 40 minutes. Remove from oven. Allow to stand about 10 minutes before cutting and serving. For a touch of crisp, delicious drama, garnish with a tangle of deep-fried frizzled leeks. Serve with a splash of light soy sauce as desired.

SERVING SUGGESTIONS: You've outdone yourself here, so keep the starter and ending simple. Start with a tangy cucumber salad, end with some cooling sweet seasonal fruit doused with a bit of ginger liqueur, and the meal's complete.

Deep, Dark, and Ducky–Braised Duck with Grapes and Peppercorns   STAR
Serves 4

Even paired with an assertive sauce, lean breast meat of duck cooked to a turn reveals its rich succulence and pleasingly gamy flavor. (With its offending layer of fatty skin removed, duck meat is as low in fat as chicken breast similarly denuded.) With a crisp mantle of roasted wild rice powder (in a playful twist on the Thai staple) amped up with some coarsely ground white pepper, this small, dark, and handsome dish fills the bill when the fare needs to be festive or your appetite calls for something slightly self-indulgent.

Served here with a silky sauce based on defatted duck stock, red wine, and smoky Armagnac brandy, a pound of skinless and boneless duck breast provides ample servings for four without breaking the bank.

Be sure to allow enough lead time to make a full-flavored stock from the duck bones and carcass. (Preparing it the day before serving is fine.) After cooling and chilling, the stock can be easily defatted by simply lifting off the solidified top layer of fat. With the stock prepared, the remaining preparations for the dish are easily accomplished shortly before serving.

1 lb. boneless duck breast, skin and any visible fat removed

2 tbsp. wild rice, roasted in 350° oven for about 10 minutes, cooled and then
     pulverized in a coffee or spice grinder

1 tbsp. coarsely ground white pepper

½ tsp. ground dried ginger

1 tbsp. fruity olive oil

2 tbsp. finely minced shallots or white part of leeks

1 large clove garlic, crushed and finely minced

1 cup Fresh Tomato Puree (page 263)

½ cup dry red wine

¼ cup Armagnac (or Cognac)

2 cups (approx.) duck stock, defatted

2 cups seedless red or green grapes

Salt to taste

THE GARNISH:

½ cup finely chopped parsley

1. Wash and dry the duck breasts. Dip the pieces of breast in a mixture of roasted rice powder, white pepper, and ginger to coat evenly. Shake off any excess.

2. Heat the oil in a heavy skillet until almost smoking. Place the duck into the pan and sear 3 minutes on each side. The surface of the meat should be golden brown and crisp. Remove to a 300° oven to continue cooking just until the breast feels slightly firm and the meat is pink inside, about 25 minutes. Do not overcook or the meat will be tough and juiceless.

3. Remove any excess fat from the skillet and add the shallots and garlic. Cook until tender but not browned, adding duck stock as needed to avoid sticking or burning. Add the tomato puree, red wine, Armagnac, and the remaining stock and cook until reduced by half. Add the grapes and cook until the stock reduces to a coating consistency and the grapes are well coated. Taste for salt.

4. Remove the duck from the oven and slice across the breast on the bias into thin strips. Mask each of 4 heated serving plates with a generous ladling of sauce. Fan duck slices on the sauce and divide the remaining sauce over each serving. Garnish with the parsley.

SERVING SUGGESTIONS: A fluffy mound of creamy cornmeal pudding enlivened with juicy kernels of fresh corn is the requisite side dish here. Some Sizzled Shiitakes (page 200) would complete the plate harmoniously. Save your best ruby, fruity red wine for this one.

A Caper of Oven-Roasted Beets   SIDE
Serves 4

For sheer visual impact, a salad featuring tender, juicy beets placed against a golden, Scandinavian-scented sauce can't be outdazzled. In a dish that's more Helsinki than Harvard, the beets' rich, smoky taste from an unorthodox roasting competes winningly here with the mustard and dill in a yogurt-based caper dressing. (Curiously, the ancient Greeks believed that the offensive smell of garlic on the breath could be mitigated by chewing on some beet roasted over hot coals.) When paired with some fine imported herring, the salad offers a perfect excuse for a glass of dry champagne.

I find that larger beets tend to be sweeter and more flavorful (although you will need to allow more oven time). Roasting enhances the natural sweetness of the vegetable and seals in all the glorious ruby color which a watery boiling often washes out.

Be sure to scrub the beet skins thoroughly. When well crisped, they make a rustically charming addition to the dish that I find irresistible. (If you prefer a more refined presentation, peel the beets after roasting.)

2 large beets (about 1½ lbs. total), tops and tails removed
Fruity olive oil to brush the beets lightly before roasting

THE SAUCE:

2 tbsp. sharp Dijon-style mustard

1 tbsp. rice vinegar

½ tsp. granulated sugar

1 cup Thickened Yogurt (page 265)

½ cup finely chopped fresh dill tops

¼ cup capers, drained

Salt and freshly ground black pepper

½ cup (approx.) freshly squeezed orange juice

THE GARNISH:

Generous bouquet of fresh dill sprigs

1 tbsp. finely grated zest of 1 orange

Golden caviar (optional)

1. Place the washed and scrubbed beets on a baking sheet. Coat them lightly with oil. Roast in a 350° oven for about 45 minutes, or until they test tender when a small sharp knife is inserted deep into the middle. Allow to cool.

2. To make the sauce, in a small bowl blend the mustard, vinegar, and sugar with a whisk. Add the yogurt and whisk until smooth. Mix in the dill and capers. Add salt and pepper to taste. Thin with enough of the orange juice to produce a sauce of light coating consistency.

3. If you wish to peel the beets, do so at this point. If not, simply slice approximately ¼" thick.

4. Coat the center of a decorative serving platter with half of the sauce. Arrange the beet slices as you wish (I like to fan them in a concentric circle). Surround with the dill sprigs. Pour the remaining sauce evenly over the beets. Sprinkle the grated orange zest on top. Spoon dollops of caviar at even intervals over the beets, if desired.

SERVING SUGGESTIONS: I like to serve this as a vibrant part of a weekend breakfast featuring smoked fish or surround it with an array of herring, caviar, and dense dark breads for a light late supper.

Dark Greens with a Bright Flavor

SIDE

Serves 4

O ceans apart, Asia and the American Deep South come together in this boldly flavored melange of mixed greens bolstered with fresh spinach. Three Stateside
favorites, cornbread, sesame (or benne) seeds, and greens, show unexpected affini-
ties for each other in this Asian-inflected vegetable dish.

Crackling-fresh cornbread croutons encrusted with toasted sesame seeds add
crunch to an otherwise melt-in-your-mouth high-fiber medley. The whole ensemble is
tied up in a neat package under a brightly flavored swath of sauce, which combines
bottled Chinese oyster sauce and a splash of Vietnamese fish sauce (*nuoc mam*) with a
generous edge of fresh garlic.

If either red-veined Swiss chard or Red Russian kale is available, by all means
include one or both in the mix. And if your garden is full of any other members of the
easy-to-grow greens, feel free to include some of them.

THE CORNBREAD:

½ cup coarse yellow cornmeal

½ cup all-purpose flour

1 tsp. baking powder

1 tbsp. sugar

½ tsp. salt

1 whole egg

1 tbsp. melted butter

1 cup Thickened Yogurt (page 265)

Butter for coating the baking pan

3 tbsp. raw sesame seeds

THE GREENS:

1 tbsp. fruity olive oil

1 bunch Swiss chard (white or red), ribs removed, well washed

1 bunch mustard greens, well washed

1 bunch fresh spinach leaves, well washed

THE SAUCE:

3 tbsp. Chinese oyster sauce

2 tsp. Vietnamese fish sauce (nuoc mam)

1 tsp. sesame oil (Japanese has best flavor)

1 tsp. sugar

1½ tsp. finely minced fresh garlic

Root Stock (see page 258) to mellow and thin the sauce (approx. ¼ cup)

THE GARNISH:

Sesame seeds, toasted in 350° oven for about 5–7 minutes, or until golden brown

1. Preheat the oven to 350°. Sift the cornmeal, flour, baking powder, sugar, and salt together into a large mixing bowl. In a small bowl, blend the egg, melted butter, and yogurt until smooth. Gently combine the dry and liquid ingredients just until mixed. Do not overmix. Pour the batter into a lightly buttered 8-inch square baking dish that has been coated with some of the raw sesame seeds. Cover the top heavily with the remaining sesame seeds. Bake for approximately 25–30 minutes, or until a toothpick or skewer comes out clean when inserted into the center of the cornbread. Allow to cool. Cut into ¾" cubes. Return cubes to oven and toast until crisped on all sides, turning them carefully to expose all sides evenly to the heat.

2. When the cornbread has been cubed and toasted, heat the oil in a large heavy skillet. Add the greens and stir-fry just until wilted. Remove to a heated serving platter.

3. Make the sauce by bringing oyster sauce, fish sauce, sesame oil, sugar, and garlic to a boil. Simmer for 5 minutes, or until garlic feels tender. Add enough stock to thin the sauce to a light coating consistency and continue cooking over low heat for 10 minutes more. Sieve the sauce and pour in a thin ribbon over the greens. Garnish with the toasted cornbread cubes and sprinkle the toasted sesame seeds generously over all.

SERVING SUGGESTIONS: I think this works especially well alongside a simply grilled fillet of salmon or trout. For a well-rounded dinner plate, augment the main entree and side dish with a basic basmati rice pilaf sweetened with slowly cooked shallots.

Muncha Buncha Mungs–Crisp Bean Sprouts in a Lime-Ginger Marinade

STARTER

Serves 4

This is an unpretentious little salad with flavors that are pure and direct. Requiring only a brief immersion in a marinade made from the brine of homemade Pickled Ginger and fresh lime juice, it can be easily assembled minutes before serving. I like to serve it as a light palate cleanser before a richly sauced entree. For a striking presentation, mound this on a shiny black platter lined with some frilly Savoy or beautifully pale Napa cabbage leaves.

1 lb. fresh bean sprouts (the whiter the better—Asian markets are the most reliable source)

4–6 large leaves Savoy or Napa cabbage

½ cup liquid from Pickled Ginger (page 273), or substitute liquid from commercially preserved ginger

Juice of 2 limes

½ tsp. dried ginger

1 tbsp. sesame oil

Salt and freshly ground Szechwan pepper

THE GARNISH:

1 tsp. white sesame seeds, toasted in 350° oven until golden brown, about 5–7 minutes

1 tsp. black sesame seeds, toasted in 350° oven to bring out flavor, about 2 minutes

1 tsp. finely chopped crystallized ginger

Thin wedges of lime

1. Wash the bean sprouts and place in a bowl of ice water for 5 minutes. Drain and dry. Line a platter with the cabbage leaves.

2. Make the marinade by combining the ginger liquid and lime juice in a small mixing bowl. Add the dried ginger and whisk until combined. Add the sesame oil and salt and Szechwan pepper to taste.

3. Pour this liquid over the sprouts and allow to stand for about 10 minutes. After marinating, drain the sprouts and place on the prepared platter. Sprinkle the sesame seeds evenly over them. Garnish with the crystallized ginger and lime wedges.

SERVING SUGGESTIONS: With its refreshingly snappy personality, this salad would stand up to most any entree just off the barbecue. Analogous to the sweet-and-sour daikon radish and carrot salad that accompanies many steamed dumplings of the dim sum breakfast, this also would act as a crunchy sidekick to Philippine Scallop Rolls (page 89) or Smoked Seafood Spring Rolls (page 211).

Sesame Mucho—A Fragrant Toss-Fry of Fennel and Artichoke Hearts in a Sesame Glaze   SIDE or STARTER
Serves 6 to 8

Stir-fry two vegetables with distinct personalities and unite them in a warm, nutty, sesame honey glaze. Then add a sneaky touch of heat thanks to the Japanese hot red pepper blend called *shichimi togarashi* (itself a mix of hot red pepper, orange peel, and the seeds of sesame, hemp, and poppy). The result is a dish that fairly vibrates with flavor far greater than its short list of ingredients would indicate.

In its own refreshing way, this is a pairing that handsomely proves that vegetables, when treated with respect, can and do transcend side-dish status. At my table, this duo always steals the show. Realizing that nothing can compete, I like to serve it with an unadorned fish or poultry entree that gains its savor merely from salt, pepper, lemon juice, and the flavor of the grill.

4 medium-sized fresh artichokes

2 tbsp. sesame oil

1 large fennel bulb, hard core removed, cut into roughly 1" pieces (about 2 cups)

2 cloves garlic, crushed and finely minced

Salt and freshly ground black pepper, to taste

1 quart Root Stock (page 258), reduced to 1 cup (you can substitute chicken stock here)

¼ tsp. shichimi togarashi (substitute crushed hot red pepper, if you must)

2 tbsp. honey

THE GARNISH:

  ¼ cup finely chopped fresh chives or scallion greens

  ¼ cup finely chopped red bell pepper

  3 tbsp. sesame seeds, toasted in a 350° oven until golden brown, about 8 minutes

1. Prepare the artichokes by removing leaves and fuzzy choke (save leaves for another use) but keeping the stem attached to the heart. Blanch in boiling water just until crisp-tender, about 5 minutes. Drain, refresh in an ice water bath, and drain again. Set aside.

2. Heat the oil in a large heavy skillet or wok until almost smoking. Stir-fry the artichoke hearts in small batches without crowding, just until outer surface browns. As they are browned, remove to a bowl. Continue stir-frying the artichoke hearts until they have all been browned. Stir-fry the fennel for about 2 minutes, or until slightly browned. Remove to the bowl with the artichoke hearts.

3. Add garlic, salt, and pepper and cook over medium heat, about 1 minute. Deglaze the pan with the reduced stock. Add the shichimi togarashi and the honey and cook until the liquid is reduced again by half. Return the vegetables to the pan, stirring gently to coat evenly with the glaze. Cook just to heat through and remove to a heated serving platter. Garnish with the chopped chives or scallion greens, red bell pepper, and sesame seeds.

SERVING SUGGESTIONS: If a main dish of fish or poultry is not what you're after, merely bring some fat Japanese *udon* noodles to the boil, drain them, and top with a generous serving of this stir-fry. Offer a good bottle of soy sauce (Pearl River Bridge brand is a safe bet) and some Pickled Ginger (page 273) on the side as do-it-yourself adornments. Japanese beer tastes wonderful with this.

Quasi Lasagna

STARTER

Serves 4

The great French chef-restaurateur Fernand Point used to say that great cooking achieves its greatness by allowing the prime ingredients in a dish to taste like themselves. This dish is a case in point. Here Napa cabbage, dead-ripe tomatoes, flavorful vegetable stock, and aged grated goat cheese or fine Parmesan are the essential four ingredients, which, when combined in this rough-and-ready, pasta-free, vegetable lasagna-in-a-bowl, make a bright and clear statement that supports his contention. A mere gloss of shallot-infused oil brushed between the layers lends a haunting sweetness. Aside from that, the ultimate success of the dish resides in the quality of the four main ingredients.

I like to make this in summer when garden-ripe tomatoes are in reach of my kitchen door (alternatively, I rely on farmer's markets, which are usually a reliable source, especially in summer).

> 1 lb. Napa cabbage, leaves left intact
> 4 medium-sized ripe red tomatoes, peeled, sliced into rounds (Roma or plum work
>   well here)
> 2 tbsp. Shallot-Infused Oil (page 269)
> Salt and freshly ground black pepper
> 1 quart Root Stock (page 258)
> 1 cup grated aged goat cheese or fine-quality Parmesan

1. Preheat oven to 350°. In a 3-quart-capacity rectangular roasting pan, arrange a layer of cabbage leaves to cover the bottom of the pan. Next layer the tomato slices, then brush lightly with the shallot oil. Continue alternating the cabbage with the tomato and brushing each layer with oil until all of the vegetables and oil are used. As you go, season lightly with salt and pepper between the layers.

2. Cover the dish tightly with foil and bake at 350° for about 35–45 minutes, or until tender (the tip of a knife should meet no resistance when inserted into the vegetables). Allow to stand for about 5 minutes. Using a wide spatula to keep the vegetable layers intact, tilt the pan and carefully pour off all liquid that has accumulated into a 2-quart heavy saucepan. Add the Root Stock and cook until reduced by half.

3. Cut vegetable mixture into large rectangular pieces and place carefully into heated serving bowls. Gently pour the reduced stock over each serving. Blanket each serving heavily with the grated cheese.

SERVING SUGGESTIONS: Quick to make, this dish would be the perfect introduction to a more ambitious entree such as Petti di Pollo Semiamaro (page 108) or Charbroiled Chicken with Afghan Aubergines (page 80). If you are opting for a less filling meal, flank this dish with platters of Carrots Slow and Sweet (page 127) and A Caper of Oven-Roasted Beets (page 158). With this trio, colors may be muted but flavors certainly are not. In any case, I like to finish with a bowl of Blushing Bartletts (page 222).

Orzo with a Greek Herb Pesto
STARTER, SIDE, or STAR

Serves 4 as a main dish; 6–8 as an appetizer or side dish

Pasta shaped like plump grains of rice provides a soothing backdrop for this melding of eggplant and tomato anointed with good olive oil. The wild herbs of Greece are represented here by a generous bouquet of fresh oregano and thyme that is turned into the powerfully herbal green pesto just before serving. The traditional Greek pairing of tangy oil-cured black olives and cubes of salty white feta here add a bit more Mediterranean flavor.

Try to find fresh herbs that are perky and brightly colored and, most of all, highly perfumed. To be sure, pinch a leaf or two between your fingers to release some of their fragrance.

THE PESTO:

    1 bunch fresh oregano, leaves only (reserve a few sprigs for garnish)
    1 bunch fresh thyme, leaves only (reserve a few sprigs for garnish)
    2 tbsp. fruity olive oil
    Water
    Juice of 1 lemon

THE PASTA:

    1½ cups orzo (or the finer-grained riso)
    2 large bay leaves
    Zest of 1 lemon
    Lightly salted water

2 tbsp. fruity olive oil

2 large cloves garlic, crushed and finely minced

4 large Japanese eggplant, cut into ½" cubes (the small black globed variety found in
Indian stores also promises a sweetly tender result)

4 red ripe Roma (or plum) tomatoes, peeled, seeded, and cut into ½" cubes
(substitute canned tomatoes, well drained and cubed, if the fresh are pallid)

Freshly ground black pepper

THE GARNISH:

4–6 oz. feta cheese, cut into ½" cubes

½ cup roughly chopped, pitted oil-cured black olives

Few sprigs of fresh oregano and thyme

1. In a food processor or blender, or by hand with a mortar and pestle, make the pesto
by pureeing the herbs with the oil and water, as needed, until smooth and pourable.
Add enough of the lemon juice to produce a sauce with a discernible tartness. (I like
to sprinkle the finished dish with more fresh lemon juice, which seems to balance the
fruity undertones of the olives and their oil and mute the occasional oversaltiness of
the feta.) Set aside.

2. Cook the pasta with the bay leaves and lemon zest in a 2-quart pot of boiling lightly salted water just until tender. Drain, discarding the bay leaves and zest, and set
aside. (If you intend to hold the pasta for more than a few minutes, lightly coat it
with oil to keep the grains separate.)

3. In a large heavy skillet, heat the oil until hot. Add the garlic and cook, stirring, just
until softened but not browned. Add the eggplant and sauté just until tender and
evenly browned, about 5 minutes. Add the tomato and stir to combine, cooking for
about 1 minute longer.

4. Add the cooked pasta and stir gently to combine. (If necessary, heat, just before serving, in a 350° oven until heated through.) Season vigorously with pepper. Mound on
a large heated decorative platter and scatter the feta and olives over the dish. Garnish
with the reserved herbs.

SERVING SUGGESTIONS: This dish with its Mediterranean flair works well either
as an entree or, in smaller portions, introducing or accompanying an uncomplicated
grilled chicken or fish dish. You might also feature it at a pasta buffet including Birds in

the Bush (page 207) and the impostor Sham Spaghetti Anti-Pesto (page 134). Fresh fruits in season presented over a bowl of ice and tiny glasses of chilled anisette or ouzo would be a fitting finale.

Fennel Gratin with a Red Pepper Ribbon   SIDE
Serves 4

Under its aromatic crust of grated Parmesan, tender slices of pale fennel borrow the spirit, if not the fat, of the classic creamed potato dish of Lyon, France's gastronomic heart. Nonfat yogurt makes a credible stand-in for the often unconscionable amounts of heavy cream used in the classical version. Transcending tradition is a ribbon of roasted red pepper puree, which adds flavor but no fat and ties up each portion of the dish into a neat, brightly colored package. Sweet anise, firm yet creamy yogurt, and nutty oven-toasted cheese all merge in a memorable congruence of textures and flavors.

For a grand variation on this theme, substitute 1½ lbs. Napa cabbage leaves for the fennel and proceed with the recipe, with one exception: when using the Napa, place a few thick coins of peeled gingerroot in the water when precooking it. Discard them and proceed as shown below.

1½ lbs. fennel, cored, feathery tops removed (reserve a few sprigs as garnish)
Fruity olive oil to coat baking dish
1 cup grated imported Parmesan cheese
2 cups Thickened Yogurt (page 265)
Salt and freshly ground black pepper
Nonfat milk

THE RED PEPPER PUREE:
1 large red pepper, stuck with 6 cloves and roasted in 350° oven until skin is lightly browned; then skinned and seeded, cloves removed
Water

1. Place the fennel in a saucepan with enough boiling water to cover. Reduce to a simmer and continue to cook over low heat until tender but still intact, about 10 minutes. (You can steam the vegetable with equal success, if you wish.) Drain and dry on absorbent paper toweling.

2. Preheat oven to 350°. Lightly oil a rectangular or square 2-quart baking dish. Layer the fennel, grated cheese, and yogurt thinned slightly by whisking in enough milk to achieve the consistency of thick buttermilk. End with a thick layer of cheese on top. Salt and pepper lightly between the layers as you go.

3. Bake at 350° for about 20–25 minutes, or until the top is golden brown and bubbling. Remove from oven and allow to cool to lukewarm.

4. While the dish is cooling, puree the red pepper in a food processor or blender, adding enough water to achieve a barely pourable consistency. Set aside.

5. In the center of each of 4 heated serving plates, pour a circle of the puree. Place a rectangular piece of the gratin, cut to fit within the circle of puree, on each plate. Pour two ribbons of puree, intersecting at right angles, on top of the squares of the gratin (the effect should look like a package tied up with a red ribbon). Garnish with a sprig of the fennel tops.

SERVING SUGGESTIONS: Nothing tops this as the side dish of choice for a crisply roasted chicken or squab. Add more fragrant excitement with a portion of Sizzled Shiitakes (page 200) and you'll never notice the starch missing from the plate. With this relatively virtuous kind of meal, dessert should be something special like Three Ring Citrus (page 238) or a thin slice of the White Chocolate Mousse Torte with Pistachios and Bitter Lime Sauce (page 240).

Rolled Buckwheat Pancakes with a Double Cache of Salmon

STARTER

Serves 8

Homey, yet luxurious at the same time, this update on the well-known Russian blini takes two forms of an underused grain, turns them into an eggless, yeast-raised batter, and when griddled, rolls them around a stuffing containing two forms of salmon—silky smoked and salty-sweet roe. Avoiding fat-laden sour cream or the even more sinfully delicious crème fraîche, this version settles for a tart dollop of Thickened Yogurt sparked with fresh dill to add gloss to the finished dish. Choose from dry champagne, icy vodka, or aquavit to wash these down elegantly.

Make the batter a day in advance and refrigerate to allow it to develop flavor overnight before cooking. Japanese or Russian markets are good, reliable, and reasonably priced sources for fresh salmon roe and sometimes smoked salmon as well.

¼ cup fine-grained kasha

⅓ cup warm water (about 90–110°)

1 tsp. active dry yeast

1 tbsp. sugar

1½ cups nonfat milk warmed to 90–110°, plus additional to thin batter before griddling

2 tbsp. unsalted butter, melted

½ tsp. salt

½ cup masa harina (fine corn flour used in Mexican cookery) or fine polenta

1 cup buckwheat flour

8 oz. salmon roe (natural-colored is preferable)

1 cup Thickened Yogurt (page 265)

Vegetable oil spray or clarified butter to cook the pancakes

4 oz. thinly sliced smoked salmon

THE GARNISH:

Feathery sprigs of fresh dill

8 oz. clarified butter (page 278), warmed (optional)

Finely chopped onion (optional)

Lemon wedges (optional)

1. Toast the kasha in a 350° oven for about 10 minutes, or until fragrant. (Although it is sold already roasted, this additional toasting deepens the flavor and, in drying it out, lends a bit of crisp texture to the final product.)

2. Blend the warm water, yeast, sugar, and milk in a large mixing bowl until the yeast and sugar are dissolved. Add the butter and salt and then blend in the masa harina, buckwheat flour, and kasha. Mix only until smooth. Cover and refrigerate overnight. Allow to come to room temperature before cooking, adding water or more milk as needed to make a batter that runs easily to coat the surface of a nonstick frying pan.

3. In a small bowl, blend the salmon roe into half of the yogurt and set aside. (If you don't mind giving away the identity of the cache, use only half of the roe here, reserving half to bejewel the yogurt that adorns the rolled pancakes.)

4. Heat an 8" nonstick frying pan. Coat the pan with the vegetable oil spray or butter and pour enough of the pancake batter to thinly coat the pan. (Stir and thin the batter with milk or water as needed.) It should not be necessary to grease the pan after each pancake. Cook for about 1 minute on each side. Invert the pancakes onto a baking sheet in a single layer and keep them warm, covered, in a 200° oven. The batter should make approximately 20 thin pancakes 8" in diameter.

5. To assemble, spoon a scant tablespoon of the salmon roe-yogurt mixture down the center of each pancake, top with a thin strip of smoked salmon, and roll tightly. Arrange on a heated serving platter or individual heated plates, 2 pancakes to a serving. Top with dollops of the remaining yogurt (and the reserved roe if you chose to reserve some) and decorate the platter with the dill. Serve with melted butter, chopped onion, and lemon wedges, if desired.

SERVING SUGGESTIONS: New Year's Eve has become synonymous in my mind with this appetizer, but any weekend brunch, with or without the champagne, would benefit from its inclusion in the menu. For an unorthodox but no less delicious accompaniment, serve these with A Caper of Oven-Roasted Beets (page 158) whose vaguely Scandinavian origins place them comfortably within the sphere of Russian-inspired foods. If you're looking for an appropriate entree to follow these, look no further than the Gorgeous Georgian Chicken (page 16). A side dish of steamed, shredded brussels sprouts or mixed cabbages would fit in here.

For dessert, escape to sunnier climes and go for broke with Lavender Honey Ice Cream with Grilled Pineapple (page 244).

Very Nearly Vietnamese Salad

STARTER or STAR

Serves 6-8 as appetizer; 4 as main dish

This is a layered salad in more ways than one. In a veritable fugue of flavors running the gamut from sweet to hot to acidic to smoky to garlicky, this is one bowl of greens that beckons you to take another bite, and another . . . .

With some added protein in the form of a julienne of home-smoked chicken breast, this is an intriguing main-dish salad. If chicken palls, choose shrimp or scallops straight from the grill for an alternate stick-to-the-ribs embellishment. Although traditionally this kind of salad is topped with fried spring rolls (*cha gio*) or crisp-edged barbecued pork, it can embrace a wide diversity of other toppings and invites you to improvise.

Here's the basic architecture: Thin, soft rice noodles alternate with layers of shredded crisp romaine lettuce and thin rounds of cucumber, which, in turn, alternate with a mixture of fresh basil, mint, and cilantro leaves. A bright shred of raw carrot is snuck in between each layer. On top of everything, finely chopped roasted peanuts and shards of fried garlic are a savory scattering that, when mixed throughout with the tart dressing, add texture and zing to the whole structure.

I like to show off its subtle stripes of color by serving this salad in clear glass bowls, with a variant of *nuoc mam* (rhymes with Look Mom) dressing in individual small bowls on the side to be mixed in at the last moment. For greatest delicacy, make the dressing just before serving. I always provide a jar of homemade Sweet Chile Vinegar (page 272) to enable each diner to spike the dressing at his or her discretion.

2 large whole chicken breasts (about 1½ lbs. total), with keel bone removed, home-smoked for 35–40 minutes (see page 276)

1 lb. tiny rice stick noodles (banh pho)

1 head romaine lettuce, cored, washed, dried, and thinly shredded

1 bunch fresh basil leaves

1 bunch fresh mint leaves

1 bunch fresh cilantro leaves

1 seedless cucumber, peeled and sliced into paper-thin rounds (about 4 cups)

2 large carrots, peeled and shredded medium fine, about 4 cups (the shreds should remain separate)

4 oz. peanuts, roasted and finely chopped

4 cloves garlic, thinly sliced and then fried in 2 tsp. flavorless salad oil until golden
   brown, drained on absorbent paper toweling

THE NUOC MAM DRESSING:
Juice of 2 oranges (about 1 cup)
Juice of 1 large lime (about 2 tbsp.)
2 tsp. fish sauce (nuoc mam)
Red chile peppers to taste
Sugar
Salt to taste
Water

THE GARNISH FOR THE DRESSING:
Thin julienne of carrot and daikon, as desired, to float in each bowl

1. Remove the skin and bones from the smoked chicken. Split each breast into halves
   and slice diagonally into thin strips. Set aside.

2. Soak the noodles in warm water for 30 minutes and then place in a pot of boiling
   water just long enough for the water to return to a boil. Drain and reserve.

3. Arrange the salad artfully in layers, beginning with the lettuce, then alternating with
   layers of herbs, cucumber, noodles, and carrots. Continue layering until all ingredients have been used. Top with the sliced chicken. Sprinkle the peanuts and garlic on
   top. Set aside.

4. Make the dressing by mixing the citrus juices with the fish sauce. Add chiles to taste,
   along with sugar and salt to taste. Add just enough water to dilute the sauce until it
   is mildly hot, fishy, and sweet. To bring the flavors into balance, you may need to
   add some of any or all of the dressing ingredients. The right way is what pleases you.
   Serve dressing on the side in individual bowls. Float julienne of carrot and daikon on
   top to garnish.

SERVING SUGGESTIONS: Start with appetizer portions of this and move on to a
steaming bowl of Thai-Dyed Seafood Soup (page 6) for a filling but not heavy pairing.
Finish with Sticky Rice Snowballs with Coconut Sauce (page 250).

Warm "Salad" of Watercress, Arugula, and Roasted Red Pepper

STARTER

Serves 4

Why cook the crunch out of salad greens? Why not? After too long a spell of pallid salads where crunch is all they have going for them, it's time for an assertive mix like this one, where any traces of bitterness are muted by a quick wilting in the sauté pan. A well-balanced dressing of soothing olive oil, red wine vinegar, and a somewhat shy puree of roasted garlic coats every dark green leaf. Punctuated by bits of roasted red pepper, the salad is then covered with a thatch of freshly flaked Parmigiano Reggiano, arguably the king of Italian cheeses. Whoever said that salads have to be cold and crunchy hasn't tasted this one.

You should have little difficulty finding watercress and arugula since they are both becoming more commonly available year round. Store them in the refrigerator in a container of water lightly tented with a plastic bag until ready to use.

1 large red bell pepper

3 tbsp. fruity olive oil, plus additional to lightly coat pepper and garlic before
   roasting

12 cloves garlic, unpeeled

1 bunch fresh watercress (about 2 cups leaves), washed and dried

1 large bunch arugula (about 3 cups leaves), washed and dried

1 tbsp. fine-quality red wine vinegar

¼ cup coarsely grated or flaked Parmigiano Reggiano

Freshly ground black pepper

1. In a preheated 350° oven, roast the pepper, whole, lightly oiled, until the skin is evenly browned, about 20–30 minutes. Place the garlic, lightly brushed with oil, in a separate baking pan and roast until tender, about 15–20 minutes. As they are done, remove from the oven and let cool until easily handled. Remove the skin of the pepper, cut in half, and remove the seeds and ribs. Chop into ½" pieces and set aside. Squeeze the soft garlic from each clove into a small bowl, mash with a fork until smooth, and set aside.

2. Remove the leaves from the watercress, discarding the stems. Remove any coarse stems from the arugula. Mix the two greens together and set aside.

3. Heat the oil in a large skillet and cook the greens over moderate heat, stirring, until just barely wilted. (Some of the leaves may appear to be uncooked. As they stand, they will wilt from the residual heat of the mixture.) Remove to a serving platter and add the garlic puree and the vinegar to the skillet. Cook over medium heat, stirring, for another minute or until the liquid thickens slightly and the vinegar no longer tastes harshly acidic. Pour over the greens and sprinkle the cheese heavily over all. Grind fresh black pepper over the salad at the table.

SERVING SUGGESTIONS: I like to awaken the taste buds with this one before a meal of Charbroiled Chicken with Afghan Aubergines (page 80) or Leek-Wrapped Grilled Shrimp with Tarama Sauce (page 142). If appetites are smaller, the Risotto Island in an Herbal Broth (page 148) would fill the bill. Either way, Blushing Bartletts (page 222) would be the hard-to-beat sweet here.

Toss-Up of Red and Yellow Peppers with Crisp Water Chestnuts

STARTER or SIDE

Serves 4

This multiethnic alliance is what you get when you take Chinese stir-frying and add a subtle Japanese accent thanks to a Spanish ingredient. Here it's sweet bell peppers that benefit from this sassy treatment, but any colorful mosaic of vegetables on hand would work just as well.

Intensely sweet and crunchy fresh water chestnuts are used here to provide textural contrast (in their absence, substitute small chunks of peeled jícama for a somewhat different effect). With no more than a flash in a well-heated pan, the strips of pepper emerge lightly coated with a sauce somehow reminiscent of Japanese teriyaki-style entrees where mirin or sweet sake is used. Here the sauce results from the mingling of Spanish sherry wine vinegar, soy sauce, and dark sesame oil united with garlic.

¾ cup fresh water chestnuts

1 large red bell pepper

1 large yellow bell pepper

2 tbsp. dark sesame oil

3 cloves garlic, crushed and finely minced (about 1 tbsp.)

2 tbsp. sherry wine vinegar

1 tbsp. dark soy sauce

Freshly ground black pepper

THE GARNISH:

2 tsp. finely chopped Chinese garlic or yellow chives (include a few buds if attached)

1. Wash and peel the water chestnuts. Place in ice water until ready to use and then drain and quarter. Set aside.

2. Halve the peppers and remove the seeds and ribs. Slice lengthwise into strips ½" wide.

3. Over high heat, heat the oil in a heavy 10" skillet until almost smoking. Add the peppers and stir-fry for 30 seconds. Add the garlic and stir for 10 seconds more, or until fragrant. Remove to a bowl, stir in vinegar and soy sauce, and cook the sauce over high heat until slightly thickened. Return the peppers to the pan and stir to coat evenly. Remove to a heated serving platter. Grind pepper to taste over the bell peppers.

4. In the same skillet, quickly stir-fry the water chestnuts just until heated through. Scatter over the peppers. Garnish with the chives.

SERVING SUGGESTIONS: With its pan-cultural personality, this side dish would neatly complement such diverse pungent entrees as Pan-Seared Bass with a Searing Melon Coulis (page 61), Sumatran Salmon with Honey Glaze (page 41), or Southwest by Southeast Saté (page 57).

Madame Sprat's Pan-Grilled Foie Gras with Cassis-Vinegar Sauce

STARTER

Serves 4

This one is for those rare celebratory times when dietary and budgetary considerations don't hover in the wings, the guests are extra-special, and the champagne is equally so. With only three main ingredients, this festive dish can be prepared in a matter of minutes just before serving. Featuring the ultimate in luxury on the tongue, here fresh foie gras (from New York State ducks) is first quickly seared, then kept warm while the pan sauce is being made. A simple deglazing of the skillet with a pour of black-currant syrup and red wine vinegar captures and intensifies all the aromas of the pan juices, producing a sauce that is subtly sweet and slightly tart. The foie gras is returned to the pan for a final glazing and is then encircled with a necklace of sauce, like liquid rubies. If you can find fresh black currants (sometimes shipped from New Zealand) or black currants in syrup (often available imported, bottled, from Poland and Czechoslovakia), use them to add a resplendent touch. If in season, either fresh blueberries or blackberries would work well here, too.

1 cup dark raisins

½ cup hot water

1 lb. fresh duck foie gras (see Superb Sources, page 290)

1 small clove garlic, finely slivered

Salt and freshly ground white pepper

⅛ tsp. ground nutmeg

1 tbsp. clarified butter (page 278)

1 cup dry red wine

3 tbsp. fine-quality red wine vinegar

1 cup bottled black currants, well drained (reserve juice for step 4 below)

2 cups Root Stock (page 258)

¼ cup sirop de cassis (black-currant syrup)

Juice of 1 lemon

THE GARNISH:

A few sprigs of fresh black currants

2 tbsp. freshly chopped parsley leaves

1. Soak the raisins in ½ cup hot water for 15 minutes. Drain, reserving the liquid to be used for the sauce (save the raisins for another use).

2. Carefully trim any visible fat, veins or spots of blood from the duck liver. With the point of a small sharp knife, insert the garlic into the liver, distributing the slivers as evenly as possible throughout. Lightly salt and pepper the liver and dust with nutmeg. (Note: At this point, for an alternative presentation, wrap portion-sized pieces of the foie gras, about 4 oz. each, in large leaves of blanched Savoy cabbage and then proceed with the packets per the recipe.)

3. Place the butter in a stovetop griddle or heavy skillet. When hot, add the liver and cook over high heat for 2 minutes. With a wide spatula, carefully turn over and cook for another 2 minutes. The liver should feel slightly firm to the touch. If overcooked, it will lose too much of its fat, leaving it dry and hard instead of meltingly tender. Remove to an ovenproof platter, cover, and place in a 200° oven to keep warm while the sauce is being made.

4. Pour off all but 1 tsp. of the fat from the skillet. Add the wine, vinegar, raisin water, and liquid drained from the bottled black currants. Cook over high heat until reduced to a mere glaze. Add the stock and cook until reduced by half. Add the sirop de cassis, lemon juice, and bottled black currants and cook until the sauce has been reduced to coating consistency. Taste for salt and adjust as necessary.

5. Gently return the liver to the pan to coat with the sauce. Then transfer to a heated decorative serving platter. Pour the remaining sauce over the liver and garnish with the fresh black currants and the parsley. Serve immediately.

SERVING SUGGESTIONS: Conceding that this kind of luxury is a hard act to follow, I suggest a salad of mixed greens, both bitter and mild, barely drizzled with fine olive oil. Serve it with the best rustic loaf of bread you can find and call it a feast. But keep the champagne coming.

CHAPTER 5

• • • • • • • • • • • • •

It's Almost All Done with Smoke and Wood

here's something comforting and complex about foods cooked over the fragrant smoke of a fire. Certainly no small part of the multisensory experience is the captivating aroma released by the foods during cooking, hinting at the tastes in store. Who can explain their appeal? Perhaps it's the subliminal link to our primitive roots that makes these foods so popular. (After all, many cuisines from which I draw inspiration have retained the basic outlines of their ancient cooking methods down to the present day with only the slightest concessions to modernity.)

Serving as inspiration for the dishes featured here are foods as diverse as the spit-roasted marinated lamb of Turkey, the charcoaled quail of Tuscany, and the primitive Mongolian hot pot. Distinct taste memories all, I think of these as primarily dishes with a sensual winter personality, with an overall taste impression reminiscent of the piercing tang of pine or spruce inhaled while deep in the woods.

Take Lusty Chicken Tamales with a Touch of Smoke (page 193) and Tea-Steeped Duck Atop a Nest of Noodles (page 198), for example, both transformed by a stay in the smoker, dishes that seem destined to be served on an icy weekend in midwinter. Stretching the definition a bit, Sizzled Shiitakes (page 200) and More Than Fair Fowl (page 183), with their inherently "smoky" character, are prepared without even a wisp of smoke. Given the subjective reality of taste perception, however, they seemed nonetheless right for inclusion here.

This is food to unleash the imagination. Digging into a steaming bowl of Porcini Mushroom Soup au Gratin (page 205) or a plate of grilled sea bass in a sauce redolent of rosemary and retsina (page 219), I can almost imagine smoke curling from a cabin chimney, high up in a winter retreat where the window panes are frosted with a lacy rime. At times like these, my appetite sharpens and I crave applewood-smoked chicken or eggplant whose skin is blistered over a crackling fire. No matter what the season, the smoke of a real wood fire (or any other kind, for that matter) lends an unforgettable layer of flavor that simply cannot be summoned from a bottle.

Fire up your wok-turned-smoker in winter or the backyard grill-with-a-cover in summer and join me in the reverie.

Key Ingredients

For conspiring to create flavors that are dusky, smoky and woodsy.

ARMAGNAC—brandy from southwest France, often considered a more robust and fiery cousin of Cognac

BALSAMIC VINEGAR—the pride of Modena (See Flavor Flash!, page 126)

BARBECUED MEATS—particularly Chinese, Korean, and Thai, available to go by the pound in many Asian markets and delis; a wonderful ingredient in spur-of-the-moment salads and soups, or for use in a utensil-free picnic, as is

BLACK BEANS, preserved fermented (Chinese)—salted beans used in Cantonese-style sauces, particularly with seafood

BUCKWHEAT GROATS (OR KASHA)—a favorite in Eastern and Middle European cooking, these are the roughly triangular fruits of the herbaceous buckwheat plant; slow-cooked onions bring out their toasty fullness of flavor

CHIPOTLE CHILES—fire roasted jalapeños, usually sold canned, in a rust-colored tomato sauce; can be extremely hot

DRIED POLISH MUSHROOMS—usually a mixture of mushrooms often rehydrated and used in soups; despite their name, now commonly imported from Chile

EARL GREY TEA—black tea flavored with essence of bergamot, the fruit of a small citrus bush; an excellent flavoring for poultry and game marinades, this tea also adds fragrance when foods are smoked over a mixture where it predominates

FINE COGNACS—with their almost smoky, full-bodied, high spirited character, these distilled brandies from France add an incomparable luxury and finesse to sauces

HOISIN SAUCE—a versatile, thick, Chinese brown sauce, composed of soy sauce, plum sauce, garlic, and sesame oil; somewhat sweet, of variable hotness; Lee Kum Kee brand is reliably good

LAPSANG SOUCHONG TEA—black tea with a pronounced smoky, almost tarry flavor, produced in Fujian province in southeastern China; when combined with dried citrus peel and aromatic spices such as star anise and cloves, the tea imparts its special flavor to a marinade for duck or goose before they are smoked

MUSHROOMS—morels, portobello, shiitake, trumpet, chanterelles, chicken-in-the-wood, other edible wild mushrooms; check with the experts first on edibility of those found in the wild

PINE NUTS—the edible seeds of certain pine cones; the best come from Italy but the Chinese varieties are a good, more economical second choice; these blond beauties are used in everything from cookies and cheese cakes to pasta sauces; a light roasting unlocks their sweet nutty flavor

RETSINA—a strongly resinated wine of Greek or Cyprus

RICE POWDER, ROASTED—jasmine or basmati rice yields the most fragrant powder; used in salads, braised meat dishes; see Flavor Flash!, page 51

RICE, WILD

SERCIAL MADEIRA—the driest wine made from grapes grown on Madeira, a group of islands 400 miles off the coast of Morocco; the Sercial variety is based on the Riesling grape of the Rhine; its sharp flavor makes it the perfect wine for sauces

SMOKED CHEESES—mozzarella, ricotta, Rambol, and Gouda are often given that extra layer of flavor; worth the journey to find

SMOKED FISH—including salmon, trout, and tuna; demand a sample before buying to be sure that the flesh is still moist, not dry due to over-smoking

SMOKED MEATS—French and Italian charcuterie, Smithfield ham, Chinese gammon

SMOKED SEAFOOD—mussels, shrimp, scallops (See How to Smoke Foods..., page 276)

SZECHWAN PEPPERCORNS (ALSO KNOWN AS ANISE PEPPERCORNS)

TREE EARS (WOOD EARS)—a Chinese fungus, available fresh or dried; even when long-cooked, these retain their pleasantly chewy texture

More Than Fair Fowl

Serves 6

For a new twist on barbecue, try this Oriental-inspired marinade on turkey, chicken, or duck. The resulting combination of sweet, tart, and smoky (grill over hard wood like mesquite for the most mellow smoky flavor) transforms even the humble low-fat turkey breast, if cooked carefully, into something sublime and succulent.

> 1 (3 lb.) boneless turkey breast; or 6 boneless duck breasts (8 oz. each); or 1 (3 lb.) chicken

THE MARINADE:
> ½ cup roasted sesame seed paste (see Flavor Flash!, next page)
> ½ cup Chinkiang vinegar (if unavailable, another rice vinegar will do)
> 1 cup soy sauce (low-sodium version is fine)
> 2" piece gingerroot, peeled and minced
> 4 cloves of garlic, crushed and minced
> 1 tbsp. sugar or honey

1. To prepare the marinade, combine the sesame paste with the vinegar in a medium-sized mixing bowl, whisking until smooth. Add the remaining ingredients and set aside.

2. For turkey or duck, prick the breasts with a sharp knife all over to allow the marinade to penetrate the meat. Place in bowl with the marinade, cover, and refrigerate for at least 1 hour, or until ready to grill (longer than overnight may result in undesirably mushy meat, however). For chicken, cut into 8 pieces. Remove skin as desired and marinate as above.

3. Prepare the grill. Allow the mesquite wood to turn white. (Check the intensity of the heat by briefly placing your hands 2" above the surface of the grill; if the heat feels intense, the grill is ready.)

4. Remove the meat from the marinade and cook as follows: The 3-lb. turkey breast will require about 25–35 minutes, turning every 7–10 minutes, with the grill covered. (If your grill does not have a cover, simply invert a roasting pan over the turkey

to retain enough heat to properly cook the meat.) For accurate cooking, it helps to use an instant read thermometer. Be careful not to prick too often or precious juices will be lost to the fire. The temperature should read about 160 when the thermometer is inserted halfway through the thickest part of the breast. The boneless duck breasts should be cooked only until slightly pink in the center. The chicken parts will take approximately 15 minutes for the breast halves and wings, 20–25 minutes for the thighs and legs.

5. While the meat is cooking, sieve the marinade to remove the minced ginger and garlic. Boil rapidly in a heavy sauce-pan to reduce to a light coating consistency. Remove the grilled meat to a heated platter, remove the skin, slice as desired. Pass the reduced marinade in a sauceboat as accompaniment.

SERVING SUGGESTIONS: This is great served with a side of Chilled Chinese Crunch (page 43). Finish the meal with a plate of Beijing Biscotti (page 234) and a steaming pot of smoky Lapsang Souchong tea.

Flavor Flash!
Roasted Sesame Seed Paste vs. Sesame Tahini

It would be hard to find two foods made from the same ingredient that are more different than the Asian sesame seed paste and the Middle Eastern tahini. They seem to approach the versatile sesame seed from opposite directions. The former, a deep brown, celebrates the nutty character of darkly roasted sesame seeds, while the latter, a pale grayish-beige, points up the oily luxury of raw sesame seeds when ground. In different degrees, each shines in cold preparations. The Asian version, sometimes labeled as sesame sauce, works especially well in salads and noodle dishes. I also like to add it to cookies like biscotti and shortbread for an especially rich toasty flavor and as a replacement for a small amount of the fat in the recipes. The Middle Eastern one combines beautifully with roasted eggplant, chickpeas, or as a component in a yogurt-based dip for crisp raw vegetables. When sweetened with honey, the ground raw seeds become the base for halvah, that spongy, crumbly confection of Turkish descent which, in its chocolate and nut-flavored forms, almost obscures its sesame origins.

> Maybe, just maybe, Ali Baba was saying more than he knew when he said "Open Sesame." The seed's wondrous taste is really revealed only when it is split, whether roasted or not.
>
> Store the roasted paste at room temperature with a thin layer of flavorless oil floated on top; refrigerated and stored in a tightly closed tin or jar, tahini will keep indefinitely.

Bird in a Bag–Aromatic Roasted Chicken in a Haunting Sauce

STAR

Serves 8

The French are definitely onto something when they prepare a fish fillet or veal chop *en papillote*. Behind what appears to be a bit of restaurant theatrics is sound culinary procedure, not to mention some keen merchandising. When foods are wrapped in parchment in close proximity to flavor-enhancing herbs, wine, or other aromatics, they literally stew in their own juices. And when the packet is opened at the table, beneath the nose of the expectant diner, a cloud of fragrant steam is released and the heads of neighboring diners turn in response to the celestial aroma. Here an ovenproof roasting bag stands in for the parchment pouch of the original version. It's opened in the kitchen to enable the cook to create a sauce by defatting and then reducing every bit of the precious pan juices produced in the slow, steam-roasting process.

The big bird is given a head start to big flavor with an overnight marination in a mostly Chinese-accented seasoned liquid. Save this one for a time when company's coming since it works best with a large roaster (weighing in at approximately 6 lbs.). I find that the sturdier meat of the bigger bird retains its texture even after long steeping in the marinade and some 2½ hours in the oven. It also absorbs the forthright flavors of hoisin, star anise, and soy sauce right down to the bone.

Tiny squabs or small Cornish hens take to this treatment nicely as well. The same overnight marination applies, but cooking times are proportionately reduced. Cooking 8 squabs (under ½ pound each) should take about 25 minutes; cooking 4–6 Cornish hens (slightly over 1 lb. each) should take about 40 minutes.

1 roaster chicken, approx. 6 lbs.

THE MARINADE:

3 cups soy sauce (preferably low-sodium version)

½ cup hoisin sauce

6 whole star anise

¼ cup honey

½ cup ruby port

¼ cup rice vinegar

8 cloves garlic, smashed but left whole

4" piece gingerroot, peeled, cut into
    ½" chunks

1. Wash and dry the chicken thoroughly. Place in a stainless steel or crockery bowl large enough to fit it comfortably.

2. Whisk all of the marinade ingredients in a large bowl, being sure that the honey is dissolved. Pour over the chicken, cover, and place in refrigerator overnight.

3. The next day, place the chicken and all of its marinade into an ovenproof roasting bag. Tie tightly. Place the bag in a large roasting pan and roast at 350° for approximately 2 to 2½ hours. When done, an instant-read thermometer should indicate 195° when inserted into the thigh (don't hit the bone when taking the bird's temperature).

4. Allow the bird to rest a bit to redistribute its juices before serving. Remove the garlic, gingerroot, and star anise from the pan juices and reserve. Skim off as much visible fat as possible (or defat using a plastic defatting cup). Pour the defatted juices into a heavy 2½ to 3-quart saucepan and reduce over high heat until the resulting liquid coats a spoon nicely (this will take about 10 minutes of supervised cooking).

Flavor Flash!
Star Anise

Native to southeastern Asia, star anise is the sun-dried fruit of an evergreen tree from the magnolia family. The highly aromatic reddish brown fruits, usually eight pointed, add a warm, spicy edge to soups, stews, sauces, poached fruit compotes, and even pastries when the spice is finely ground. Its sweet licorice-like aroma and flavor announce their presence in the five-spice powder used freely in Chinese cooking. (The rough proportions to use here are: 3 parts black peppercorns, to 2 parts each of fennel seeds and cinnamon, to 1 part each of cloves and star anise.) If kept in a cool, dark place, in a glass jar with a tight-fitting lid, a supply of star anise (or the five-spice powder, for that matter) will keep indefinitely. A little of either goes a long way.

5. Carve the bird into serving-sized pieces, remove the skin if desired, and nap with the sauce. Garnish the platter with the reserved garlic cloves, gingerroot, and star anise.

SERVING SUGGESTIONS: Sesame Mucho—A Fragrant Toss-Fry of Fennel and Artichoke Hearts in a Sesame Glaze (page 163) and a well of plain, steamed jasmine rice for each plate are all this dish needs to be complete.

Wild Rice Pancakes
SIDE

Serves 4

When is a rice not a rice? When its botanical name is *Zizania aquatica*, better known as wild rice. The grains from this tall aquatic grass impart a wonderfully earthy note to these crisp pancakes. Their smoky edge evokes for me the depths of a forest after a spring rain. These are not only a great brunch dish but also a savory complement to any roast fowl. Don't forget these when Thanksgiving rolls around.

    1 cup wild rice
    8 cups water
    1 tsp. salt
    2 bay leaves
    6 oz. can of water chestnuts, well drained, chopped coarsely; or 1 cup diced jícama
    2 oz. Smithfield ham (with any encircling fat removed) or Chinese gammon, finely
        chopped
    ½ cup dried currants, soaked in warm water until puffed, then drained
    1 egg, beaten
    1 tbsp. flour, to coat waxed paper
    2 tbsp. olive oil, for sautéing the pancakes

1. Cook the wild rice, covered, in a medium saucepan with the water, salt, and bay leaves until tender, about 30 minutes. The cooking liquid should all be absorbed. If not, drain the rice well before mixing with the water chestnuts (or jícama), ham, drained currants, and egg.

2. With wet hands, divide the mixture evenly into 8 mounds and flatten into round pancakes. Place on floured wax paper as you proceed. Heat the olive oil in a heavy sauté pan and cook the pancakes for about 2 minutes per side, about 4 at a time, until well browned and crisp on the outside. Keep warm in a 250° oven until ready to serve.

SERVING SUGGESTIONS: I like to serve these with Pepper-Crusted Turkey Steak (page 65) or Grilled Turkey Paillard with Honeyed Rhubarb Ginger Sauce (page 20) on a cool spring evening. When special company's coming, end the meal with subtle, sophisticated Tahitian Tarts (page 235), redolent of flowery vanilla.

Kasha Rutti-Frutti

SIDE

Serves 4

T hanks to the proliferation of farmer's markets, truly fresh-from-the-farm produce is within reach nearly everywhere around the country. Summer, of course, holds the showiest riches, although in my part of the world the other seasons have their own special delights.

Where I live we are blessed by one purveyor whose dazzling array of lovingly dried fruits never fails to capture my heart and stomach every time I pass by. In particular, I look forward to the time when, about a month after fresh apricots appear for their fleeting stay on produce shelves, their dried-but-not-dry counterparts arrive at the market. Even though I lay in a supply in the freezer to get through the intervening seasons, I never seem to keep enough on hand. (See Superb Sources, page 292.)

Looking for a poultry go-with, I decided to build a side dish that would celebrate the apricots' chewy perfumed tartness. Pairing toasted buckwheat, which, botanically speaking, is the fruit of an herbaceous plant, with that other vaunted fruit of my dreams seemed a viable marriage. Attempting to conserve a dwindling supply, I devised this dish to prove that a mere cup of something wonderful can go a long way. One nutty grain, two superlative dried fruits and a quartet of full-flavored root vegetables make up the sublime arithmetic. Try this with slices of juicy turkey breast roasted at high heat in a foil packet. I find that toasting the kasha before cooking lends an appealing smokiness and accentuates its nutty flavor and aroma; likewise, roasting the root vegetables heightens their natural sweetness and deepens the flavor of the dish.

1 medium-sized rutabaga, peeled and cut into ¼" cubes (about ¾ cup)

1 medium-sized turnip, peeled and cut into ¼" cubes (about ¾ cup)

1 sweet potato, peeled and cut into ¼" cubes (about 2 cups)

2 medium-sized carrots, peeled and cut into ¼" cubes (about ½ cup)

2 tbsp. olive oil

1 large onion, finely chopped (about 2 cups)

1 cup kasha

2 cups Root Stock (page 258)

Salt and freshly ground black pepper

1 cup dried apricots, soaked in hot water to plump, cut into ¼" cubes

½ cup golden raisins, soaked in hot water for 5 minutes to plump and then drained

2 egg yolks, lightly beaten

Oil to coat molds

THE GARNISH:

4 large leaves Romaine lettuce

1 cup coarsely chopped toasted blanched hazelnuts

1. Preheat the oven to 350°. Lightly coat the rutabaga, turnip, sweet potato, and carrot cubes with 1 tbsp. oil. Roast until just tender and a bit crusty and brown, about 10–15 minutes. Set aside.

2. In a heavy sauté pan, cook the onion in the remaining oil just until tender but not browned.

3. Toast the kasha at 350° just until fragrant, about 5 minutes. Add to the onions in the pan. Cook, stirring over moderate heat, to coat the grains with oil. Add the Root Stock and cook covered at the merest simmer for about 15 minutes, or until the kasha is tender but not pasty. The stock should be fully absorbed by the kasha. (If not, drain excess.) Salt and pepper to taste.

4. Stir in the vegetables, apricots, and raisins and mix lightly. Quickly stir in the egg yolks and then pack tightly into lightly oiled 1-cup timbale molds or muffin tins. Cover with foil and bake at 350° for about 15 minutes. Keep warm.

5. Blanch the lettuce in boiling water just until slightly wilted. Drain and quickly submerge in ice water. Drain and dry. Set aside.

6. Invert molds onto warm serving plates or a platter lined with the romaine. Serve garnished with a generous dusting of hazelnuts.

SERVING SUGGESTIONS: Any simply roasted fowl would work grandly with this as a side dish. Or you might stuff and roll boneless chicken breasts and poach them in Root Stock if company's coming.

Smoky Chicken Packets Steamed in Banana Leaves   STAR
Serves 4

Is there life for the banana (and its cousins) beyond the cereal bowl? Most definitely. This entree features the broad, dark green leaves of one member of the banana family and the fruit of another. For me it evokes the sultry tropics, from Asia to South America, where members of the banana bunch are staples in everything from soup to dessert.

Sticky rice, whether or not enhanced with other ingredients, shows up both sweetened and un-, enveloped in a wrap of banana leaves in much of Southeast Asia. Half a world away in the Yucatan state of Mexico, banana leaves enclose locally caught fish grilled over hot coals. For at least two hundred years, Mexican cooks have understood the virtues of wrapping foods in banana leaves before cooking. As true now as then, the leaves preserve the moisture of the item being cooked without added fat, prevent burning or overcooking, and impart an extra hint of flavor to boot. Around Christmas each year, the leaves replace the dried corn husks used in making tamales.

Here the matte, jade-colored leaves lend their own musky note to a filling of smoky shredded chicken embedded in coconut-scented sticky rice. Bronze, baked plantains with a garlicky glaze extend the banana's haunting fruity intensity to a side dish that can turn any unadorned grilled chicken or fish preparation into something quite wonderful.

Using nitrite-free and salt-free home-smoked chicken (the procedure is easier than you might suspect) adds another unforgettable layer of flavor in a dish that only *tastes* complex. Do a few steps in advance (smoking the chicken and preparing the dipping sauce) and the final assembly will be a tropical breeze. Be sure to buy plantains whose skins are blackened from room-temperature ripening, with flesh that yields easily to light pressure. The ripe fruit will be yellow with the faintest blush of pink, a color that reminds me of the first glow at sunset.

> 1 lb. boneless smoked chicken, equal parts light and dark meat (see page 276 for smoking procedure)
>
> 1¾ cups uncooked sticky rice (about ¾ lb.)
>
> 2 cups Mock Coconut Milk (page 267)
>
> Salt and freshly ground white pepper
>
> 1 lb. banana leaves (available frozen in most Asian markets)

THE BAKED PLANTAINS:

> 1 lb. ripe plantains, peeled, halved, and cut into 2" lengths
>
> ½ cup Root Stock (page 258)
>
> 6 cloves garlic, crushed and roughly chopped
>
> ½ cup palm sugar
>
> Salt and ground white pepper to taste

THE DIPPING SAUCE:

> 2" piece gingerroot, peeled
>
> 3 cloves garlic, peeled
>
> ½ cup light soy sauce
>
> ½ tsp. Thai chile sauce
>
> 1 tsp. honey
>
> 1 tsp. vinegar
>
> 2 tbsp. chopped cilantro leaves

1. Shred the chicken and set aside in a bowl.

2. Cook the rice in a mixture of half of the Mock Coconut Milk combined with ¾ cup water. Cook, covered, over low to moderate heat in a heavy saucepan for about 15 minutes. Most of the liquid will have been absorbed. Add the remaining Mock Coconut Milk to the rice. Mix the chicken gently into the rice. Add salt and pepper to taste. Set aside.

3. Center a heaping cupful of the chicken-rice mixture on each banana leaf. Fold two sides over the filling. Then fold in the ends to create a neat, compact package. You can tie the packets closed with kitchen string, if necessary. Place as many packets in

the steamer rack as can be accommodated in a single layer. Set the rack in the steamer over boiling water. Cover the steamer and steam for about 15 minutes, or until the point of a knife feels hot when inserted into the filling. Remove from the steamer and keep warm and covered in a 200° oven. Continue to steam the remaining packets until all 8 have been steamed.

4. In a heavy skillet, place the plantains in a single layer. Add stock, garlic, sugar, salt, and pepper and bring to a boil over medium heat. Reduce heat to a simmer and cover, cooking about 10 minutes more, or until the plantains test tender when a knife is inserted into them. Remove the plantains to an ovenproof dish and reduce the pan liquid over high heat just until it will coat a spoon lightly. If too thin, cook carefully to reduce further. If too thick, add a bit of stock. There should be about 1 cup of liquid remaining after cooking. If not, adjust by adding enough stock to equal one cup. Pour over the plantains, turn them to coat evenly in the sauce, cover the dish, and keep warm in a 200° oven.

5. Make the dipping sauce by blending gingerroot, garlic, soy and chile sauces, honey, and vinegar to a smooth consistency in a food processor or blender. Stir in the cilantro and reserve.

6. To serve, place two packets on each plate with a portion of well-sauced plantains on the side. Provide an accompanying decorative bowl of dipping sauce for each person. When serving the packets, cut the strings (if any) and unwrap. The banana leaves are not eaten. Dip the chicken-rice filling into the sauce.

SERVING SUGGESTIONS: A salad of crunchy jícama, red pepper, and avocado in a lime vinaigrette would complement this dish nicely. For an appropriately tropical finale, a small scoop of Vietnamese Coffee Ice Cream (page 232) would send me to creamy caffeine contentment.

Lusty Chicken Tamales with a Touch of Smoke

Serves 6 as a main course, 8 as an appetizer   STARTER or STAR

When fresh corn is out of season, I like to make this northern Mexico-inspired dish featuring masa harina, which to me tastes and smells more like corn than corn itself. It's made from dried corn kernels first treated with lime and then finely ground.

The stuffing for the steamed corn husks is a mosaic of smoked chicken, raisins, green olives, and toasted almonds all lightly bound with a tomato salsa, hottened up with fire-smoked chipotle chiles. Considerably friendlier to the heart than the traditional lard-laden versions, this cool-weather dish sneaks in a rough puree of golden acorn squash to hold the masa together with little discernible difference in texture from its Mexican forebears. Chicken and chicken stock are the lower-fat alternatives to the pork meat and pork-derived stock used in the classic *cocina*.

THE SAUCE:

2 tbsp. fruity olive oil

1 cup finely chopped onion

8 cloves garlic, crushed and minced

4 cups Fresh Tomato Puree (page 263)

4 cinnamon sticks

1 tsp. ground cumin

2 cups cilantro leaves

Salt and freshly ground black pepper

4 chipotle chiles, drained of excess sauce and finely chopped

THE CORNMEAL PASTE:

1 medium-sized acorn squash (about 1½ lbs.)

4 cups masa harina

2½ cups (approx.) Gingery Chicken Stock (page 259)

THE FILLING:

1½ cups smoked chicken, light and dark meats mixed in the proportion of your choice (see page 276 for directions on smoking)

½ cup dark raisins, plumped in hot water for 5 minutes and drained

½ cup slivered almonds, toasted in 350° oven for 5 minutes until golden brown

½ cup large green olives, pitted (hotly spiced olives from Israel work particularly
   well)

3 oz. dried corn husks (about 24) soaked in hot water for 5 minutes to soften

8 cinnamon sticks

THE GARNISH:

1 bunch fresh cilantro leaves

1. Heat the olive oil in a heavy saucepan and cook the onion and garlic until tender but
   not browned. Add the tomato puree, cinnamon sticks, cumin, and cilantro. Cook
   over low heat for 20 minutes, stirring occasionally. Add salt and pepper to taste.
   Remove the cinnamon sticks and discard. Blend in chipotles. Set aside half of the
   sauce to serve with the tamales.

2. For the masa mixture, bake the acorn squash in a 350° oven for about 35–40 minutes or until tender. (Or microwave for about 12–15 minutes at high power.) Cut in
   half, scoop out seeds and discard. With a spoon, scoop the flesh into a bowl.
   Discard the skin.

3. Beat the squash until smooth, adding the masa and stock alternately until the mixture is smooth but somewhat liquid. Add more stock as needed.

4. To make the filling, fold the chicken, raisins, almonds, and olives into half of the
   tomato sauce.

5. Center about 1 tbsp. of the masa mixture on each softened corn husk. Spoon about
   1 tbsp. of the chicken mixture over the masa. Fold in sides of the husk to enclose the
   filling, then fold in top and bottom.

6. Place the filled corn husks upright in the rack of a steamer. Intersperse 8 cinnamon
   sticks among the tamales. Cover with a damp paper towel. Place over boiling water
   in the steamer, cover, and steam over low heat for about 2 hours, adding hot water
   to the steamer as needed.

7. Serve hot from the steamer with some of the reserved sauce on each plate. Garnish
   with cilantro leaves.

SERVING SUGGESTIONS: Start with a crisp salad of seedless cucumber and fresh pineapple splashed with Tropical Vinegar (page 271). End with a refreshing goblet of frozen seedless grapes, slightly thawed (the more colors the better), doused with a bit of cassis-tinged dry champagne.

Napa-Kasha Nests Afloat in Cabbage Essence   STARTER

Serves 4

Although strictly speaking, nothing in this East-West fusion touches the smoke of a wood or charcoal fire, the overall taste impression this dish produces reminds me of the dark and almost mysterious *je ne sais quoi* of smoked foods. Hence its inclusion in this chapter.

More apt to be a staple in Middle European pantries than Far Eastern ones, buckwheat groats, unexpectedly pivotal in this Chinese-accented dish, are well toasted here to reveal their nutty side. (I like to blend coarse and fine versions to yield a lighter texture in the final dish.)

Subtly smoky Chinese star anise gets double billing here—first in the filling and then more quietly in the hoisin-tinted cabbage essence that surrounds the neat Napa cabbage-wrapped packages when served. (Commonly found, hoisin sauces vary widely in spiciness from brand to brand. Taste a few and decide which blend you like, noting the source and brand name for future reference.)

Drawing again from the Chinese pantry, sweet sausage, pulverized dried shiitake mushrooms, and ground Szechwan peppercorns contribute to the overall smoky edge of the dish. A chop of carrots adds a bit of color. Slowly sautéed onions, slivered fresh gingerroot, garlic, and the merest hint of sesame oil conspire to impart fragrance to a hearty, though delicate, cool-weather dish that marries East and West, with each partner having an equal voice, despite an ingredients list that seems to give the Orient the upper hand.

½ cup fine-grained kasha
¼ cup coarse-grained kasha
12 whole leaves Napa cabbage

THE COOKING LIQUID FOR THE KASHA:

2 cups water

Napa cabbage trimmings

1 tbsp. sesame oil

2" piece gingerroot, sliced into thin rounds

THE STUFFING:

2 large dried shiitake mushrooms

3 whole star anise

4 oz. Chinese-style sweet sausage, casings removed, cut into ¼" cubes

2 large cloves garlic, crushed and then finely minced

1 small onion, finely chopped (about ¼ cup)

1 medium-sized carrot, cut into ¼" cubes (about ¼ cup)

½ tsp. kosher salt

½ tsp. freshly ground black peppercorns

2 eggs, lightly beaten

Oil or vegetable oil spray to coat the molds

THE CABBAGE ESSENCE:

¼ head Napa cabbage, thinly shredded (about 1 cup)

¼ small head white cabbage, thinly shredded (about 1 cup)

4 whole star anise

4 cups water

2½ tbsp. hoisin sauce (or less if you prefer less spicy result)

THE GARNISH:

2" piece gingerroot

Green part only of 2 scallions

1. Toast both types of kasha on a baking sheet for 20 minutes in a preheated 350° oven. (When properly toasted, it should smell almost but not quite burnt.) Place in a heavy sauté pan and reserve.

2. Trim the Napa cabbage leaves to a length 2" longer than the height of the molds used. (Save trimmings to flavor the cooking liquid for the kasha.) Place in a pot of boiling water and cook until flexible. Do not overcook. Drain, refresh under cold running water, and set aside to dry.

3. In a 2-quart saucepan, bring 2 cups water, cabbage trimmings, sesame oil, and gingerroot to a boil. Add this liquid to the sauté pan containing the kasha, stir once and cook the mixture covered over low heat for about 10 minutes, or until the grains are tender and all the liquid has been absorbed. Fluff with a fork and let stand, covered.

4. Pulverize the shiitake mushrooms and star anise in a spice grinder until fine.

5. Cook sausage over medium heat in a separate sauté pan until it begins to exude some of its fat. Add the garlic, onion, and carrot and cook until tender but not browned. Add the mushroom, star anise powder, salt, and pepper. Cook over low heat, stirring, until the mixture is fragrant, about 2–3 minutes. Add to kasha. Add the eggs and stir to blend. Reduce oven temperature to 325°.

6. Lightly oil (or spray with vegetable oil) four 1-cup-capacity timbale molds or muffin cups. Line the bottoms and sides of each with the cabbage leaves, allowing approximately 2" overhang to be used to seal in the filling at the top of the molds. Fill with kasha mixture and enclose with overhanging cabbage leaves. Cover each mold with foil and place in a water bath with enough water to reach halfway up the sides of the molds. Bake for 45 minutes at 325°.

7. While the molds are baking, make the cabbage essence. In a 2-quart saucepan, bring shredded Napa and white cabbage, star anise, and 4 cups water to a boil. Reduce heat to a simmer and cook for approximately 35 minutes. Remove star anise. Add hoisin sauce to taste.

8. Peel the gingerroot and slice paper-thin. Stacking slices, cut into fine julienne strips. Slice the scallion greens into long, thin julienne strips.

9. Run a knife around the inside edge of each mold and remove the timbales from the molds. To serve, ladle one-fourth of the cabbage essence into each of 4 wide shallow soup bowls. Carefully center one timbale in each bowl. Garnish with some of the julienned gingerroot and scallions.

SERVING SUGGESTIONS: This would make a comforting beginning for a meal of Pepper-Crusted Turkey Steak (page 65) with a side of Bitter Greens in a Honey-Lemon Drizzle (page 25).

Tea-Steeped Duck Atop a Nest of Noodles   STAR

Serves 4

Redolent of sweet spice and a tinge of smoke, this Oriental-inspired dish takes the best part of the duck, its breast, and marinates it in a brew of smoky Lapsang Souchong tea. Then the meat is smoked in a wok disguised as a stovetop smoker and served julienned atop a nest of fresh, slightly chewy eggless water noodles (sold fresh in the refrigerated cases of most Asian markets). With its boldly flavored sauce based on soy sauce, cinnamon, and star anise, the dish can stand alone as a fragrant room-temperature treat. If you'd like to really go all out, some unctuous melt-in-the-mouth seared duck foie gras would be a luxurious but sublime counterpoint to the leaner breast meat featured here.

This makes an impressive focal point for a glistening buffet that includes a variety of noodle dishes, spring rolls, dumplings, and the like.

1 lb. boneless duck breast, skin removed

THE MARINADE:

2 cups strong-brewed Lapsang Souchong tea

1 tsp. sugar

1 tsp. salt

2 cloves garlic, crushed and minced

Grated zest of 1 orange

Sesame oil for coating the duck before it is smoked, and for coating the noodles after they are cooked

INGREDIENTS FOR STOVETOP SMOKING (SEE PAGE 276)

THE SAUCE:

1 cup light soy sauce

2 whole star anise

1 cinnamon stick

1 dried red hot chile, crushed

2 tbsp. honey

1 tbsp. Chinkiang or balsamic vinegar

Salt to taste

12-oz. package of eggless Chinese or Japanese water noodles

THE GARNISH:

½ cup chopped green part of scallion

Few sprigs of fresh cilantro

1 tbsp. white or black sesame seeds, toasted lightly in moderate oven for 3 minutes

1. Mix the marinade ingredients in a stainless steel or crockery bowl. Place the duck breast in it to marinate for 2 hours, covered, at room temperature. Remove from marinade, wipe dry, and set aside.

2. Set up wok as described on page 276.

3. Lightly coat the duck breast with the sesame oil. Fit the wire rack in the wok. Place the reserved duck breast on the rack. Pinch the foil overhang from the wok and its lid together to create a tight seal. Turn the heat to high and heat the wok until smoke begins to emerge, about 5 minutes. Continue smoking for about 8 minutes longer. Allow the wok to cool before opening it. Remove the duck and cook further in a 350° oven, for about 7 minutes, or as needed, until the breast feels slightly squishy and is still pink when cut, indicating medium doneness. Check frequently to avoid over-cooking. When done, remove to a plate, cover and set side.

4. To make the sauce, bring the soy sauce, star anise, cinnamon, and chile to a boil in a heavy 1-quart saucepan. Sieve out solids and return the liquid to the pan. Add the honey and vinegar. Bring the sauce to a boil again and cook to reduce to a light coating consistency. Add salt to taste, if necessary. Set aside.

5. Cook the noodles in a large pot of slightly salted boiling water for about 10 minutes, or just until they are somewhat resistant to the bite when tested. Drain and coat lightly with sesame oil. Mound noodles on a decorative serving platter. Slice the duck meat across the breast on a diagonal into thin julienne strips. Arrange the duck on top of the noodles. Pour the sauce in a thin drizzle over the duck. Garnish with the scallions, cilantro, and sesame seeds.

Sizzled Shiitakes

SIDE

Serves 4

Although the overall taste impression of this dish qualifies it for inclusion here, no smoke from a wood or any other kind of fire plays a part in its actual cooking. It only seems that way. When gently prepared, these meaty mushrooms project a slightly smoky character—and in this treatment, doubly so. Like two opposite sides of the same coin, fresh and dried Japanese shiitakes work together to celebrate the mushroom's quintessential woodsy character, with the locally grown fresh version lending texture and the dried contributing most of the flavor.

Here's a dish that's long on flavor and short on preparation time. It will share the spotlight as comfortably with an assertively sauced fillet of beef as with a roasted chicken heavily encrusted with herbs, or even a delicately poached salmon. Served generously atop a plate of perfectly cooked fresh pasta, the mushrooms are thrust front and center. The idea here is to let the hauntingly musky, somehow ancient perfume of the mushrooms shine through. Enhancements are straightforward and few; nothing more than a soft touch of mellow roasted garlic, a mere coating of fragrant olive oil, and a gloss of vegetable stock come between the mushrooms and the palate.

The method is refreshingly simple: singe some large fresh mushrooms over high heat, thereby leaving the insides tender, juicy, and meaty. Reduce the liquid used to soak the dried mushrooms to serve as a sauce. To complete the plate, serve a few almost blackened, grilled shallots for a smoky-sweet side note.

For a slightly sharp variation on this theme, substitute large brown, thick-capped portobello mushrooms for the shiitakes. Insert thin slivers of fresh garlic to taste into the broad mushroom caps before searing, and elaborate the sauce with ¼ cup of fine Sercial, the driest wine of Madeira. Made from the Riesling grape of the Rhine, Sercial has a characteristic caramel tang, which adds another layer of smooth complexity to the sauce.

Fruity olive oil to coat the pan when searing the fresh mushrooms and to brush on
     the garlic and shallots before cooking

6 shallots, peeled and halved

6 large cloves garlic

2 oz. dried shiitake mushrooms

Cool water to soak the dried mushrooms

½ lb. fresh large shiitake mushrooms (remove any tough stem ends and save for
     another use)

Salt and freshly ground black pepper

½ cup Root Stock (page 258)

THE GARNISH:

A few sprigs of assorted fresh herbs, as available (basil, rosemary, thyme, oregano, or chives)

1. Brush the shallots lightly with oil and cook until almost black in a heavy skillet coated lightly with oil. Brush the garlic cloves with oil and place in a 350° oven for about 20–25 minutes, or until skins are lightly browned and the garlic feels soft when squeezed lightly. Squeeze the garlic out of its skin and mash to a smooth puree. Set shallots and garlic paste aside.

2. Place the dried mushrooms in a bowl of cool water to cover. Allow to soak for approximately 30 minutes. Sieve the liquid and reserve. (I like to save the soaked mushrooms and use within a day as a soup base, or as part of the cooking liquid in a risotto or pilaf.)

3. Quickly rinse the fresh mushrooms and pat dry. Salt and pepper lightly. Heat enough olive oil to coat the bottom of a heavy skillet lightly. When the pan is almost smoking, sear the mushrooms, a few at a time, just until they are slightly browned, stirring in the softened garlic. Remove mushrooms to a pan and cover to keep warm in a 200° oven.

4. Over high heat, quickly reduce the liquid from soaking the dried mushrooms and the stock until it barely coats a spoon. Stir in any juices that may have collected in the dish containing the cooked fresh mushrooms. Correct salt and pepper as necessary and then mask the mushrooms with the sauce. Surround with the shallots. Garnish the platter with a bouquet of mixed fresh herbs.

SERVING SUGGESTIONS: This one fits in handily on the plate with any grilled meat, poultry or fish dish or can be called on to crown a plate of plain pasta, cooked *al dente*. If there any leftovers, chop them into bite-sized pieces, add more Root Stock (retrieved from the freezer, of course!) and as much heavy cream as your conscience will allow and you will have a soup of unsurpassed suavity in the time it takes to set the table.

Salmon Tournedos with a Smoky Surprise and a Celadon Sauce

STAR

Serves 4

If, like me, you love salmon and asparagus, you will be rewarded fourfold by this refined treatment featuring two forms of the king of all fish and two of the liliaceous spears. Each spring when the first tender shoots of asparagus arrive in the markets, I celebrate with this elegantly unpretentious dish.

Using well-marbled, glisteningly fresh fish, a soupçon of the best quality smoked salmon you can find, and a few deft cuts of a sharp boning knife, you can reconfigure the common salmon steak. What results is an oval packet of boneless fish camouflaging at its center a sliver of the Scottish smoked variety. The whole construction is poached in a pristine fennel-scented fish stock. Enclosed in plastic wrap, the tournedos are suffused lightly with smoke and then served on the palest green sauce of pureed asparagus.

> 4 salmon steaks, about ½" thick, each weighing approx. 8 oz.
>
> Salt and freshly ground white pepper
>
> 2 oz. finest quality Scottish smoked salmon, thinly sliced (other less subtle varieties will do)
>
> 1 bunch fresh asparagus (thin or medium spears are the least fibrous), about 1 lb.
>
> 1 quart Fresh Fish Stock with Fennel (pages 260–262), sieved of all solids
>
> 1 tbsp. unsalted butter
>
> 2 tbsp. Thickened Yogurt (page 265)

THE GARNISH:

> 1 oz. fresh salmon caviar (optional)

1. Bone the salmon steaks by inserting a sharp boning knife close to the backbone. Release the meat from the bone by cutting close to the bones that lie along the inside of the steaks. Remove any visible fat or darkened flesh. Then remove the skin from each comma-shaped fillet by placing each fillet skin side down on the cutting board. Holding the knife parallel to the board, cut with a gentle sawing motion to separate the skin from the meat. Lightly salt and pepper the two comma-shaped pieces.

2. Place the two thicker ends of the "commas" side by side with the thin belly ends radiating outward in opposite directions. Enclose a sliver of smoked salmon between these ends and form the fish into a compact oval by wrapping each thin belly end around the thicker end of the other piece. Wrap each tournedos in plastic wrap. Prick the wrap in a few places with the point of a sharp knife and set aside.

3. Remove the tips from the asparagus and reserve. Bring the stock to a boil. Reduce to a simmer and add the asparagus spears and cook until tender enough to puree easily, about 20 minutes. Remove the asparagus from the stock and set aside. Poach the salmon in the simmering stock, covered, for about 8–10 minutes, or until the fish feels slightly springy to the touch. Do not overcook or it will be dry. Remove from the stock, unwrap, place in an ovenproof dish and keep warm, covered, in a 200° oven.

4. Place the stock in the container of a blender or food processor along with the cooked asparagus spears and any liquids that may have collected in the dish containing the salmon. Puree until smooth. Add the butter and the yogurt and process just until blended. Add salt and white pepper to taste. Keep warm.

5. Blanch the asparagus tips in a small amount of boiling lightly salted water. Drain and place on absorbent paper. (They may also be steamed, if you prefer.)

6. Mask a decorative, heated serving platter with half of the sauce. Place the tournedos on the sauce. Pour the remaining sauce over the salmon. Garnish each portion with the asparagus tips and a small dollop of salmon caviar, if desired.

SERVING SUGGESTIONS: Start with the clear, refreshing zing of a Fennel-Orange Salad (page 18). Continuing in the smoky vein, and providing just the right textural counterpoint, a Mixed-Grain Pilaf with a Touch of Smoke (page 215) would be my choice to partner the fish.

Slightly Smoked Eggplant and Company
with Roasted Shallot Yogurt Sauce   STARTER

Serves 4

The usual litany of vegetables associated with Provençal cookery—eggplant, tomato, and sweet bell pepper—is represented here but with an enlivening difference. They are treated to a faint wisp of smoke in a wok-turned-smoker before being combined in a sauce that's easy to like even when not limiting fat intake. In fact, the only fat that enters this boon to dieters comes in the form of olive oil, which is used to anoint the vegetables with a feather-light brushing before they are smoked.

I like to serve this do-ahead dish at room temperature as part of a casual, family-style spread where the cook can sit down at the same time the guests do. I always count on the long, thin Japanese eggplant to ensure the sweetest-tasting end result.

INGREDIENTS FOR STOVETOP SMOKING (SEE PAGE 276)

3 medium-sized Japanese eggplants (about ¾ lb. total), peeled and halved

4 fresh ripe Roma or plum tomatoes (about ½ lb. total), blanched in boiling water for about 3–4 minutes and well drained on absorbent paper toweling

1 medium-sized sweet red bell pepper, oven roasted for about 15 minutes at 350°, then skin removed

Fruity olive oil to brush the vegetables lightly before smoking them

Salt and freshly ground black pepper

1 cup Roasted Shallot Yogurt (page 265)

THE GARNISH:

A few basil leaves, sliced into long strips

3 shallots, peeled and thinly sliced, pan-fried in ¼" of canola or peanut oil until golden brown, then drained (optional)

1. Set up the wok-turned-smoker on the stovetop (page 276). Brush the vegetables lightly with the oil and set on a rack or screen that will fit into the wok. Heat the wok until smoke is produced. Open the lid, place the rack of vegetables inside, and cover tightly. Continue heating the wok over high heat for an additional 3 minutes. By that time, the vegetables will have acquired a light smoky fragrance and, in the case of the eggplant, a light golden browned surface. Remove vegetables from the smoker

and continue to cook in a preheated 450° oven on a heavy baking sheet just until tender. (The length of time in the oven will vary depending on the vegetables and how
much cooking they received in the smoker. Check frequently and remove from the
oven when they test done.)

2. Lightly salt and pepper the vegetables, then gently combine with the Roasted Shallot
Yogurt. Garnish with the basil and/or the pan-fried shreds of shallot.

SERVING SUGGESTIONS: I like to make a meal out of this when combined with
other vegetable celebrations such as Sham Spaghetti Anti-Pesto (page 134) and Fennel
Gratin with a Red Pepper Ribbon (page 168).

Porcini Mushroom Soup au Gratin   STARTER or STAR
Serves 4

When they're fresh, wild mushrooms have an alluring fragrance that can fill a room.
Even if they have been frozen, they will unleash most of their potent aroma when
thawed. Interfering as little as possible with their wild seasonal magnificence,
here's an eclectic soup where Italian mushrooms, French smoked cheese, and Indian flatbread are linked to create a bowl of soup that can easily stand alone as a satisfying meal.

Atop a broth thick with slices of fragrant caps and stems floats an impossibly thin
flake of toasted chapati, which itself supports a crust of molten cheese. As a finishing
touch, a silvery green leaf of slightly charred fresh sage with its sharp minty taste and
slightly bitter edge adds its own special intrigue. I like to present this in single-portion-
sized ramekins (8"–9" diameter) that can go from counter to oven to table nonstop with
the seared sage leaf on top.

If fresh wild mushrooms aren't available, use half the quantity of the dried variety.
Soak them in cool water until soft, drain, and slice, discarding any tough stems. Sieve
the resulting soaking liquid through cheesecloth and use to replace an equal quantity
of the stock.

For the cheese, choose any full-flavored smoked variety of Gouda, mozzarella, or
raclette (my personal favorite for this purpose). Taste before you buy to make the right
choice.

1 tbsp. butter

¾ cup thinly sliced onion

2 tsp. Forest Fragrance (page 137)

2 oz. fresh porcini mushrooms, brushed clean (if frozen, thaw in a bowl in order to retain any juices that exude from them)

2 quarts Root Stock (page 258)

Salt

4 whole-wheat chapati, toasted until crisp (you may substitute pita, split horizontally)

2 oz. smoked cheese, grated

THE GARNISH:

4 whole large fresh sage leaves, brushed lightly with vegetable oil

1. Melt the butter in a 3-quart (or larger) saucepan. Add the onions and cook over low heat until tender but not browned, stirring occasionally. Add the Forest Fragrance and cook, stirring, for another minute.

2. Add the mushrooms and stock. Simmer the soup for 30 minutes over low heat. Salt to taste, bearing in mind the saltiness of the cheese that will be used on top.

3. Divide the soup evenly into 4 serving bowls. (The dish can be prepared in advance to this point and refrigerated. When ready to serve, remove from the refrigerator and proceed with the next step.)

4. Top each bowl with a round of toasted chapati and cover with grated cheese. Place the bowls on a baking sheet with sides in a preheated 350° oven for about 20–25 minutes, or until cheese is melted and soup is hot.

5. While the soup is heating in the oven, use tongs to carefully hold the sage leaves over an open flame (or close to the heat source of the oven broiler) until slightly charred. They should be pleasantly aromatic. Garnish the top of the soup with the sage and serve immediately.

SERVING SUGGESTIONS: With the mere addition of a brightly flavored salad of mixed greens and additional toasted plain chapati, this dish becomes the focus of a filling meal. If you have been prescient enough to have made a double batch of Vietnamese Coffee Ice Cream (page 232) recently, come to a sweet conclusion by pressing the leftovers into service.

Birds in the Bush–Smoked Capellini Nests   STARTER

Serves 4

With "birds" fashioned from nut-brown fried garlic set atop thin strands of smoked pasta "nests" and "eggs" of roasted garlic puree adding avian authenticity, this dish gives the lie to the old adage about "a bird in hand." An assertive sauce of fresh tomato and gingerroot competes gamely with the smoky tang of the pasta and is undaunted in the presence of garlic, which here is twice tamed; in one case, carefully fried, and in the other, slowly roasted for maximum mellowness.

Make this when you have an audience whose members have a lively imagination and like a mild dose of humor along with bold foods.

THE ROASTED GARLIC PUREE (THE "EGGS"):

1 large head garlic

1 tsp. olive oil plus additional for brushing the garlic before roasting

1 tsp. lemon juice

THE "BIRDS":

2 large cloves garlic, sliced into long thin slivers

2 tbsp. flavorless salad oil

THE SAUCE:

2 lbs. ripe red tomatoes, blanched in boiling water for about 3 minutes to facilitate removal of skin, peeled and seeded and cut into $\frac{1}{2}$" cubes

3" piece gingerroot, peeled and finely minced

1 red chile, seeded and finely chopped

Pinch salt

Pinch sugar

10 oz. capellini pasta (thin spaghetti)

FOR THE SMOKING APPARATUS:

1 cup white rice

$\frac{1}{2}$ cup granulated sugar

1 cup loose black tea

Peel from 1 large orange or 2 small tangerines

6 whole star anise

2 large cinnamon sticks

½ tsp. whole allspice

1. In a preheated 350° oven, roast the head of garlic, which has been first brushed lightly with olive oil, for about 20–25 minutes, or until tender. Remove from oven. Allow to cool slightly, then peel the garlic. In a food processor or blender, puree garlic along with lemon juice and 1 tsp. olive oil until perfectly smooth. Place in a parchment pastry bag for ease of arranging in small egg-shaped dots on the "nests." (Alternatively, use a small spoon to arrange them.) Set aside.

2. To make the "birds," in a small sauté pan, cook the garlic slivers in the oil just until golden brown. Drain on absorbent paper toweling and set aside. Reserve the flavored oil for another use.

3. Lightly oil four metal 1-cup-capacity molds and set aside.

4. In a small heavy saucepan, cook the tomato, ginger, and chile over low heat until thickened, stirring occasionally to avoid burning, about 5 minutes. Add salt and sugar. The sauce should have a tart, sharp flavor.

5. Cook the pasta in a large pot of lightly salted boiling water just until tender. Do not overcook. Drain pasta. Immediately fill the molds with the pasta, packing it down firmly. Cover with foil and keep warm while you assemble the stovetop smoker.

6. On each of two lengths of aluminum foil 18" long, place half of the ingredients for smoking listed above. Using one of the prepared pieces of foil, set up the wok-turned-stovetop smoker as shown on page 276. Heat the wok over high heat. As soon as the first wisps of smoke begin to issue from the wok, place the molds containing the pasta on a rack inside the wok and smoke for about 20 minutes. After the first 10 minutes, remove the piece of foil with the burned ingredients used in smoking and quickly replace with the second piece of foil containing the remaining smoking apparatus mixture. Over high heat, continue smoking the pasta nests for another 10 minutes. (For a less smoky final product, reduce the smoking time as desired.)

7. On each of 4 heated serving plates, arrange a circle of tomato sauce. Invert the smoked pasta nests onto the sauce. Pipe or spoon three or four "eggs" on the top of each nest. Place the garlic "birds" beside the "eggs." Serve immediately.

SERVING SUGGESTIONS: To balance out the labor-intensive nature of this starter, I would suggest a follow-up entree such as a whole herb-roasted chicken (or bone-in-breast for quicker results) or Pepper-Crusted Turkey Steak (page 65), neither of which would be burdensome. A Toss-Up of Red and Yellow Peppers with Crisp Water Chestnuts (page 175) would add a colorful crunch to the plate. For dessert, simply serve a plate of the best fruits found in the market.

Steamed Rice in Bamboo Leaves with Shiitakes and Smoked Salmon   STARTER
Serves 4

Take one Oriental cooking method—steaming using a very Oriental, flavor-imparting wrap of bamboo leaves encasing a mixture of Oriental mushrooms—and Occidental smoked salmon, and you have a decidedly tasty foreign exchange. Don't splurge on the best smoked salmon for this one, since lesser versions will suffice. Before preparing this, make your trip to the local Asian grocery worthwhile by stocking up with bulk purchases of soy sauces (sweetened and not), Oriental vinegar, and any seasonal case-lot produce featured in addition to buying the dried bamboo leaves, shiitakes, and jasmine rice specified below.

For the most fragrant results, allow at least a half hour of leisurely steaming once the packets are assembled.

THE RICE:
1¾ cups water
1 cup uncooked jasmine rice
½ tsp. salt

THE SWEET-SOUR SAUCE:
1 cup assorted fruits from Tropical Vinegar (page 271); or 1 cup chopped fresh
    pineapple, mango, and papaya, in proportions as desired
Sugar
Pinch of hoisin sauce

THE FILLING:

1½ oz. fresh shiitake mushrooms

1 oz. dried shiitake mushrooms

Salt

3 oz. sliced smoked salmon

4 tsp. ketjap manis (or substitute 1 tbsp. soy sauce combined
    with 1 tsp. dark molasses)

16 dried bamboo leaves

Kitchen string

1. In a 2-quart heavy saucepan, bring the water to a boil. Add the salt and rice. Reduce the heat to a simmer and cook covered for approximately 18 minutes, stirring once or twice during the first few minutes of cooking. When done, all the liquid should have been absorbed. Allow to stand, covered, while you prepare the sauce.

2. Make the sauce by draining fruit from Tropical Vinegar. (Add more fresh fruit and vinegar to refresh the vinegar.) Cut fruit into bite-sized pieces. Place in a small heavy saucepan with enough sugar to balance the tartness (taste as you add the sugar to decide how much). Cook over low heat just until glazed. If the fruits have been marinated in vinegar for a while, they will dissolve into a kind of chutney when cooked with the sugar. Blend in just enough hoisin sauce to color the sauces lightly.

3. To make the filling, wash and dry the fresh mushrooms. Slice into thin strips and set aside. Soak the dried mushrooms in cool water to cover for about 15 minutes, or until soft. Remove any tough stems (reserve with the soaking liquid for another use) and slice into thin strips. Combine with the fresh mushrooms. Salt lightly.

4. Slice the smoked salmon into long thin strips and set aside.

5. Soak the bamboo leaves in warm water until pliable. Drain.

6. With hands moistened with water, shape eight 4-inch round patties of rice, each about ½" thick. (Leftover cooked rice makes a wonderful breakfast treat cooked with milk and sweetened with ripe banana and a few pitted dates.) Arrange equal amounts of the mushrooms and smoked salmon on 4 of the patties, spoon the ketjap manis over the salmon, and top with the remaining patties. Press to seal in filling.

7. Place two bamboo leaves side by side, slightly overlapping. At right angles to these, place two more leaves, again side by side, slightly overlapping. Center the rice patty over the area where the two sets of leaves intersect. Enclose the filling tightly by bringing the ends of each set of leaves over it, tucking them under the filling where necessary. Continue folding each of the remaining leaves over the filling. Tie diagonally with kitchen string to secure the packets. Set packets on a rack or in a bamboo steamer. Set aside.

8. Bring enough water to a boil to reach just below the rack or bamboo steamer when placed inside a wok. (Alternatively, you can use any other large cooking vessel with a tight-fitting lid to approximate a steamer.) When the water has come to a vigorous boil, place the rack or steamer in the wok. Use foil, if necessary, to seal the lid tightly to the base of the wok, and steam for 30 minutes, adding more boiling water as needed. Remove steamer from heat and keep covered.

9. With sharp kitchen shears, cut an X into the top of each packet, allowing each diner to open the packet just before eating. Serve with the fruit sauce.

SERVING SUGGESTIONS: More than Fair Fowl (page 183), Village Baked Chicken (page 150) without its noodle accompaniment, or restaurant or store-bought barbecued chicken or duck would tastefully extend the Eastern borders of this meal. Serve store-bought green tea ice cream garnished with frozen green seedless grapes, slightly thawed, and cups of flowery chrysanthemum tea for a soothing finish.

Smoked Seafood Spring Rolls with Serendipi-Tea Dipping Sauce   STARTER

Serves 8 as an appetizer

Ranging from East to West, many classical cuisines exploit the magic of pastry wrapped foods. Whether it's French puff pastry or Middle Eastern filo for savory and sweet delights, Vietnamese rice wrappers for *cha gio* or *banh cuon*, or wheat and egg based coverings for use in Chinese *dim sum*, Korean *mandu*, and Japanese *gyoza*, the pleasurable ease of eating such morsels without benefit of fork or knife cannot be denied. If, as in this case, the filling is something beyond ordinary, the wrapper, whether crisp or soft, is relegated to the role of a mere conveyance for the delights contained within. The filling here, which features smoked seafood, becomes even more special if you smoke the shrimp and scallops yourself. (Read how on page 276.)

In fact, depending on the kind of wrapper used and level of concern about fat in your diet, this dish may be prepared in one of several ways: steamed if the Vietnamese-style rice wrappers are used, or fried if pan-Asian spring roll pastry is used. (To complicate matters further, the latter can also be steamed.) If time allows, try them all three ways. But by all means, set aside enough time to prepare the Thai tea-based dipping sauce to experience a marriage of tastes that seems heaven-made. The visuals are not bad either. (The recipe can be halved if desired, but any extra spring rolls may be frozen uncooked for future use, and these *are* addictive.)

THE WRAPPERS:
    16 rice-paper wrappings (Vietnamese banh trang) or
    8 wheat-flour spring-roll pastry wrappers, 8" square (I prefer the Tee Yih Jia brand
        manufactured in Malaysia, imported via Singapore)
    6 cups finely shredded Savoy cabbage (ordinary cabbage or Napa cabbage may be
        substituted)
    3 medium-sized carrots, peeled and finely shredded (about 2 cups)
    2 tbsp. Shallot-Infused Oil (page 269)
    1 tbsp. crushed and finely minced garlic
    1 tbsp. finely minced gingerroot
    1½ oz. fresh shiitake mushrooms, washed, dried well, and thinly sliced (reserve the
        stems, if tough, for another use)
    Chiles to taste, drained and seeded, from Sweet Chile Vinegar (See page 272), finely
        chopped
    1 tsp. cornstarch dissolved in 1 tbsp. cold water, plus enough to lightly dust the tray
        containing the completed spring rolls
    4 oz. smoked shrimp, peeled, deveined, and finely chopped
    4 oz. smoked scallops, finely chopped
    1–2 egg yolks, lightly beaten
    Salt (amount will vary depending on the saltiness of the smoked seafood)
    Egg white to seal the spring rolls if using spring-roll pastry wrappers
    Oil for frying

Vegetable oil spray to lightly coat the steaming rack

2 cups Serendipi-Tea sauce (See Flavor Flash!, next page)

THE GARNISH:

1 bunch fresh cilantro

1. In a heavy large skillet, sauté the cabbage and the carrots in the shallot oil, stirring constantly until wilted and lightly browned, about 5 minutes. Add the garlic and gingerroot and sauté, stirring, for another minute. Add the mushrooms and cook another minute. Stir in the chiles, cornstarch, smoked shrimp and scallops, and enough egg yolk to bind the mixture lightly. Salt lightly and set aside.

2. If using the rice wrappers, moisten them one at a time in a bowl of warm water just until pliable. Place about 2 tbsp. of the filling on the center of each. Tightly enclose the filling by bringing the bottom edge of the wrapper up and over the filling. Then fold each end in tightly over the filling (the left and right sides as they face you), ending with the top edge, and roll up like a cigar. As they are completed, place on a baking sheet dusted lightly with cornstarch.

3. If using the spring-roll pastry wrappers, follow the same procedure as above, but brush a bit of egg white along the edges of the wrapper to seal tightly as they are being overlapped.

4. To fry the spring-roll pastry wrappers, heat enough oil to reach 3" up the sides of a heavy saucepan until the temperature reaches 325° on a deep-fry thermometer. Test the temperature by dropping a piece of the wrapper into the oil. It should brown almost immediately and float to the surface. When ready, drop several spring rolls at a time into the oil and fry until golden brown. Remove to absorbent paper toweling and place on a rack in a 200° oven to keep them warm. When all have been fried, transfer to a heated serving platter and serve immediately with the Serendipi-Tea Sauce. Garnish with the cilantro.

5. To steam either the rice wrappers or spring-roll pastry wrappers, bring enough water to a boil in a wok or other large pot that has a tight-fitting lid and can be fitted with a rack. Arrange spring rolls on the rack that has first been sprayed lightly with vegetable oil. Steam covered for about 15 minutes, or until the pastry feels light and the spring rolls feel hot to the touch. Arrange on a heated serving platter and serve immediately with the dipping sauce. Garnish with the cilantro.

SERVING SUGGESTIONS: Deep fried, these are a natural for any stand-up cocktail party or as part of an eclectic buffet of finger foods. Whether fried or steamed, they also make a stunning introduction to a meal of simply grilled fish served on a bed of bitter and mild greens. Finish with a citrus-based dessert such as Broiled Oranges with Brown Sugar-Lime Glaze (page 255) or Grilled Fruit Salad with Fresh Berry Coulis (featuring oranges and grapefruit) (page 254).

Flavor Flash! *Thai Tea—Serendipi-Tea Sauce*

MAKES ABOUT 1½–2 CUPS

You've heard of egg in your beer? How about some tea in your dipping sauce? Not just any tea but cha thai, the familiar saffron-colored tea of northern Thailand, flavored with roasted corn, vanilla, and star anise. Traditionally, it's served iced, sweetened and topped with a Rorschach blot of light cream—an effective antidote to searingly hot foods or weather.

Captivated by its intense color and flavor (even when unsweetened) and having the vague feeling that its use need not be confined to a beverage glass, I boiled down an overly potent batch with some sugar to the consistency of maple syrup. And I happened upon what I call Serendipi-Tea Sauce. In its new guise, it becomes a wonderful dip for Smoked Seafood Spring Rolls, wrapped Vietnamese style, steamed in rice-paper wrappings, or fried to a shattering crispness in an eggless wheat pastry (see above recipe). One bite and the latter crackle like the thinnest sheet of wintry ice on a pane of glass. In either case, the smoky filling pairs felicitously with the flowery zing of the sauce. Here's one simple culinary caper that yields a complexly flavored result.

When enlivened with the kick of added star anise, cardamom, and fresh gingerroot, the unsweetened brew can also be the basis for an intriguing marinade for chicken breasts cooked on a smoking outdoor grill.

To make the dipping sauce: Use an automatic drip coffee pot to brew the tea by placing 1 cup of loose cha thai into the coffee filter. Measure 1 quart of water and let it brew. Add 8 whole star anise, 2 tsp. green cardamom pods, crushed, and a 4" piece of gingerroot, crushed and sliced. Allow to steep until cool. Sieve. At this point the liquid may be used for a marinade as noted above. To proceed with the preparation of the Dipping Sauce, add 1 cup sugar. Boil the liquid over high heat to reduce by half or until it reaches the consistency of a thin syrup. Allow to cool and store in a tightly closed glass jar. This keeps for about one month refrigerated.

Mixed-Grain Pilaf with a Hint of Smoke   SIDE
Serves 4

Reduced to their essence, pilafs are casseroles based on rice that has been washed repeatedly or, in some cases, soaked overnight to remove starch to ensure that each grain remains separate in the finished dish. In a kind of give-and-take of flavors, pilafs are frequently cooked right on top of the meat stews they are designed to accompany. Most contain onion, but elaborations often include dried fruits, nuts, and basic vegetables such as carrots and tomato. Seasonings may range from garlic and cumin to allspice and dill. But generally it's a dish where your freedom to invent and personalize is limited only by the breadth of your pantry and your imagination.

Here's a version that reconnects with its 700-year-old ancestor from the nomads of central Asia, where the aroma of smoke surely permeated the grains by virtue of the rather primitive cooking method used—a fire pit surmounted by a large round wok-like vessel called a *qazan,* in which the grains were cooked. Lacking the *qazan,* modern versions of which are still used today, I suggest using a roomy wok to steam-cook the rice-less ensemble of grains that make up a largely golden mixture. The key here is a tightly fitting lid. (If your wok allows less than a hermetic seal, join the base to the lid with a ribbon of foil crimped tightly against the wok.)

Standing in for the rice are quinoa, with its faintly asparagus-like fragrance and high protein content, millet, barley, bulgur, and couscous. By introducing each variety to the pot in turn according to the time it takes to cook, you need only one pot to accomplish the task and the flavors are commingled in the process, percolating up and down through the layers of grain. Eggplant and dried shiitakes (or other dried Oriental mushrooms of your choice) are added from the outset to imbue the mixture with their own sweet and smoky character. When the ingredients have cooked to their proper tenderness, they are then wrapped in a foil packet and kept warm, awaiting a return to the wok for a brief smoking, which lends yet another layer of flavor to this new version of an old dish.

½ cup millet

½ cup quinoa, rinsed and drained

2 tbsp. fruity olive oil or butter

1 cup finely chopped onion

6 cloves garlic, crushed and finely minced

¼ cup barley

Root Stock (page 258), Gingery Chicken Stock (page 259), or water

½ cup bulgur

½ cup couscous

6 medium-sized Japanese eggplant, peeled and finely chopped (about 3 cups)

2 oz. dried shiitake mushrooms, soaked in warm water until softened, drained and finely chopped

1 tsp. Forest Fragrance (see page 137)

Salt and freshly ground black pepper

Ingredients for smoking (see page 276), plus 6 whole green cardamom pods

1 quart additional Root Stock or Gingery Chicken Stock, reduced by half, to pour over the grains when served

THE OPTIONAL GARNISH:

Assorted unsprayed edible flowers (pansies, calendulas, nasturtiums, or roses are particularly effective here)

1. In a preheated 350° oven, toast the millet and quinoa in two small baking pans for about 10 minutes, or until fragrant. Set aside.

2. Heat the oil or butter in the wok. Add the onion and cook over low heat until translucent and tender. Add the garlic and cook, stirring, for another minute. Add the barley and stir. Add enough stock to barely cover. Cook covered over low heat just until tender, about 30 minutes. Add the millet and quinoa and enough stock just to cover. Replace lid and cook without stirring for about 15 minutes, or until the grains look puffed and are tender to the bite. Add the bulgur and couscous and steam for another 7–10 minutes, or just until tender, adding more stock as necessary just to moisten.

3. Stir in the eggplant, mushrooms, and Forest Fragrance. Add just enough stock to prevent the bottom layer of grains from sticking to the wok. Cover tightly to steam for about 20 minutes, or until eggplant and mushrooms are tender. Add more stock as needed to continue generating steam within the wok to complete the cooking of the eggplant and to tenderize the mushrooms. Add salt and pepper to taste. Remove mixture and wrap in a large piece of foil. Keep warm in a 200° oven while you prepare the smoking apparatus.

4. Line the wok with foil and add the ingredients for smoking. Heat, covered, just until wisps of smoke escape from the wok. With a small knife, prick the foil wrapping

around the grain mixture in several places. Place the packet on a rack inside the wok. Cover tightly and smoke over high heat for about 2 minutes. Remove from heat and allow the packet to remain inside the wok for 5 minutes more. Taste it to check the smokiness. If it seems too faint to your taste, add some new rice, sugar, and aromatics to the smoker, heat over high heat and return the packet to the smoker for a few minutes more after the first wisps of smoke appear. (Reheat in a 350° oven as necessary before serving.) Mound pilaf on a heated decorative serving platter. Serve with the reduced stock, heated. Garnish with a border of flowers, if desired, strewing a few petals randomly over the grains as well.

SERVING SUGGESTIONS: Double the recipe and serve as a main dish with a sauceboat of reduced stock and nothing more than a plate of ripened, room-temperature cheeses, crusty bread and, with advance planning, Star Anise-and-Lemon Poached Apples with Almond-Aniseed Crisps (page 242) for dessert.

Chestnuts Times Two Plus

SIDE

Serves 4

With the advent of vacuum packing, this dish can transcend its wintertime slot on the calendar of seasonal foods. Sold in glass bottles and conveniently preroasted and (best of all) peeled, these nuts from a tree belonging to the beech family here lend their inimitable richness to a rough puree of potato. Whether on the winter holiday table or not, they are a sublime accompaniment to roasted domesticated or wild fowl. Piped through a pastry bag fitted with a large star tip, this becomes a fine ruffled bed for stir-fried, garlicky brussels sprouts, broccoli, or broccoflower. Providing the finishing touch is a sweet crunch of home-smoked fresh water chestnuts, whose brownish skin color when unpeeled and roughly similar shape are all they share with the tree-borne variety.

1 cup fresh (or canned, drained) peeled water chestnuts, lightly sprinkled with
    granulated sugar and smoked for 5 minutes after the first wisps of smoke appear
    escaping from the wok (page 276)
12 oz. fresh chestnuts or 9 oz. bottled shelled, peeled chestnuts
Olive oil, if using fresh unshelled chestnuts

1 tsp. roasted garlic puree (See Birds in the Bush, page 207)

1 medium russet or Idaho potato, peeled, boiled until tender (reserve cooking liquid, kept warm at a simmer in a saucepan)

2 tsp. unsalted butter

Salt and freshly ground white pepper

THE GARNISH:

2 tsp. finely chopped parsley leaves

1. Roughly chop the smoked water chestnuts and set aside.

2. If using bottled chestnuts, proceed to step 3. If using fresh chestnuts, use a small, sharp knife to cut an X in the flat side of each nut. Coat lightly with olive oil. Cook in a heavy skillet over high heat, shaking pan occasionally. Remove from the heat and place in a 350° oven for 10 minutes more, or until the skins look well browned and the incisions made in the nuts have opened, exposing the nut. Remove from the oven and allow to cool long enough to handle them. Remove and discard the fuzzy, reddish brown skin under the hard exterior shell.

3. Place chestnuts in a food processor or blender and process, adding enough of the potato cooking water to produce a smooth, fairly soft puree. Mash the potato by hand with a potato masher or put through a potato ricer. Do not overprocess or the mixture will become unpleasantly gluey. Mix the garlic into the chestnut puree and then combine with potato and butter. Add salt and pepper to taste. Pipe or spoon mixture onto a heated serving platter. Top with the chopped smoked water chestnuts. Garnish with chopped parsley.

Fragrant Fish Cooked in Rosemary-Scented Smoke with a Glistening Retsina Sauce   STAR

Serves 4

With its piney personality, fresh rosemary is a natural partner for this fish with its sauce based on the Greek wine retsina (predominantly white, from the Savatiano grape), whose name implies its resinated edge. Dating from a time three thousand years ago when the Greeks stored their wines in vessels corked with resin derived from the native Aleppo pine, retsina has retained its pleasantly sappy flavor to the present day, although nowadays pine resin is added to the wine itself during fermentation to produce that distinctive flavor.

In Greek cuisine, retsina is served traditionally with zesty and somewhat oily foods. In line with that tradition, I like to use succulent sea bass, shad, or butterfish for this smoky herbal treatment.

To achieve the complex layering of flavors that takes this dish out of the realm of simple Greek cooking, the fish is prepared in two steps. First, the fillets receive a surface charring in a white-hot cast-iron skillet. Then they are quickly transferred to a heated smoker for their final cooking. The sauce can be made in advance, reheated before serving, and then spooned over the fish at the table to add just the right perfumed, glistening touch at the last minute.

Icy cold retsina is the only choice to consider when pouring wine to go with this.

2 lbs. sea bass, shad, or butterfish fillet, skin removed

Salt and freshly ground black pepper

Fruity olive oil

Ingredients for smoking (see page 276) plus 1 large bunch fresh rosemary

THE SAUCE:

2 cups Greek retsina wine (white)

2 cloves garlic, crushed and finely minced

2 tbsp. fruity olive oil

THE GARNISH:

8 lemon wedges

A few fresh rosemary sprigs

1. Wash and dry and then lightly salt and pepper the fish fillets. Dip them in the olive oil briefly and allow excess to run off.

2. Heat a large cast-iron skillet until it is white-hot (test by flicking a drop of water in the pan; it should evaporate immediately). Carefully place the fish in a single layer in the skillet and cook for 1 minute on each side, turning with a wide spatula. (The fish should not appear fully cooked at this point since it will receive more cooking in the smoker.) Continue to char the fish in batches, as necessary, until all the fish has been charred. Prepare the smoker as noted on page 276, with the addition of the fresh rosemary. Begin heating the smoker over high heat as you finish charring the last of the fillets.

3. Place the charred fillets on the rack inside the smoker, cover the smoker tightly, and allow to smoke for about 8–10 minutes. (It is difficult to be precise here because the amount of actual cooking time during charring and the thickness of the fillets will determine how much longer the fish needs to cook in the smoker.)

4. While the fish is smoking, bring the wine to a boil in a small heavy saucepan. Add the garlic and continue cooking until the liquid is reduced by half. Pass through a sieve and whisk in the olive oil.

5. Place the fish on heated plates, garnish with lemon wedges and rosemary. Spoon the sauce over each serving at the table.

SERVING SUGGESTIONS: Start with a salad of My Fave Favas (page 87) and accompany the entree with crusty, oven-roasted red-skinned potatoes and rounds of broiled tomato. Bitter Greens in a Honey-Lemon Drizzle (page 25) would also qualify as a stellar side dish here.

CHAPTER 6

Not-So-Sweets

I f, when dining out, before even ordering appetizers, you fast-forward in your mind to dessert, take heart—you're not alone. I, for one, feel that no meal, whether eaten out or in, is complete without a "little something sweet." Scanning the dessert list, I like to anticipate what will satisfy my sweet tooth at meal's end. Surrendering to that impulse, I propose this small but diverse collection of postprandial sweets, seven that place fruits center-stage, six that offer creamy comfort, four that are frozen (plus two bonus frozen desserts-in-a-glass), two that are pastry-based, and one nearly flourless torte.

Designed with the timid first-time dessert maker as well as the seasoned pastry cook in mind, each of these sweets is a celebration; some, for example, like Fabulous Figues Fourrées (page 245) and Prickly Pear Sorbet (page 248), celebrate a seasonal specialty; others, such as Lime Flan with Cajeta Sauce (page 246) and the Chocolate Semolina Pudding with Spiced Coffee Syrup (page 252) are notable for their rich interplay of textures and flavors.

Each one is designed to add gloss to everything from the simplest alfresco picnic to the confirmed sybarite's *grand dîner à deux* by candlelight. Most of them are completely or partially doable in advance, so they will allow you to spend a leisurely coda away from the kitchen. The cleanup can wait.

Blushing Bartletts
Serves 4

The combination of fragrant pears gently cooked in a lime-scented red wine syrup makes a memorable, not-too-sweet finish to a fall feast. The slightly sweetened, crisped polenta lends a crunchy contrast to the soft fruit, with the dried fig stuffing adding additional texture.

4 almost ripe Bartlett pears
Juice of 2 lemons to keep the pears from browning

THE POACHING SYRUP:

2 cups dry red wine
1 cup sugar
Peel of 1 lime
2 cinnamon sticks
½ tsp. whole black peppercorns, wrapped in a cheesecloth bag and tied

THE POLENTA:

1 cup fine yellow cornmeal
2 cups water
1 tbsp. sugar
1 tbsp. sweet butter
¼ tsp. cinnamon

THE STUFFING:

1 cup dried figs
Juice of 1 large orange
¼ cup hazelnuts

1. Peel the pears and remove the cores with a small sharp knife. Drop them into a bowl of water mixed with the lemon juice.

2. For the poaching syrup, bring the wine and sugar to a boil with the lime peel, cinnamon sticks, and peppercorns. Add the pears and cook at a simmer for about 10 minutes, or until pears are tender but not mushy. Remove the pears from the liquid and let cool. Set aside. Sieve the poaching liquid and set aside.

3. To cook the polenta, mix the cornmeal with a small quantity of water to avoid lumping. Place this mixture in a heavy saucepan, add remaining water and sugar and cook until thick, stirring with a wooden spoon constantly to keep the mixture smooth. Blend in the butter and the cinnamon and stir until the butter is melted. Pour polenta onto a greased baking sheet (the mixture should be spread to a thickness of approximately ½") and place under the broiler until browned, about 7 minutes. Watch carefully to avoid burning. Set aside to cool.

4. To make the stuffing, finely chop the figs and soak them in the orange juice for about 15 minutes. Toast the hazelnuts in a 350° oven for about 10 minutes, or until their skins are well browned. Rub the nuts in a clean towel to loosen the papery skins. Chop nuts coarsely. Drain the figs (discarding any leftover orange juice) and combine with the nuts. Reserve.

5. To finish the sauce, reduce the red wine poaching liquid over high heat until it coats a spoon, about 8 minutes. Watch carefully to avoid burning.

6. Stuff the pears with the fig-nut mixture.

7. Nap the serving plates with a thin pool of sauce. Cut cooled polenta into 3" rounds with a biscuit or cookie cutter, and place one on each serving plate. (Save any leftover polenta to turn into a hot breakfast cereal or slightly sweet dinner side dish.) Place a pear over the polenta and nap generously with the remaining red wine sauce.

Couscous Charlotte with Persimmon Sauce

Serves 4

Typically served as a delicate starch accompaniment to fragrant Moroccan stews of poultry or meat, couscous here takes on a somewhat unaccustomed role at the end of a meal in a fall specialty. Made in tall molds, charlottes traditionally consist of cooked fruit surrounded by slices of toasted, buttered bread or cake. Diverging from the traditional in two ways, these charlottes substitute the grain for the bread or cake, and instead of a fruit filling per se, mix the fruit right into the grain.

Similar to rice pudding without the fat and cholesterol, this dessert can cap a broad range of entrees with flavor accents from the Near to the Far East. Touched with sweet cinnamon and cloves, lightened with meringue, and bound with a puree of tart apple, a mere ounce of cooked couscous per serving gives just enough body to hold the whole tremulous thing together. Bits of toasted almond, golden raisin, and candied tangerine peel are the supporting players. Providing a brilliant, naturally sweet backdrop is a puree of ripe persimmon with whiffs of vanilla, lemon, and rum. (Dried apricots stand in well when persimmons are not in season.) Serve this warm for the most gossamer treat. Note that the slightly flattened Fuyu variety of persimmons are sweet when still hard. The heart-shaped Hachiya variety, however, must be ripened until mushy to develop its characteristic flavor and sweetness. Be aware that the latter may take as long as two weeks to ripen sufficiently, so plan accordingly.

TO COAT MOLDS:

1 tsp. butter

2 tsp. sugar

THE COUSCOUS:

$\frac{1}{2}$ cup water

1 tbsp. sugar

$\frac{2}{3}$ cup (about 4 oz.) uncooked couscous

2 medium-sized tart apples (Pippins or Greenings are my choice), quartered with
skin, cores, and seeds

1 tsp. ground cinnamon

$\frac{1}{4}$ tsp. ground cloves

3 tbsp. golden raisins, soaked in hot water for 5 minutes to plump, drained, and then finely chopped

2 tsp. finely chopped candied tangerine peel (see page 432 for method)

¼ cup slivered almonds, toasted in 350° oven for 5 minutes, then chopped into ¼" pieces

4 egg whites

1 tsp. sugar

Pinch salt

2 cinnamon sticks, broken in ½" pieces

½ tsp. butter to coat foil

THE PERSIMMON SAUCE:

3 small ripe Fuyu or Hachiya persimmons, peeled, top leaf and stem removed, cut into ¼" cubes (about 1½ cups)

2" piece lemon zest

1 tsp. pure vanilla extract

1 tsp. dark rum

½ tsp. lemon juice

THE GARNISH:

1 tbsp. finely chopped toasted almonds

1 tsp. finely chopped candied tangerine peel

1. Coat four 1-cup metal timbale molds or muffin cups with butter and sugar. Set aside.

2. Bring water and 1 tbsp. sugar to a boil in a small saucepan. When boiling, stir in couscous. Turn off heat and allow to stand covered for 5 minutes. Stir with a fork to separate grains. Turn out onto a flat surface in a thin layer. Allow to cool.

3. Cook apples in enough water to avoid sticking, just until tender, about 5 minutes. (Cooking the fruit with skin on adds natural pectin to the mixture and helps to stabilize the charlottes when unmolded.) Pass apples through a food mill to separate pulp from cores, skin and seeds. Add cinnamon and cloves and stir to blend. Add raisins, tangerine peel, and almonds.

4. With a whisk, beat egg whites with 1 tsp. sugar and pinch of salt until soft peaks form. Lightly fold into the couscous mixture. Immediately turn into prepared molds. Set a

piece of cinnamon stick on top of each mold. Cover with foil that has been lightly buttered. Place molds in the rack of a steamer and fill steamer pot with enough water to reach halfway up the sides of the molds. Cover pot and steam for 20 minutes. Let cool to lukewarm.

5. To make the sauce, reserve ½ cup of persimmon cubes in a small bowl. Cook the remainder in a heavy saucepan over moderate heat with the lemon zest and a scant ¼ cup water, just until easily mashed. Remove lemon zest. Puree fruit in a food processor or blender. Add the vanilla, rum, and lemon juice, and then fold in the reserved persimmon cubes.

6. Nap 4 large dessert plates with a pool of the sauce. Unmold the charlottes by running a small thin knife around the edges of the molds. Center the charlottes on the persimmon sauce. Garnish with a sprinkle of the toasted almonds and tangerine peel.

Ah! Sweet Mystery Torte
Serves 6

This is a chic little brown number that proceeds from the standard Austrian formula for a flourless chocolate cake and branches out to East Asia for its hint of ginger and to the Caribbean for the mellow rum syrup that douses the cake before icing. With ground almonds standing in for most of the flour and a fine dice of dried apricots adding moisture, this is a cake that is surprisingly light for all its richness. Serve it at room temperature.

For the most ethereal texture, make this as close to the time you are serving it as possible. Strong coffee complements the subtle cross-cultural blend of flavors nicely.

Butter or vegetable oil spray and flour to lightly coat cake pan
8 oz. fine-quality bittersweet chocolate, coarsely chopped
4 oz. unsalted butter
2 tbsp. flour
1 tsp. baking powder
1 cup ground blanched almonds
6 eggs, separated

¾ cup plus 2 tbsp. granulated sugar

1 tsp. pure vanilla extract

1 tbsp. finely diced crystallized ginger

3 tbsp. finely diced dried apricots, soaked in hot water for 5 minutes, drained

THE RUM SYRUP:

2 tbsp. granulated sugar

1 tbsp. water

1 tbsp. dark rum

THE CHOCOLATE GLAZE:

8 oz. bittersweet chocolate

½ cup sour cream

Unsweetened cocoa

1. Preheat the oven to 350°. Lightly coat an 8" springform pan with butter or vegetable oil spray and then lightly coat with flour, shaking out any excess.

2. In a heatproof bowl set over simmering water, melt the chocolate and butter together. Stir until smooth. Set aside. Sift the flour with the baking powder twice and combine with the almonds.

3. In the bowl of an electric mixer, beat the egg yolks with ¾ cup of the sugar until light and lemon-colored. Blend in the chocolate-butter mixture and the vanilla. Lightly fold in the almond-flour-baking powder mixture, ginger, and apricots until evenly distributed.

4. Beat the egg whites until frothy. Add the remaining 2 tbsp. sugar and continue beating until stiff but shiny peaks form. Do not overbeat or the mixture will be dry. Thoroughly but gently, fold the whites into the batter, retaining as much air as possible. Pour the batter into the prepared pan and bake for approximately 35 minutes. The cake is done when a toothpick or metal skewer inserted into the center comes out clean. Do not overbake or the cake will be dry. Let cool. Remove from the pan and invert cake onto a cooling rack.

5. Make the rum syrup by bringing the sugar and water to a boil. Cook only until the sugar is dissolved, about 30 seconds. Let cool and stir in rum.

6. Make the glaze by melting the chocolate in a heatproof bowl set over simmering water. Stir to melt evenly. Remove from heat and blend in sour cream. Let stand until cool but still liquid.

7. Prick the cake all over with a skewer or toothpick and then brush with half of the rum syrup, allowing it to be absorbed before brushing on the remainder. Pour the glaze evenly over the cake, spreading with a spatula as necessary to smooth it. Scrape up any glaze that has run off the cake, reglaze as needed, and place the remaining glaze in a pastry bag fitted with a fine tip. (To decorate the torte, I like to use a disposable parchment paper cone with its pointed end snipped, which allows a fine tracery of the glaze to be extruded.) Pipe a fine crosshatch design on top of the cake, sieve a light dusting of cocoa over the cake and place on a decorative serving plate.

Suite of Pears in a Zingy Ginger Dunk

Serves 4

From the end of summer through fall into winter, pears of all sizes, colors and shapes vie for space on produce shelves. Some, like the common Bartlett or fat Comice varieties, must be ripened to tender bruisability to be enjoyed. Underripe, these are tasteless, so plan ahead to allow for room-temperature ripening. Others, particularly the round, almost spicy, speckled Asian pear-apples and their kin, are ready to eat when crisp and still green. (Tsu Li, Ya Li, and Twentieth Century varieties are particularly prevalent in Asian markets.) The marvel of these is that they retain their winning crispness and shape even when cooked, as some of them are here in a fragrant not-too-sweet syrup of ginger, cinnamon, and lemon.

As a celebration of seasonal variety, here's a trio of pears, some cooked, others peeled and raw, for dipping in a snappy ginger-laced yogurt sauce. For a bit of do-it-yourself sweet-tooth satisfaction at the dinner table, you might serve the array of pears on an attractive platter, family style. For each person provide a small deep bowl of the Ginger Dunk with a mound of crushed toasted hazelnuts on the side. Fresh quince may be used instead of pear and poached as shown in the recipe for a different but equally delicious conclusion to a meal.

2 Asian pear-apples (about 1 lb. total)

2 Bartlett or Comice pears (about 10 oz. total), ripened until just soft to the touch
    and fragrant

2 ripe Bosc pears, or other brown-skinned variety (about 10 oz.)

1 cup granulated sugar

2 cups water

2 pieces peeled gingerroot, 2" long

2 pieces cinnamon bark, 2" long

2 pieces lemon peel, yellow part only, 2" long

2 cups Thickened Yogurt (page 265)

THE GARNISH:

Juice of 1 large lime (about ¼ cup)

1 cup hazelnuts, toasted, skins removed

1. To prepare a poaching syrup, bring the sugar and water to a boil in a heavy 2-quart
   saucepan. Reduce to a simmer and add the gingerroot, cinnamon, and lemon peel.
   Cook for 10 minutes. Add 1 of each of the varieties of pear, peeled, cored, and sectioned lengthwise. Simmer for about 8 minutes, or until the fruit is translucent. Let
   cool in the syrup. When cool, remove the pears and allow to drain in a colander.

2. Reduce the syrup over high heat until slightly thickened. Let cool and combine with
   the Thickened Yogurt. Refrigerate in a covered bowl until serving time.

3. Just before serving, peel, core, and slice the remaining pears. Arrange these and the
   poached pears on a serving platter. Squeeze the fresh lime juice evenly over the
   pears. Divide the Ginger Dunk into 4 equal portions in small serving bowls. Divide
   the toasted hazelnuts evenly among 4 small side dishes. Allow each person to compose the dessert according to his or her own preference.

Grilled Pineapple and Banana in Sugarcane Juice Glaze, with Coconut Crunch Topping

Serves 4

Not as sweet as its name suggests, the freshly pressed juice of sugar cane (grown in tropical climates from Florida to the West Indies, and from Mexico, Central and South America to India) is the vanilla-honeydew scented nectar that becomes a marinade and then a glaze for the fruits used here. It's worth the search to locate a source for the juice. By itself, it makes an invigorating, addictive drink. (Other than Florida, Texas, and Louisiana, the only states in the continental United States where sugar is a cash crop, the best source for fresh cane and juice would be Hispanic markets, especially those with a clientele of Caribbean origin. Don't substitute the thin, wan canned versions imported from Southeast Asia.) If efforts fail, switch to an equally delicious variation on this theme by using bottled passion-fruit juice or frozen passion-fruit puree (more easily found at most Hispanic or Asian markets), which is then sweetened with a vanilla-scented sugar syrup. (To make the simple sugar syrup, boil ½ cup each of granulated sugar and water until the sugar dissolves. To make it vanilla-scented, place one fresh vanilla bean, split lengthwise, in the syrup as it cooks. Allow flavor to infuse for about 15 minutes. Then remove the bean, wash and dry it and reserve for another use. Lacking a vanilla bean, allow the simple syrup to cool and stir in 1 tsp. pure vanilla extract.)

Be sure both the pineapple and bananas are perfectly ripe before you proceed. Use unsweetened flaked coconut (available at most Asian and Indian stores) for the Coconut Crunch Topping—its flavor is preferable to the sweetened variety. Although painstaking to extract, the meat of fresh coconut would be even better.

> 2 large ripe bananas
> 1 medium-sized ripe pineapple
> 2 cups fresh sugarcane juice; or a combination of 1½ cups bottled passion-fruit juice
>   mixed with ½ cup of simple sugar syrup flavored with vanilla bean or pure
>   extract to taste
> 1 cup unsweetened flaked coconut
> 1 egg white
> Unsalted butter
> Granulated sugar

Juice of 1 lime
1 cup Thickened Yogurt (page 265)
Pinch each of allspice and cloves

1. Peel the bananas and slice lengthwise and then into 4 pieces each. Peel the pineapple and halve. Remove the core. Slice each half lengthwise into 8 wedges. Place the fruit in a bowl with the sugarcane juice.

2. Make the Coconut Crunch by combining the coconut with the egg white, lightly beaten. Pour onto a baking sheet lined with lightly buttered foil. Sprinkle mixture heavily with granulated sugar. Bake in a 325° oven for 20–25 minutes, or until golden brown. Set aside.

3. Line the broiler pan with lightly buttered foil and preheat the broiler. Remove the fruits from the marinade. Arrange them on the foil-lined pan and place the pan 2" from the flame or heating element. Watching carefully, broil until bubbling and lightly browned. Artfully arrange fruit on each of 4 heated serving plates. Quickly reduce the marinade to a thick glaze and pour the glaze evenly over the fruits. Sprinkle with the lime juice. Top with the Coconut Crunch and a dollop of yogurt. Dust with the allspice and cloves and serve immediately.

Flavor Flash!

Liquid Nirvana—Passion Fruit-Coffee Shake

Throwing caution to the winds is easy when two tropical flavors combine in a sublime but simple dessert-in-a-glass. This frosted concoction celebrates not one but three of my passions—good strong coffee, passion fruit juice, and sweetened condensed milk. When you pair freshly brewed Colombian coffee and the musky ripeness of passion fruit with a hint of condensed milk providing the link between the two, you'll arrive at nothing less than lingering luxury on the palate. With each sip, you will be surprised by the pleasantly bitter jolt of the coffee, which prepares your palate for more of the haunting ripeness of the passion fruit.

   If you have access to fresh passion fruit, so much the better. If not, frozen passion-fruit puree or readily available frozen tropical juice concentrate (usually composed of pineapple, banana, and passion-fruit juices) will work just fine. Here's the secret to the sublime.

To serve 4, whirl the contents of a 12-oz. can of tropical fruit concentrate (pineapple, passion fruit and banana—the passion-fruit flavor predominates even in this heady tropical mix) with 2 cups of cold, strong, freshly brewed coffee. (If you are using seeded fresh passion-fruit pulp or frozen puree, use a mere ½ cup of either and add 1 cup cold water to the mix when blending and proceed as follows.) Add 2 cups ice cubes and ½ cup sweetened condensed milk and blend just until the ice is fully dissolved. Pour into tall frosty glasses, grate a sprinkling of nutmeg on top, garnish with a spear of fresh pineapple or frozen banana if desired, and serve immediately. Be ready to be transported.

Tropical Times Two–Vietnamese Coffee Ice Cream with Mango Sauce
Makes 1 quart

Variously known as *caphe sua da* in Vietnamese, *cafe filtre,* and French coffee, in any language this holdover from the period of French colonial rule in Southeast Asia means espresso with a strong caffeine kick. Traditionally made in individual servings with the help of a neat metal filter containing a screw that compacts the grounds, the coffee slowly drips into a glass containing some sweetened condensed milk. (Like its European model, it's also served straight—no sweetening, no milk.) When all of the water has dripped through, the table ritual continues as the mixture is stirred with a long spoon and then poured over a tall glass of ice.

From such inspiration comes a dessert that takes this luxury-in-a-glass one step further. Here enriched like a custard with egg yolks and cream, the blended coffee becomes the base for a serious coffee lover's frozen sweet. In fact, serving coffee after this would be redundant.

For the roundest flavor, hunt down the finely ground Vietnamese-style espresso available in most Asian markets (normally sold in 8-oz. cans). While you're there, check the produce bins for ripe mangoes nearly bursting with juice, which make the best sauce for this untypical tropical coupe. I use Lyle's Golden Syrup, the refined English sweetener, which seems to intensify the natural mellow sweetness of the mangoes.

2 cups heavy cream

½ cup finely ground espresso coffee, Vietnamese style

1 whole cinnamon stick

1 can (14 oz.) sweetened condensed milk

4 egg yolks, lightly beaten

Pinch salt

THE MANGO SAUCE:

2 ripe mangoes, about 1 lb. each

Juice of ½ lime (about 2 tbsp.)

Lyle's Golden Syrup to taste

THE GARNISH:

Cubes of fresh mango (optional)

1. In a heavy 2-quart saucepan, bring the cream, espresso, and cinnamon to a boil. Remove from heat and allow to infuse for 30 minutes. Pass through a fine sieve into a large stainless steel bowl. Add the condensed milk and the egg yolks and set the bowl over a pot of boiling water (the water should not touch the bottom of the bowl). Cook, whisking constantly, until the mixture lightly coats a spoon. Sieve into a clean bowl set over a bowl of ice, and cool quickly, stirring occasionally. Add the salt and freeze in an ice-cream freezer until firm. (Alternately, the mixture can be frozen in ice-cube trays until firm, then processed in a food processor or blender until smooth and then stored in the freezer.) Remove to a container with a tightly fitting lid and freeze overnight to ripen the flavors.

2. To make the sauce, peel the mangoes. Over a bowl to catch the juices, scoop the fruit from the skins and scrape any flesh that clings to the pit. Add the lime juice and transfer the mixture to a blender or food processor. Puree until smooth. Sieve to remove any remaining fiber. Sweeten lightly with the Golden Syrup. Refrigerate until ready to serve.

3. To temper the ice cream to scoopable consistency, place it in the refrigerator about a half hour before serving. Scoop into well-chilled bowls or slightly frosted goblets. Pour some of the mango sauce over each serving, scatter cubes of mango over each portion, if desired, and serve the remaining sauce in a sauceboat.

Beijing Biscotti with Kumquat Dipping Sauce
Makes about 3 dozen cookies

After a heavy meal rich with creamy sauces, these little crunchy bites satisfy handily. Redolent with toasted almonds and sesame, made conveniently ahead, these twice-baked cookies will keep well stored in a tin with a tight-fitting lid. Relying on another Oriental favorite, the accompanying zesty sauce (also doable in advance) uses fresh or bottled kumquats to great effect. Leftovers of this make a fine spread for bread, muffins, or, best of all, French toast.

2 tbsp. sesame seeds

½ cup (about 2 oz.) blanched slivered almonds

1½ cups all-purpose flour, sifted

1 tsp. baking powder

1 tsp. ground ginger

¼ lb. unsalted butter, softened

1 tbsp. roasted Asian sesame paste

¾ cup granulated sugar

2 eggs

2 oz. crystallized ginger, finely chopped

1 tsp. pure vanilla extract

Vegetable oil spray or butter for greasing baking sheet

THE GLAZE:

1 egg yolk, lightly beaten with 1 tsp. water

Granulated or coarse-crystal sugar (also known as sanding sugar)

THE SAUCE:

10 oz. fresh or water-packed kumquats, drained (if using syrup-packed fruit, drain it
    and reduce the sugar in the cooking syrup below accordingly)

1 cup water

½ cup granulated sugar

½ cup fresh orange juice, about 2 medium oranges

1. On a heavy baking sheet, toast the sesame seeds and almonds in a 350° oven until golden brown, about 8 minutes, stirring occasionally. Do not burn. Set aside.

2. Sift the flour, baking powder, and ginger and set aside.

3. With an electric mixer or in a food processor fitted with a steel knife, cream the butter and sesame paste with the sugar until fluffy, scraping occasionally with a spatula. Add the eggs, crystallized ginger, and vanilla and beat until light, about 2 minutes. Add the dry ingredients and mix until just combined. Add the almonds and sesame seeds and mix until evenly distributed.

4. On a lightly floured surface, with floured hands, form the dough into 4 rolls each measuring 8" by 1½". Be sure to compact evenly to remove any tunnels or air holes that may have formed during shaping. Place on a lightly greased heavy baking sheet leaving 1" between rolls. Brush the surfaces with the egg glaze, and sprinkle lightly and evenly with the granulated sugar. Bake in a 350° oven for about 25 minutes. (The rolls may have cracked on top—that's OK.) Remove from oven and allow to cool 5 minutes. Then with a sharp knife, slice them on the diagonal into ½" thick cookies. Return to the baking sheet, cut sides down, and bake for another 7 minutes, or until golden brown. Turn off oven and allow the cookies to crisp further in the oven for about 7 minutes longer. Remove from oven and cool on a rack.

5. For the sauce, halve the kumquats and remove any pits. Bring the water and sugar to a boil and add the kumquats. Cook for about 5 minutes. Skim off any foam that rises to the surface. Reduce the heat to a simmer and cook for another 8 minutes, or until the fruit is tender. Transfer to a blender or food processor and puree, adding enough orange juice to achieve a sauce with an easily pourable consistency. The sauce should taste pleasantly tart. Allow to cool. Serve the biscotti on individual plates with small bowls of the room-temperature sauce as accompaniment.

Tahitian Tarts
Makes 6 (4" by 1") tarts

Like the richest coconut custard pie you've ever tasted, this is essentially a baked vanilla-scented custard in a crust. Only here, the coconut flavors not only the filling but also the buttery short pastry that contains it. With its nutty flavored crust, smooth tremulous middle, and surface crazed with burnt sugar, this is one velveteen habit that's hard to break.

THE COCONUT CRUST:

$3/4$ cup unsalted butter

$1/4$ cup granulated sugar

1 egg yolk

1 tsp. pure vanilla extract

$1/2$ cup (about 2 oz.) unsweetened shredded coconut

$2\frac{1}{4}$ cups all-purpose flour

THE CRÈME BRÛLÉE FILLING:

$1/2$ cup heavy cream

1 cup milk

1 vanilla bean, split lengthwise

$1/2$ cup (about 2 oz.) unsweetened shredded coconut

$1/2$ cup sugar

5 egg yolks

Granulated sugar for caramelizing the tops of the tarts

1. To make the crust, cream the butter and sugar together in a food processor or in an electric mixer until pale and fluffy. Add the egg yolk and vanilla and beat until well blended. Add the coconut and the flour and mix just until the flour disappears. Form into a rough ball, flatten into a disk about 1" thick, and refrigerate, covered with plastic wrap, for about an hour. When chilled, roll out on a lightly floured surface into a sheet about $1/3$" thick. Fit into six 4"-diameter tart molds with removable bottoms. Chill until firm. Prick with a fork and bake on a baking sheet in a preheated 350° oven for about 20 minutes or until dry and just beginning to turn pale golden brown. Remove from oven and set aside.

2. Make the filling by bringing the cream, milk, vanilla bean, coconut, and $1/4$ cup of the sugar to a boil in a heavy saucepan. Remove from the heat and allow flavor to infuse for about 30 minutes. Sieve into a stainless steel bowl and whisk in the egg yolks lightly beaten with the remaining sugar. Do not overbeat or the mixture will be over-aerated and pocked with air bubbles instead of dense and smooth. Sieve again and transfer into a measuring cup with a pouring spout. Reduce the oven temperature to 275°.

3. Place the baking sheet of tart shells on the rack in the oven and carefully pour the custard filling into each tart, dividing it equally. Bake for about 35 minutes, or until the custard feels firm to the touch. Allow to cool, then chill in the refrigerator until cold.

4. Just before serving, sprinkle the sugar evenly over the surface of the custard. To protect the exposed edges of the crust on each tart, cover with templates made from squares of aluminum foil with circles of slightly less than the diameter of the tarts cut out. Place under a preheated broiler, about 2" from the heating element or flame, and melt the sugar. Reposition as needed, watching carefully to avoid burning. When evenly browned, remove from broiler and serve.

Flavor Flash! *Vanilla*

The flavor of vanilla is due to a miracle of nature made more miraculous by the intervention of man. Only two out of the fifty vanilla orchid species produce edible vanilla beans, and one, *Vanilla tahitensis*, is a laboratory-bred cousin of the original plant, *Vanilla planifolia*. The fruit of not just any tropical orchid vine, the vanilla bean must be carefully fermented to create the highly prized perfumed intensity we associate with vanilla extract. Even the ancient Totonacs, populating the Gulf Coast region of Veracruz, Mexico, knew the importance of hand pollination (given the poor odds that natural pollinators would happen by in sufficient numbers to do the job). As much as a thousand years ago, they knew the secret of unlocking vanilla's sensational scent through the ripening process. Nowadays, vanilla orchid cultivation is limited to tropical environments within 25 degrees of the Equator, with Madagascar (producing so-called "Bourbon" beans) followed by a close second, Tahiti, as the top vanilla-producing countries. Alas, the vanilla-worshiping Totonacs of Mexico are no longer prime producers and Mexican vanilla, priced at suspiciously low prices, has gotten a bad name—and often deservedly so. Often it is not true vanilla at all but a synthetic version, often diluted with coumarin, a potentially toxic compound. With its less than requisite 35 percent alcohol content, Mexican "pure vanilla extract" is best avoided in favor of the real thing.

In their cured bean form, soft, moist Tahitian vanilla beans are worth searching for—their intense fragrance justifies the luxury of their price. With proper handling, they can be counted on to continue lending their inimitable aroma to much more than dessert even with repeated use. After using to infuse a sauce or custard, simply wash and dry them—and then refrigerate them, well wrapped until the next use.

A final note: The word is still out on vanilla's aphrodisiacal powers, although the Aztecs and Europeans of Renaissance times were true believers. But in its pure form there's no doubt that vanilla ranks right up there with finely crafted chocolate, a frequent partner at dessert time since the 16th century in Spain. Who can resist the romance of either one of these alone, or in combination? (See Superb Sources, page 291, for a mail-order supplier.)

Three-Ring Citrus
Serves 4

In this confection, which only *looks* complicated, three layers of fragile shortbread alternate with layers of creamy citrus curd and tower above a tartly sweet cranberry puree tinged with black-currant syrup. With the main components under your belt, the last-minute construction work is child's play. I like to follow a fish or seafood entree with this one in early winter when citrus fruits are in high season. For the curd, experiment with the juice of different varieties of orange, lemon, and the whole range of citrus with easy-to-zip-off skins for subtle variations on the basic one given here.

THE SHORTBREAD PASTRY:

½ recipe of 2-4-6-8 Dough with Citrus Variation (page 439), using:

Zest of 1 lemon

Zest of 1 lime

1" strip of grapefruit zest

THE CITRUS CURD FILLING:

Strip each of lemon, lime, and grapefruit rind, measuring ½" by 1"

1 cup granulated sugar

1 tbsp. plus 2 tsp. lemon juice

2 tbsp. lime juice

4 tbsp. grapefruit juice

6 egg yolks

¾ cup unsalted butter

THE CRANBERRY COULIS:

¾ cup fresh or frozen cranberries

⅓ cup granulated sugar

½ cup water

1 tbsp. pure maple syrup

1 tbsp. sirop de cassis (black-currant syrup)

Confectioners sugar

THE GARNISH:

1 each of assorted sweet citrus (orange, grapefruit, tangerine, etc.), peeled, pith
    removed, sliced between the membranes into seedless sections

Fresh mint leaves (optional)

1. Make the pastry with the above noted additions. Chill and roll into a sheet ¼" thick.
   With a cookie or biscuit cutter of 3" diameter, cut into rounds. Place on a heavy baking sheet and prick the dough rounds lightly with a fork. Gather the scraps of dough
   together into a ball and reroll as necessary to produce 12 pastry rounds. Chill until
   firm. Bake in a preheated 275° oven for about 40 minutes, or until golden browned.
   Let cool and set aside.

2. Make the citrus curd by placing all of the ingredients in a stainless steel or crockery
   bowl set over, but not submerged in, a pot of boiling water. Whisking constantly,
   cook over high heat until the curd thickens, about 3–4 minutes. Remove from the
   heat and set over a bowl of ice water to cool quickly, stirring occasionally. When
   cool, refrigerate, covered, until firm.

3. Make the cranberry coulis by combining the cranberries, sugar, and water in a heavy
   2-quart saucepan. Bring to a boil and cook just until the cranberries pop. Remove
   from the heat and puree in a blender or food processor until smooth. Blend in the
   maple syrup and sirop de cassis. Allow to cool, then place in the refrigerator to chill
   until cold.

4. To assemble, sprinkle 4 of the shortbread rounds heavily with confectioner's sugar.
   Set aside. Spoon a 6" circle of the sauce on each of 4 large dessert plates. Place one
   round of shortbread on each. Using a pastry bag fitted with a star tip, pipe a layer of
   citrus curd on each cookie. Place another pastry round on top of the curd and pipe
   more curd on these rounds. Top with the reserved, sugar-dusted pastry rounds.
   Serve, garnished with citrus wedges and mint leaves.

White Chocolate Mousse Torte with Pistachios and Bitter Lime Sauce

Serves 8

Cake and mousse become fused here in a balance of crunch and cream. Often perceived as cloyingly sweet, white chocolate here is undercut with a tangy sauce of lime juice and zest, which adds a satiny gleam to the plate. Assemble the cake a day in advance and allow textures and flavors to meld fully (refrigerate and cover well—a cake plate with a dome lid is best).

THE RUM SYRUP:

½ cup granulated sugar

½ cup water

1 tbsp. dark rum

THE CAKE:

1 cup (about 4 oz.) shelled raw, natural pistachios

⅓ cup plus 1 tbsp. granulated sugar

½ cup all-purpose flour

½ tsp. baking powder

Pinch salt

Butter or vegetable oil spray to coat the baking pan

4 oz. unsalted butter

2 eggs, separated

THE MOUSSE:

8 oz. fine-quality white chocolate, finely chopped

1¼ cups heavy cream

½ cup (about 2 oz.) finely chopped shelled raw, natural pistachios, to coat the finished cake

THE BITTER LIME SAUCE:

Juice and grated zest of 2 limes

Rum syrup, remaining after the cake layers have been brushed

1 tsp. Lyle's Golden Syrup (or light corn syrup)

1 tbsp. cornstarch dissolved in 2 tbsp. cold water

1. To make the rum syrup, bring the sugar and water to a boil. Cook just until the sugar is dissolved. Allow to cool slightly and blend in the rum. Set aside to cool further at room temperature.

2. Preheat the oven to 350°. In a food processor or blender process half of the nuts with 1 tablespoon sugar until finely ground, reserving the other half to garnish the cake. Do not overprocess into a paste. Sift the flour, baking powder, and salt into a bowl and set aside.

3. Lightly coat an 8" springform pan with butter or oil. Cream the butter with the sugar until pale-colored and light. Add the egg yolks and beat until incorporated. Fold in the nuts and the sifted dry ingredients.

4. Whip the egg whites until foamy. Add 2 tsp. sugar and beat until stiff peaks form. Fold the whites into the batter and pour into the prepared pan. Smooth the top of the batter with a spatula. Bake for 15 minutes, or until the cake feels firm and is lightly golden. Let cool in the pan. With a knife, release the sides of the cake from the pan and invert onto a rack. With a long, serrated knife, slice the cake horizontally into two thin layers. Brush both layers lightly with some of the rum syrup (there should some syrup left, to be used later in the Bitter Lime Sauce.) Place one cake layer on a heavy cake cardboard cut to fit the cake.

5. To make the mousse, place the chocolate in a heatproof bowl. In a small heavy saucepan, bring ½ cup cream to a boil. Pour the hot cream into the chocolate and stir with a wooden spoon until fully melted and smooth. Set aside. With a whisk, rapidly beat the remaining ¾ cup cream until it holds soft peaks. Chill the white chocolate and cream mixture (this mousse base is sometimes referred to as a white chocolate ganache) over a bowl of ice water, stirring and scraping the bowl well to ensure that no lumps are forming. Just as the mousse base starts to thicken, gently but thoroughly fold in the whipped cream. Remove from the ice and set aside. In a food processor or blender, process the reserved nuts to a fine powder and reserve.

6. Make the sauce by bringing the lime juice and zest to a boil along with the reserved rum syrup. Add the Golden Syrup and cornstarch and cook until the sauce thickens. Pass through a sieve and set aside.

7. To assemble the cake, spread half of the mousse evenly over the cake layer set on the cardboard. Place the second cake layer on top of the mousse and spread the remaining mousse over it and evenly on the sides of the cake. Smooth with a spat-

ula dipped into hot water. Press the reserved chopped nuts evenly over the top and sides of the cake. Set onto a decorative cake plate and refrigerate, removing it from the refrigerator about 20–30 minutes before serving. Serve the cake slices over a small pool of Bitter Lime Sauce. Serve any remaining sauce in a sauceboat.

Star Anise-and-Lemon Poached Apples with Almond-Aniseed Crisps
Serves 4 (allowing for extra cookies)

This is for those times when a light, finely nuanced dessert is in order. Try to find full-flavored, crisp-fleshed apples like Braeburn, Fuji, or Mutsu for best results here. (More and more, Chile is exporting tasty specimens of these varieties to our shores.) Even the sometimes insipid Golden Delicious variety, when fragrant, will hold up well in this treatment, adding their own light vanilla scent to the dish.

When making the cookies, experiment with fennel seeds in place of the aniseed called for in the recipe to see which flavor you like best. I sometimes like to combine the two varieties for a pleasing nutty, powerfully licoriced taste. For an amusing touch, present the cookies as crunchy "stems" for the apples.

Water (enough to come halfway up the sides of the apples when placed in the saucepan)
1/3 cup granulated sugar
6 whole star anise
Zest of 1 lemon, peeled from lemon in strips
1 1/2 tbsp. fresh lemon juice
4 medium-sized apples, cored, top half of peel removed

THE COOKIES:
1 tbsp. aniseed
1 cup (about 4 oz.) blanched slivered almonds
2/3 cup granulated sugar
1/2 cup unsalted butter, melted
2 egg whites

2 tbsp. all-purpose flour
1 tsp. pure vanilla extract
Vegetable oil spray or butter to coat baking pan

1. In a heavy saucepan just large enough to accommodate the apples snugly in a single layer, bring the water, sugar, star anise, lemon zest, and lemon juice to a boil. Add the apples and boil for 3 minutes. Reduce the heat to a simmer and cook covered for about 15 minutes, or until apples are tender but not disintegrating. With a slotted spoon, remove the apples to a serving bowl and set aside. Sieve the cooking liquid and return to the saucepan to reduce over high heat for about 8 minutes, or until slightly thickened. Pour over apples and set aside.

2. In a small heavy skillet, toast the aniseed over medium heat until fragrant. Cool slightly and grind in a spice or coffee grinder.

3. In a food processor or blender, grind the almonds with the sugar until fine. Remove to a mixing bowl and blend in the aniseed, butter, egg whites, flour and vanilla.

4. Preheat oven to 375°. Lightly coat a heavy baking sheet with vegetable oil spray or butter. Spoon the cookie batter, by tablespoonfuls, onto the sheet, thinly spreading it with the back of the spoon dipped into hot water. Since these cookies do not spread during baking, fit as many on the sheet as possible, allowing only about ½" in between. Bake for about 9–10 minutes, reversing the position of the baking sheet after the first few minutes of baking to ensure even browning. If desired, while they are still warm, roll the cookies around a wooden dowel to form cigarette shapes, and when fully cooled, carefully remove from the dowel. If they harden too quickly, return them to the warm oven for a few seconds to soften and then roll.

5. Serve the apples with a bit of the reduced poaching liquid with a cookie inserted into each. Serve some of the remaining additional cookies on a decorative platter of their own. Store the leftover cookies in an airtight container.

Lavender Honey Ice Cream with Grilled Pineapple

Makes about 1 quart; serves 6

It's no surprise that bees are attracted to the fresh clean scent of purple lavender, which carpets the gentle hills in Provence in the summer. What results from that attraction is an incomparably fragrant, opaque pale honey that's perfect alone as a spread for bread or as a sweetener in everything from custards to vinaigrette. Highly touted for its medicinal and cosmetic uses, here it flavors the honey that imparts a haunting sweetness to a custard base for an ivory-colored ice cream. Warm wedges of sweet/tart fresh pineapple, marked by a white-hot grill, cut through the richness of this frozen treat.

If lavender grows in your garden and the season is right, by all means accent the dish with a flowering sprig.

> ¾ cup (about 6 oz.) lavender honey
> 1 cup heavy cream
> 1½ cups whole milk
> 1 cup buttermilk
> 6 egg yolks, lightly beaten
> Pinch salt
> 1 medium-sized sized pineapple, about 3 lbs. (to yield about 18 oz. usable fruit)
> Granulated sugar

1. Bring the honey, cream, milk, and buttermilk to a boil. Place the egg yolks in a large stainless steel or crockery bowl. Temper the yolks by whisking in about 1 cup of the hot liquid. Return this tempered mixture to the saucepan and continue cooking over low heat until the mixture lightly coats a spoon. Sieve into a large bowl, set over a bowl of ice, to cool quickly. When cool, freeze in an electric ice-cream machine or, lacking that, place the bowl in the freezer and stir occasionally until the mixture has reached the consistency of a soft ice cream.

2. Remove the leaves and peel from the pineapple. Cut in half and remove the core. Slice into spears ½" thick. Coat lightly with the sugar. Heat a heavy cast-iron skillet or stovetop griddle until hot. Grill the pineapple until slightly caramelized, turning once during cooking. Set aside.

3. Temper the ice cream to scoopable consistency and place a large scoop on each of 4 frozen plates or in frosty goblets. Garnish each serving with approximately 4 wedges of pineapple.

Fabulous Figues Fourrées–Stuffed Fresh Figs
Serves 4

In the dog days of summer, when highly perfumed fruits crowd the produce shelves of all markets, fresh figs seduce with their almost sensual sweetness. When perfectly ripe, they fairly burst with sticky sweet juice and yield to gentle pressure. So how to improve on perfection? Read on for this startlingly simple path to summer bliss.

    16 large perfectly ripe fresh figs, stems removed
    6 oz. soft mild fresh goat cheese (Montrachet is a good choice)
    6 tbsp. brown sugar
    ½ cup fresh basil leaves, lightly packed, sliced into long slivers

Preheat the oven to 400°. Place the figs on a cutting board, stem side up. Remove the stem and cut an **X** into the fruit through the stem end, halfway down the fruit. Place a dollop of goat cheese inside each fig, then re-form the fruit to enclose the cheese. Sprinkle with the brown sugar and bake in a single layer for about 5 minutes, or until the cheese oozes. Remove from the oven and shower the figs with basil. Serve immediately, 4 figs per person, while cheese is still molten.

Frozen Mango Cream
Serves 4

Drawing upon *lassi,* a traditionally liquid form of Indian refreshment made from mangoes and yogurt, this nonfat sweet is beguilingly easy to make, looks great on the plate, and brings a welcome chill to the mouth after a chile workout. For the most luscious results, be sure to use highly perfumed, ripe, or even overripe fruits that feel heavy for their size. A bit of dark rum is included to keep the mixture from freezing too hard.

2 large mangoes, about 1 lb. each

1 cup nonfat plain yogurt

1 tbsp. dark rum

THE GARNISH:

Freshly grated nutmeg

A few Brazil nuts, dark skins removed, grated (optional)

4 lime wedges

1. With a small sharp knife, make a shallow straight cut around the middle of each mango, from one end to the other. With a spoon, working over a bowl, free the fruit from the skin, producing two similar oval shells. Carefully scrape out any pulp that clings to the skin. Using crumpled aluminum foil, make 4 nests to hold the shells upright during freezing.

2. Puree the fruit in a food processor or blender with the yogurt and the rum. When well blended, pour into the mango shells and freeze until almost solid, about 45 minutes (actual time needed depends on your freezer). If too solid, remove from the freezer and place in the refrigerator to soften for about 15 minutes before serving. When ready, it should be easy to spoon.

3. Sprinkle grated nutmeg and nuts over each portion and serve with wedges of lime on the side.

Lime Flan with Cajeta Sauce
Serves 4

Here's a dreamy, soul-satisfying cross between velvety cheesecake and gently baked custard that yields an improvement on each. With a rumor of lime and cinnamon in the background, this make-ahead dessert cannot claim low-fat status but every calorie and gram of fat are worth it. Its sauce is made by heating some bottled *cajeta*, a thick caramel made of goat's milk and sugar that have been slowly cooked to creamy perfection, often used by Mexicans as a spread for bread or spooned straight from the jar as a confection. (Many varieties, made instead from cow's milk, are available in most Hispanic markets.)

THE CARAMEL TO LINE THE MOLDS:

   1 cup granulated sugar

   ¼ cup water

   Juice of 1 large lime

THE CUSTARD:

   2 cups heavy cream

   Zest of 4 limes

   2 whole cinnamon sticks

   4 oz. cream cheese (those without stabilizing gum work best)

   ¾ cup granulated sugar

   6 egg yolks

THE SAUCE:

   4 oz. bottled cajeta

1. To make the caramel, cook the sugar, water, and lime juice in a small heavy saucepan, without stirring, until the mixture turns a deep golden brown. Swirl the pan occasionally to distribute the heat evenly throughout the mixture. Do not burn. Immediately pour into four 1-cup ovenproof molds. Using heat-resistant gloves or potholders to grasp the molds, swirl the caramel to coat the bottom and sides evenly. Place the molds in an ovenproof pan about 4" deep and set aside.

2. In a 2-quart heavy saucepan, bring the cream to a boil with the lime zest and cinnamon sticks. Watch carefully to prevent boiling over. Remove from heat and allow to infuse for 30 minutes. Sieve out solids and reserve the liquid.

3. In a large bowl, beat the cream cheese with the sugar until smooth. Stir in the egg yolks and then, without aerating, blend in the reserved cream. Sieve and then transfer the mixture to a pitcher to pour into the prepared molds. Place the pan containing the molds on the middle rack of a preheated 325° oven. Pour the mixture into the molds (each mold should contain about ¾ cup of the mixture). Pour boiling water into the pan to reach halfway up the sides of the molds. Bake for about 30 minutes, or until the custards feel firm and are lightly browned. Remove from the oven and allow to cool at room temperature. When cool, chill until cold, covered, in the refrigerator, preferably overnight.

4. Just before serving, heat the cajeta in a small heavy saucepan over low heat, just until pourable, watching carefully to avoid burning.

5. Run a blunt knife around the inside of each mold and then invert onto serving plates. Drizzle some of the warm cajeta over each serving.

Prickly Pear Sorbet with Saguaro Shortbreads
Makes 1 quart sorbet and approx. 8 cookies

From a seemingly inhospitable environment blossoms the fruit of the Opuntia and nopal cactus with a flavor that can only be described as fresh, almost sweetly vegetal. Oval shaped, about 4" long and covered with a shiny greenish skin mottled with patches of white, orange, or red, depending on the variety, the prickly pear (also known as the cactus pear, or *la tuna*, in Spanish) is a specialty commercially grown in the American southwest (including California), Mexico, and Chile, available in Mexican *mercados,* and increasingly in upscale supermarkets, roughly from July through March.

I like to use the red variety with deep magenta-colored flesh. After peeling, the fruit, with a texture somewhat like that of kiwi, is then pureed and sweetened with a simple sugar syrup. For an added taste surprise, bits of bittersweet chocolate, masquerading as the seeds that have been removed from the fruit, are introduced to the mixture during freezing. Served on the side, buttery cookies, shaped like the emblematic multipronged saguaro cactus, add a smile to the lips.

One note of caution: Handle the fruits with care when peeling to avoid being stuck by the invisible cactus spines that lurk in the skin.

THE SHORTBREAD:
½ recipe 2-4-6-8 Dough (page 279) with 2 tbsp. Indian white poppy seeds added to the butter during creaming

Vegetable oil spray or butter to coat baking sheet

1 egg yolk, mixed with 1 tsp. water for the glaze

Coarse crystal sugar (also known as sanding sugar)

THE SORBET:
3 large, red-fleshed prickly pears (about 1 lb. total)

1 cup granulated sugar

½ cup water

Zest of 1 lemon

2½ tbsp. lemon juice

¼ tsp. pure vanilla extract

1 oz. bittersweet chocolate

Chilled tequila to serve over the sorbet (optional)

1. Roll the prepared dough into a sheet ¼" to ⅓" thick. Cut a paper template into a three-pronged cactus shape with the central prong the longest (about 4" from base to top) and the two prongs on either side, curving outward and upward, about 2" from the base. The tops of each prong should be rounded. Place the template on the dough and cut out the cookies, removing the scrap and rerolling as needed to produce 8 cookies. As you cut them out, place the cookies carefully on a heavy baking sheet that has been lightly coated with vegetable oil spray or butter. Brush evenly with the egg glaze and sprinkle lightly with coarse sugar. Bake in a preheated 325° oven for about 10–12 minutes, or until lightly browned and firm to the touch. Set aside on a rack to cool.

2. To make the sorbet, peel the fruit carefully with a small sharp knife and set aside. In a small heavy saucepan, bring the sugar, water, and lemon zest to a boil. When the sugar has dissolved, remove from heat. Allow to infuse for about 15 minutes. Sieve the syrup. Puree the fruit (there should be about 1½ cups) with the sieved syrup in a blender or food processor until smooth. Pass through a fine sieve set over a stainless steel or crockery bowl, pressing hard on the solids to extract as much pulp from the mixture as possible. Add the lemon juice and vanilla and place in freezer. Freeze, stirring occasionally and scraping the sides of the bowl well, until the mixture has started to set, about 1 to 1½ hours, depending on your freezer.

3. In a small bowl set over boiling water, melt the chocolate. While still liquid, pour it in a thin stream into the sorbet, whisking constantly. It will harden immediately into small flecks. (If you have an ice-cream machine, freeze the mixture in it according to the manufacturer's directions. Halfway through the freezing, add the melted chocolate quickly in a thin stream, while the machine is running.) Cover the sorbet tightly with plastic wrap and return to the freezer to complete the freezing, about ½ hour. Like most homemade sorbets and ice creams, this is best served the same day it is made for creamiest texture and brightest flavor and color.

4. With two spoons, first dipped into hot water, form oval scoops of the sorbet and place them on frozen dessert plates or in frosted stemmed glasses. Set one or two cookies beside the sorbet. At the table, pour some tequila over the sorbet, if desired.

Sticky Rice Snowballs with Coconut Sauce
Serves 4

Here a fragment of an idea from Roman cookery is transferred to a Southeast Asian idiom to produce an untraditional treat with a whole range of textures, from creamy to crunchy. Prompted by the Italian appetizer *supplì al telefono,* deep-fried rice croquettes stuffed with cheese, which derive their name from the "wires" of stringy melted cheese, in this dessert an intensely flavored core of chopped fruit is surrounded with fragrant jasmine rice slowly cooked in coconut milk. The resulting baseball-sized spheres are then gently steamed instead of fried and served warm, swathed in a creamy coating of slightly sweetened coconut milk for a comforting ending to any light meal. When it comes to rice and coconut, white-on-white can be exciting. Here two whites don't make a wrong.

For a good mix of fruits, choose one tart fruit, such as prunes or apricots, to balance the sweeter varieties. For best results, be sure the fresh fruits are fragrant and ripe and the dried fruits are moist.

THE RICE:

³⁄₄ cup uncooked jasmine rice

1 cup unsweetened coconut milk (substitute Mock Coconut Milk, page 267, if you wish)

½ cup water

2 tbsp. granulated sugar

1 whole egg, lightly beaten

THE FRUIT STUFFING:

3 whole pitted dates, finely chopped (about 2 tbsp.)

¼ cup finely chopped fresh pineapple

2 tbsp. chopped pitted prunes or dried apricots

¼ cup finely chopped fresh or dried papaya (if available, substitute white-fleshed fresh Babcock peaches)

Butter or vegetable oil spray to coat foil to wrap rice snowballs

THE SAUCE:

2 cups unsweetened coconut milk

¼ cup granulated sugar

1 soft Tahitian vanilla bean split lengthwise, or 1 tsp. pure vanilla extract

THE GARNISH:

½ cup flaked unsweetened coconut

1. In a heavy, covered 2-quart saucepan, bring rice to a boil. Reduce heat to low and cook rice over low heat in the coconut milk and water with the sugar until tender and all the liquid has been absorbed. When done, transfer the rice to a baking pan and spread to a thickness of about ½" to facilitate cooling.

2. In a small bowl, combine the fruits and set aside.

3. Lightly coat 4 sheets of aluminum foil, each measuring 8" square, with butter or vegetable oil spray and set aside. Mix the lightly beaten egg into the rice. Using two spoons, and hands moistened with water, form the rice into balls, each about 2½" to 3" in diameter, placing one quarter of the fruit mixture in the center of each and enclosing the fruit fully with the rice, filling in with additional rice as necessary. Wrap the balls in the aluminum foil by bringing the opposite corners of the squares together and twisting the foil to create a topknot that tightly seals the foil packet. Prick the packets with a sharp knife in several places and place on a steamer rack or in a bamboo steamer and steam, covered, over boiling water for about 30 minutes. (Add more boiling water to the steamer as needed.) When done, keep the packets warm in the covered steamer while the sauce is being made.

4. To make the sauce, bring the coconut milk and sugar to a boil along with the vanilla bean and cook over high heat, stirring occasionally, until reduced to coating consistency, about 5 minutes. Remove the vanilla bean, wash well, dry, and save for another use. If you are using vanilla extract, allow the sauce to cool and then stir in the extract.

5. Toast the coconut for the garnish in a 350° oven for about 8 minutes, stirring occasionally, until golden brown. Watch carefully to avoid burning.

6. Warm 4 serving plates. Pour some of the sauce on each plate. Carefully unwrap the foil packets and center one snowball on each plate. Pour the remaining sauce over each portion. Garnish with the toasted coconut.

Chocolate Semolina Pudding with Spiced Coffee Syrup

Serves 4 generously

Resting ethereally on the plate, this is something like a cross between the most down-home mud pie and an elegant warm souffle. Composed mostly of fine melted chocolate but lent structure with a few eggs and some ground walnuts, it gets its pleasant bit of grit from semolina, the granular, hard wheat flour from which the best pasta is made. With its coffee sauce as smooth as glass and just as shiny, this airy pudding seems to levitate from plate to spoon to mouth with only the slightest nudge from the person behind it. Try it when caffeine and calories don't matter.

Butter or vegetable oil spray to coat the mold

Semolina to line the mold

6 oz. fine-quality bittersweet chocolate, roughly chopped

4 oz. unsalted butter

½ cup strong brewed coffee

½ cup plus 4 tsp. semolina flour

1 tsp. baking powder

Pinch salt

3 whole eggs

½ cup granulated sugar

⅓ cup (about 1½ oz.) ground walnuts

THE COFFEE SYRUP:

1 cup strong brewed coffee

½ cup granulated sugar

6 whole cloves

1 cinnamon stick

THE OPTIONAL GARNISH:

Softly whipped unsweetened heavy cream (optional)

1. Preheat the oven to 350°. Lightly butter or oil an ovenproof 1-quart glass bowl or baking dish. Sprinkle with semolina and shake out excess.

2. Melt the chocolate and $\frac{1}{2}$ cup butter in the top of a double boiler, stirring occasionally until smooth. Remove from heat. Add the coffee and set aside. Sift the semolina, baking powder, and salt and set aside.

3. In a large bowl, whisk the eggs and the sugar just until blended. Blend in the chocolate-butter mixture and stir to combine. Add the dry ingredients and the nuts and mix just until smooth. Pour into the prepared bowl or dish and set in a pan with enough boiling water to reach halfway up the sides of the bowl. Bake for 45–50 minutes. When done, the pudding will have a crack on top and should have a slightly soft center. Do not overbake or it will be dry. Allow to cool to lukewarm.

4. To make the syrup, in a heavy 1-quart saucepan, bring the coffee, sugar, cloves, and cinnamon stick to a boil. Cook without stirring just until the mixture is reduced by half. Sieve and let come to room temperature. Transfer to a serving pitcher.

5. Unmold the pudding onto a decorative serving platter. With a large serving spoon, scoop portions onto each of 4 serving plates. Pour a ribbon of the syrup around each serving. Garnish with whipped cream, if desired.

Flavor Flash!
Frozen Banana Shake

A simple summer cooler that I can't live without couldn't be easier to prepare. Merely whirl a peeled, frozen, about-to-turn-overripe banana in the blender with 1 cup of nonfat milk, a healthy pour of real vanilla extract, a few ice cubes, and presto! You'll have a low-fat treat that only tastes like an indulgence. I always keeps a few extra bananas on hand in the freezer, so I'm ready when the craving strikes.

If you want to treat yourself to something extra-special, prepare it with stubby Manzano (also known as baby or finger bananas), those Lilliputian luxuries (about 3" long) available in many Asian and Hispanic markets. Somehow the flavor of these is even more intense and sweeter than the standard variety.

Not to give them short shrift, but these last two desserts are designed for those times when you've outdone yourself preparing Starters, Stars, and Sides. Not so much recipes as ideas, these require only a good eye in ferreting out the truly best produce of the season and, with little effort, you can achieve a dessert with clear, direct, and satisfying flavor. I like to think of these as shortcuts that transform essentially off-the-shelf ingredients into something more highly evolved.

Grilled Fruit Salad with Fresh Berry Coulis
Serves 4

For this one, carefully select the ripest, most fragrant array of fresh fruits with an eye to including at least one tart variety (such as grapefruit), one sweet (don't forget grapes), one soft (figs, mango, or melon, in season), and one hard (apples or Asian pears seem never out of season). This selection is merely a snapshot of what looked best in the produce aisles one day when the arrival of unexpected guests demanded a sweet conclusion to an ultimately labor-intensive meal.

2 tart apples, peeled, cored, and cut into eighths

½ fresh pineapple, peeled, cored, and sliced into spears 2" x 4" x ½" thick

1 medium-sized papaya, halved, seeded, peeled, and sliced into wedges ½" thick

1 small ripe but slightly firm avocado, peeled, pit removed, sliced into thick wedges

1 seedless orange, peeled, pith removed, sliced into segments between membranes

Several bunches of seedless red or purple grapes, left on stem

Pure maple syrup (to coat the fruit)

Vegetable oil spray to coat cooking surface

Granulated sugar to sprinkle lightly on fruit

THE BERRY COULIS:

12-oz. package fresh or frozen cranberries cooked with ½ cup granulated sugar, pureed and sieved; or 2 pints fresh raspberries, pureed and sieved to remove seeds; or 14½-oz. jar Swedish lingonberries in sugar, pureed and sieved, if desired, to remove seeds

THE GARNISH:

Wedges of lime

Fresh mint leaves

1. Lightly coat the fruit with maple syrup. Lightly coat the grill with the oil and heat until it is almost white-hot. (A drop of water should evaporate instantly upon contact with the hot surface.) Cook the fruits in the order listed, removing each to a heat-proof serving platter as it is grilled. They should have some visible marks from the grill but should not appear burned or blackened.

2. When all the fruits have been cooked, arrange them attractively on the platter and sprinkle lightly with sugar. Place under broiler, about 2" from the heating element, just until the sugar has melted evenly, turning the platter as necessary. Remove from the broiler and serve with a pitcher of the berry coulis. Garnish the platter with lime wedges and mint leaves.

Broiled Oranges with Brown Sugar-Lime Glaze

Serves 4

The name nearly says it all, but gives no idea of just how good this simple dessert is, with its underpinning of chunky tart apples.

2 medium-sized tart apples, peeled, cored, and roughly chopped

4 seedless oranges, peeled, pith removed, cut into sections between the membranes (taste for sweetness and adjust the amount of brown sugar below accordingly)

2½ tbsp. freshly squeezed orange juice

¾ cup Thickened Yogurt (page 265)

½ cup light or dark brown sugar

4 tsp. freshly squeezed lime juice

THE GARNISH:

4 whole blanched almonds, lightly toasted in 350° oven for about 8 minutes, or until golden brown

1. Cook the apples in a small heavy saucepan over low heat until just tender, stirring occasionally. Drain any excess liquid and discard. Set the apples aside.

2. Preheat the broiler until hot. Set the broiler rack about 2" from the heating element. Spoon some of the cooked apple into the bottom of each of 4 ovenproof dishes (shallow tempered glass bowls work well). Place the orange wedges in a pinwheel design on top of the apples. Sprinkle the orange juice over each serving.

3. In a small bowl, whisk the yogurt, brown sugar, and lime juice until smooth. Pour over each serving, napping the orange segments evenly.

4. Place the dishes on the broiler rack for about 10 minutes, or until the mixture is bubbling and evenly browned. Reposition the dishes under the broiler as needed to glaze evenly. When done, the yogurt should have the texture of a soft custard. Carefully remove dishes from the broiler and place an almond in the center of each pinwheel. Allow to cool slightly before serving.

Flavor Flash! *Chile Powder on Fresh Fruit*

How can you improve on the sweet fruitiness of a ripe cantaloupe, honeydew, or papaya? Take your cue from the street vendors of tropical Mexico—cool down and turn the heat up at the same time. Try dusting some dried chile, preferably chile pequin (or cayenne pepper powder) over the chilled fruit and you will be pleasantly surprised at how sweet suddenly tastes sweeter when juxtaposed with the mouth-searing heat of any *Capsicum frutescens*.

CHAPTER 7
• • • • • • • • • • • • • • •

Back-of-the-Book Recipes

These are the workhorses, basic preparations, many of which inspired or were inspired by the main recipes in the chapters preceding. Most are easily prepared in advance (recommended batches and storage strategies are indicated where appropriate), some stored for long keeping, others made a day or so before use and then called upon as needed. Some are crucial components with useful variations; others add the welcome final transforming touch to a dish; still others present basic techniques that are used repeatedly throughout the book.

Although by no means intended as a thorough catalog of preparations and techniques (refer to the Recommended Reading List on page 293 to round out the picture), these may nonetheless be applied to a myriad of dishes beyond the borders of this book. They are easily mastered, and with frequent use they will become like indispensable words in the vocabulary of a new language.

Root Stock (Vegetable Stock)
Makes approx. 4 quarts

A staple in my pantry, this stock is a fat-free shortcut to big flavor in everything from soups and vegetable Sides to salad dressings, pasta Stars, hot or cold vegetable tonic drinks, and even vegetable sorbets. Make a large batch and lay in a supply in your freezer on a day when you intend to spend a lazy afternoon at home. No need to take this recipe as gospel—feel free to double up on one vegetable if any one of the specified ingredients is unavailable, although the character of the resulting stock will vary according to the substitutions. I find that the amounts prescribed below produce a balanced stock with a depth of flavor that lingers pleasantly on the palate.

If the stock is to be reduced for use in a specific recipe, salting it at the outset will result in a disproportionate amount of salt in relation to the amount of liquid. Therefore, to allow for the greatest versatility of usage, it's best to add salt to taste at the last moment.

1 bunch parsley root, finely diced, leaves removed
1 large celery root, finely diced, stems and leaves removed
4 large carrots, finely chopped
1 bunch parsnips, finely chopped
1 bunch celery, finely chopped, leaves included
1 bunch leeks, well washed, finely chopped
4 quarts water
Salt to taste when using

1. Place all vegetables in a large pot or roasting pan and cover with the water. Bring to a boil quickly and then cook at the barest simmer for at least 3 hours. Make sure the liquid does not evaporate. The vegetables should float freely in the liquid at all times during the cooking.

2. Pour the liquid through a sieve, pressing hard on the solids. (Save the vegetables for a tasty puree, which works well as a soup thickener or ready-made sauce when thinned with some of the Root Stock.) Let cool and then refrigerate or freeze.

NOTE: An alternate, more intensely colored version of this stock can be made by first roasting all the vegetables in a 350° oven for about 35–45 minutes, stirring occasionally to ensure even browning. Scrape the browned vegetables into a large pot or roasting pan and proceed as above.

Gingery Chicken Stock
Makes approx. 1 quart, highly concentrated

I like to have a batch of this on hand in the freezer at all times to give depth of flavor to soups, sauces, and vegetable stir-fries. Three things to bear in mind: (1) Use fresh, well-washed chicken backs, necks, and wings (save the breasts, legs, and thighs for a main dish). (2) Don't stint on the vegetables or aromatics; use a generous chop of celery, carrots, and leeks to create a well-balanced brew. (3) To add the sharply defined ginger flavor that is the signature of this stock, use firm gingerroot with no signs of mold or wrinkled skin, which could be an indication of improper handling or old merchandise, hence weak or off flavor.

For compact storage in the freezer, I recommend reducing the volume of the broth severely by quickly cooking it over high heat after the first hour of simmering. In that way, you can store in a single ice-cube tray enough to reconstitute up to 2 quarts of stock. To keep the salt-to-liquid ratios in line, remember to salt the stock to taste at the time you use it.

    8 lbs. chicken necks, backs, and wings, skin removed
    4 quarts water
    1 large bunch of celery, with tops, roughly chopped (about 8 cups)
    4 large carrots, roughly chopped (about 6 cups)
    2 large leeks, well washed, roughly chopped (about 6 cups)

THE BOUQUET GARNI:
    4 sprigs fresh parsley, crushed to release flavor
    4 bay leaves
    6 whole allspice
    6 whole cloves
    1 tbsp. fresh thyme (or 1 tsp. dried thyme)
    6 cloves of garlic, peeled and crushed
    ½ tsp. whole black peppercorns, crushed
    6" piece gingerroot, peeled, sliced into thin coins and crushed

1. Place the chicken parts in a large stockpot. Cover with the water and rapidly bring to a boil. Skim any scum that rises to the surface. Add celery, carrots, and leeks and reduce the heat to a simmer.

2. Using a 4" square of cheesecloth, wrap the parsley, bay leaves, allspice, thyme, garlic, peppercorns, and gingerroot. Tie tightly with kitchen string. Allow enough string to attach the bouquet garni to one handle of the pot. Lower it into the pot and cook, at a simmer, for 1 hour. Remove and discard packet.

3. Pour stock through a fine-meshed sieve set over a large heatproof bowl. Press hard on the solids and then discard them. Pour the stock back into the stockpot and cook over high heat until the liquid is reduced to one-quarter of its original volume. (Note the level of the stock at this point for reference.) Let cool to room temperature. When cool, place in the refrigerator covered overnight to allow the fat that rises to the surface to congeal.

4. Next day, skim off every trace of visible fat. Pour into clean ice-cube trays, cover, and freeze. When frozen, the cubes of stock should be stored in a plastic freezer storage bag with a tight closure. Remove as many as needed and reconstitute each 1-oz. cube with ½ cup water. Salt to taste.

Basic Fresh Fish Stock
Makes 2 quarts

With its herbal accents and fresh fish taste, this stock is a simple and direct route to highly flavored soups and sauces. Since it doesn't require long cooking, you can make this fresh on the day you want to use it. For the cleanest-tasting results, be sure to choose heads and bones from nonfatty, mild-tasting fish like sea bass, red snapper, striped bass, or whitefish. Before using the fish heads, remove the red gills and wash the bones well to remove any clinging bits of blood, which will otherwise tarnish the purity of the stock's flavor. If lack of time is an issue, you can make this in advance, sieve out the solids and store, well covered, in the freezer for up to a week with no appreciable change of flavor.

> 5 lbs. heads and bones from nonfatty, impeccably fresh fish
> 3 quarts water
> 2 cups dry white wine

½ cup white wine vinegar

2 stalks celery, roughly chopped (about ½ cup)

2 medium carrots, peeled and roughly chopped (about ½ cup)

2 large onions, roughly chopped (about 2 cups)

2 leeks, split, well washed, and roughly chopped, about 1 cup (use green and white parts)

THE BOUQUET GARNI:

½ bunch fresh parsley

1 spring fresh thyme (or 1 tsp. dried thyme)

2 bay leaves

2 cloves

½ tsp. black peppercorns, crushed

Salt to taste (see note below)

1. Place the well-washed heads and bones in a large stockpot with the water. Bring to a boil quickly, skimming any scum that rises to the surface.

2. Add the wine and vinegar. Add the celery, carrots, onions, and leeks.

3. Using a 4" square of cheesecloth, wrap the parsley, thyme, bay leaves, cloves, and peppercorns and secure tightly with kitchen string. Allow enough string to attach the bouquet garni to one handle of the pot. Lower it into the pot and cook, at a simmer, for 30 minutes. Remove and discard packet.

4. Pour the stock through a dampened cheesecloth-lined sieve, pressing hard on the solids. Remove any fat that floats on the surface. Cool to room temperature. If using the same day, refrigerate until ready to use. Otherwise, freeze, well covered, for up to a week.

NOTE: I recommend adding salt to the stock at the time of its final use. This gives the cook flexibility in using the stock— either as a simple reduction sauce, or a more highly elaborated soup.

VARIATION I. *Fresh Fish Stock with Fennel*

Add 2 large bulbs of fresh fennel, about 4 cups chopped, to the basic recipe. Cut fennel into rough chunks, feathery tops and all, and with a heavy meat cleaver or wooden mallet, crush it just before adding to the stock. With its almost sweet licorice-scented edge, this stock serves especially well as the base for sauces accompanying grilled fish and seafood.

VARIATION II. *Fresh Fish Stock with Herbs*

When its end use calls for an herbal inflection, I simply add a generous amount of fragrant fresh herbs to the basic stock according to what the garden holds at the time. (Thankfully, supermarkets nowadays are a reliable source for hothouse herbs of all kinds if space, time, or the color of your thumb won't allow your own personal plot or pots of green.) Just before using, add 2 cups of any one or a combination of the following: basil, cilantro, dill, oregano, lemongrass, mint, parsley (flat leaf has the most flavor). Before turning this into a soup or sauce, remove the herbs by sieving the stock.

VARIATION III. *Well-Rooted Fresh Fish Stock*

When used in a sauce, this stock flavored with root vegetables complements steamed shellfish such as scallops, crab, shrimp, and lobster. To accentuate the vegetal notes in the stock, add 2 cups chopped, peeled parsley root and/or celery root after the first 15 minutes of simmering. At the end of the cooking time, sieve these out along with the rest of the solids.

VARIATION IV. *Citris-Flavored Fresh Fish Stock*

This variation is particularly winning as the base for sauces served with richer, fattier kinds of fish including shad, butterfish, and salmon. Here's how: During the last few minutes of cooking add 1 cup of the brightly colored peel of a well-scrubbed lemon, orange, lime, or grapefruit, or any combination of these. Be careful to avoid including any of the bitter white pith that lines the skin. After the short infusion, sieve out the peel and discard.

Fresh Tomato Puree

Makes approx. 1 quart

Capture the savor of summer by using the reddest, ripest, most flavorful tomatoes you can find (or grow). Choose firm varieties in which the pulp-to-seed ratio is high and the level of acidity in the juice is low. Shop the farmer's markets for the greatest variety, and taste widely to find the best flavor. By all means, if golden varieties, which tend to have a lower acidity and are proportionately well priced, are available, buy some of those to throw into the mix. Consider even cherry tomatoes (prolific, though seedy, Sweet 100s, for example, lend their own fruity charm to a puree when used as part of the total poundage).

Freeze this in airtight containers or fill ice-cube trays with the mixture, freeze and then pop them out, and store in airtight freezer bags to carry a bit of July all the way to the following June.

Salt, pepper, and fresh herbs should be added when you use the puree. If time, ambition, and harvest allow, you can easily increase the recipe in direct proportion to the amounts given below. Of course, cooking times for larger amounts will increase accordingly.

1 tbsp. olive oil
6 large cloves garlic, peeled and crushed
8 lbs. fresh tomatoes, any woody cores removed, cut into quarters
Enough water to prevent the tomatoes from burning before they surrender
    their juices

1. In a heavy saucepan, heat the olive oil until very hot. Add the garlic, stirring constantly. Cook just until light brown. With a slotted spoon, remove the garlic from the pan and discard. Add the tomatoes and water and cook until the mixture comes to a boil.

2. Reduce the heat to a simmer and cook until the tomatoes have disintegrated, about 30 minutes.

3. Pour through a fine-meshed sieve and reserve the liquid. Process the solids in a food mill fitted with a fine disc. (Use a food processor here if you like.) There should be no seeds or skins in the resulting puree. If necessary, pass the mixture through a fine sieve again.

4. Return the sieved mixture along with the reserved liquid to a clean heavy saucepan and cook over medium heat until reduced to a thick puree, about 20–30 minutes. Stir frequently as the water in the mixture evaporates to avoid burning. When thickened, remove from the heat, allow to cool to room temperature, then refrigerate or freeze. Add salt and pepper to taste and fresh herbs, if desired, at the time you use the puree.

Curry Blend
Makes ½ cup

Although prepackaged blends of curry spice take up space on shelves of supermarkets all over, I much prefer the homemade variety for its unsurpassed freshness and subtlety. It's indeed worth the bit of extra effort it takes to customize your own spice blend. It's simply a matter of getting on sniffing terms with your local Indian grocery and investing in a small electric spice or coffee grinder (a mortar and pestle will do if you have the muscle for it). I find that I can never have too many glass jars with tightly fitting lids on hand for storage of the whole spices and the resulting curry blends. By the way, be kind to your spices (whole or ground) and store them in a cool, dark place.

The first time out, you may want to follow my recipe exactly to give you a point of reference. Later, when you concoct your own blend you can modulate the amount of heat it will generate by simply varying the amount of black peppercorns and/or ginger you use. You can also alter the amount of sweet spices according to your preference for sweet over heat. A greater amount of sweet spices (cloves and cinnamon) will result in a more mellow, less obviously hot blend. No need to follow strict rules here.

There are as many curry blends as there are serious cooks who use them. Each one has a slightly different proportion of aromatic spices to hot ones. Experiment to find the right balance for your palate.

½ tsp. whole cloves

1" piece cinnamon stick

½ tsp. seeds from green cardamom pods

½ tsp. coriander seeds

1 tsp. fenugreek seeds

1 tsp. cuminseed

2 tbsp. ground dried ginger

1 tsp. turmeric

1 tbsp. whole black peppercorns

1. Toast the cloves, cinnamon, cardamom, coriander, fenugreek, and cuminseed in a heavy skillet until aromatic. Do not brown.

2. Grind in a spice or coffee grinder until fine. Add ginger and turmeric and blend. Grind peppercorns separately and add to the spice blend. Trial and error will help you decide how much to use.

Thickened Yogurt

Makes approx. 3½ cups (exact yield depends on water content of yogurt used)

L istening to your conscience and reducing fat in your diet is a lot easier when using this nonfat enrichment in soups, sauces, dressings, and spreads. I like to prepare a quart at a time and have an adequate supply on hand. Allow the yogurt to drain overnight for best results. The technique is foolproof and simple.

1 quart nonfat yogurt

1. Set a fine-meshed sieve lined with dampened cheesecloth over a stainless steel or crockery bowl. Empty the contents of a 1-quart container of nonfat plain yogurt into the sieve. Cover the whole apparatus well with plastic wrap. Place in the refrigerator overnight.

2. The next day, remove the thickened yogurt from the sieve and place in a clean glass container. Cover tightly and refrigerate. This will keep for up to 2 weeks. If you wish, you can save the nutritious whey that has drained from the yogurt for use in fruit shakes, breads, biscuits, or scones.

VARIATION I. *Roasted Shallot Yogurt*

Makes approx. 1 quart

A warm-weather essential, this is a mellow addition to gently cooked sauces and dressings and can stand alone as a nonfat dip for a plate of crunchy crudités or smoky grilled vegetables. It's also hauntingly delicious as a last-minute adornment for grilled turkey cutlets or fish. Try it as a spread on toasted flatbreads such as Middle Eastern pita or Indian chapati. I particularly like to use it as a melting mantle for a crisp-skinned baked potato. The acidic tang of the yogurt is neatly balanced by the intensified sweetness of the shallots. The merest touch of fruity sherry wine vinegar adds a mellow note, which lingers as a pleasant aftertaste.

8 oz. peeled shallots
2 oz. garlic
1 Recipe of Thickened Yogurt (page 265)
1 tsp. sherry wine vinegar
Salt and freshly ground white or black pepper

In a preheated 375° oven, roast the shallots and garlic until tender and golden brown, about 15 minutes. Peel and then puree in a food processor or blender until smooth. Add to yogurt and blend in vinegar and salt and pepper to taste. Store refrigerated in a tightly covered glass container. For maximum brightness of flavor, use within 1 week.

VARIATION II. *Roasted Garlic Spread*

Makes approx. 1 quart

A kind of golden aioli with a minute amount of good fruity olive oil, this aromatic sauce, served cold or at room temperature, works as a base for salad dressings and lends a spark to a whole range of slowly roasted and quickly grilled poultry, meats, fish, and seafood. When thinned to a pourable consistency with some earthy, full-flavored Root Stock (page 258), it becomes an addictive dressing for just about any impromptu seasonal salad. I especially like this over a plate of peppery arugula and slivered fennel. Even with its low-fat virtuousness, this sauce doesn't make me feel deprived.

8 oz. peeled garlic cloves
1 tbsp. high-quality fruity olive oil
1 recipe Thickened Yogurt (page 265)
Juice of 1 medium lemon
Salt and freshly ground black pepper to taste

1. Coat the garlic with the olive oil and roast in a preheated 350° oven for about 20–25 minutes, until golden brown and tender. Stir occasionally to avoid uneven browning. Do not allow to burn or the sauce will turn bitter. Let cool.

2. In a food processor or blender, puree the garlic to a smooth paste. Add to the yogurt. Blend in lemon juice. Salt and pepper to taste. Refrigerate in a tightly covered glass container. This keeps about 1 week before losing its freshness of flavor.

VARIATION III. *Light Aioli Dressing*

Makes approx. 2½ cups

Here the traditional fat-laden emulsion of garlic, egg yolks, and fine olive oil is streamlined. Fat- and cholesterol-conscious cooks and consumers can indulge relatively guiltlessly. A soupçon of a highly flavored olive oil goes a long way to help make this sauce more than a little reminiscent of its Provençal parentage.

½ cup Root Stock (page 258)

½ recipe Roasted Garlic Spread (page 266)

Salt and pepper to taste

Whisk the Root Stock into the Roasted Garlic Spread. Taste for salt and pepper. Store in a tightly covered glass container. For optimal flavor, mix this just before using.

Mock Coconut Milk

Makes 1 quart

Although nothing beats the real thing for smooth, creamy richness, this impostor lends a convincing coconut flavor to cooked foods without the fat and cholesterol. Essentially a white sauce based on nonfat milk thickened with cornstarch, this is best made no more than a day before using for maximum brightness of flavor. Scour the shelves of your nearest Asian or Indian markets to find the clear coconut extract with the truest nutty mellowness.

4 tbsp. cornstarch

1 quart nonfat milk

1–2 tsp. coconut extract, depending on strength of extract used

2 drops pure vanilla extract

1. Dissolve the cornstarch in ½ cup of the milk. In a heavy saucepan, bring the remaining milk to a boil over moderate heat. Add the cornstarch mixture and continue cooking, whisking until smooth and thick. Pass through a fine sieve if there are any lumps.

2. Allow to cool and then blend in the coconut and vanilla extracts. The coconut flavor will intensify after an hour. Refrigerate well covered.

Chile-Spiked Oil
Makes 1 pint

Especially at the end of summer and on into early fall, when many varieties of chiles have ripened on the vine into a deep burnished red, I like to make this fire-powered oil. When the hot peppers are slowly browned in a combination of peanut and safflower oils, they give up their heat to the oil but acquire a warm, almost nutty quality as well. Once it has cooled, I pour this into sterilized glass jars and top it with a hint of dark sesame oil to round things out. Store at room temperature in a cool, dark place. To keep the flavors bright, it's best to make this a pint at a time.

In warm weather, when the thought of serious cooking is out of the question, drizzle some of this liquid fire on a plate of leftover pasta, and toss with a scattering of crushed peanuts and scallions. Garnish with a shred of crisp daikon or jícama and break out the beer.

    1 cup peanut oil
    1 cup safflower oil
    1 cup mixed whole hot peppers, including serranos, chile pequin, and
        jalapeños, in whatever proportions you choose

In a heavy 2-quart saucepan, heat the oil over medium heat until hot. Add the chiles, reduce heat to low, and cook for 20 minutes or until chiles have browned slightly. Sieve when cool and store in a sterilized glass jar with a tight-fitting lid.

Shallot-Infused Oil

Makes 1 pint

To boost flavor in quickly steamed vegetables, grilled poultry, or seafood salads, or hot pasta dishes, this easy-to-make flavored oil, found in the pantry of Southeast Asian cooking, concentrates all the sweet oniony essence of the shallot when slowly browned.

I recommend using a flavorless oil such as canola or safflower to act as the medium here to transfer all the shallot's warm flavor to whatever dish is its beneficiary. Olive oil, normally the choice in my recipes, with its sometimes intrusive personality, would contribute one fruity flavor too many here.

Make this a few days before you wish to use it in order to allow its fullness of flavor to evolve. To produce a richly flavored Garlic-Infused Oil, follow the procedure shown below using the peeled cloves from 2 heads of garlic, about 4 oz.

2 cups flavorless vegetable oil (either canola or safflower work best)
1 lb. shallots, peeled and thinly sliced
Pinch salt

1. In a heavy saucepan, heat 2 tbsp. of the oil. Add the shallots and cook slowly over low heat until softened. Raise the heat to medium and cook the shallots until lightly browned. Stir constantly and watch carefully to avoid burning.

2. Remove shallots to a sterilized glass jar. Pour the remaining oil over the mixture and allow to cool thoroughly before covering tightly. Store in a cool, dark place. After about a week, I like to remove the shallots from the oil and use them to impart added depth of flavor to marinated pickled vegetables or salad dressings.

Freshly Minted Oil

Makes 1 quart

I like to use this highly concentrated, twice-infused oil as a last-minute brush-on for toasted chapati, those thin, chewy Indian flatbreads. A little also goes a long way in a cooling vinaigrette for a roasted medley of hot and sweet peppers. Crisp, sweet cucumbers take kindly to a light anointing, too. Tiny roasted new potatoes paired with some slow-cooked shallots become an impromptu salad when dressed with a drizzle of the oil sharpened with a bit of white wine vinegar.

Find the freshest, greenest, and most fragrant mint you can buy (either or both the peppermint or spearmint varieties will do). Wash and dry well before using. Don't forget to crush the stems to release their volatile oil before plunging them into the heated oil.

   2 large bunches of fresh mint
   1 quart flavorless cooking oil (soy, safflower, or canola works best)
   6 whole black peppercorns, crushed
   4 large cloves garlic, crushed

1. Chop the mint leaves and stems and set aside.

2. In a heavy saucepan, heat the oil to 190°. Add half the mint and simmer for 5 minutes. Let infuse until cool. Pass through a fine sieve and discard the solids.

3. In the same saucepan, heat the sieved oil again until it reaches 190°. Add the remaining mint, peppercorns, and garlic. Simmer for 5 minutes more. Let infuse again until cool. Sieve, discarding solids, and pour into a clean glass jar with a tightly fitting lid. Store in a cool, dark place and use within 1 month for maximum flavor.

VARIATIONS:

I. For a citrusy edge, add the leaves and crushed stems of 6 long stalks of fresh lemongrass in step 2 and proceed as above.

II. For some friendly fire, toss a few red-hot Thai chiles into the oil in step 2 and proceed as above. Oxymoronically speaking, this is the coolest heat you will find.

Tropical Vinegar

Makes 1 ½ quarts

With its heady perfume, this is more a fruity infusion than a vinegar. Somewhat golden in color, it adds a refreshing bite to sauces, bastes, marinades, and salad dressings. When it's added to a coconut milk or curry-accented soup or sauce, its bright acidic zing seems to bring the predominating flavors into sharper focus, mellowing and intensifying them at the same time.

Choose ripe but not overripe fruit and a tried-and-true white wine vinegar for the best boost. I like to make this about 1 week before using to allow the fullest fruit flavors to emerge and marry. Store in the refrigerator for the safest keeping. As you use it, replace the vinegar to keep the fruits covered at all times.

1 large ripe papaya, peeled and seeded, cut into 1" pieces (about 2 cups)

1 large ripe mango, peeled and seeded, cut into 1" pieces (about 2 cups)

½ medium-sized ripe pineapple, peeled and cored, cut into 1" pieces (about 2 cups)

Granulated sugar to lightly coat the fruits

2 quarts white wine vinegar

2 tbsp. dark rum

1. Place the prepared fruits in a stainless steel bowl. Lightly sugar just to coat. Let stand about ½ hour until they give up some of their juices.

2. In a non reactive heavy saucepan, bring the vinegar to a boil. Pour the boiling vinegar over the fruits in the bowl. Allow to stand 1 hour at room temperature. Add the rum.

3. Pour into sterilized glass jars with tight-fitting lids and refrigerate. After one week, pour through a fine sieve fitted with a dampened piece of cheesecloth. After sieving, discard the solids and return the liquid to clean jars. The liquid will be somewhat cloudy. Store in the refrigerator.

Sweet Chile Vinegar

Makes about 1 cup

Here's a homemade, somewhat sweet, variant of what lurks in bottles on the tables of many Asian (particularly Vietnamese) restaurants known for their spice-inflected dishes. Just the thing to perk up a too-timidly spiced soup or to add zing to a pan-fried noodle dish, this brew is easily made using the freshest, firmest chile peppers you can find (a combination of milder serranos and jalapeños ignited with a few tiny green Thai peppers is one way to go). Taste widely and wisely to find the right chile complement for your palate. Double or triple the recipe as you wish. Refrigerated, this keeps indefinitely

> Assorted chiles, about 1 oz. (red and green, if you wish)
> ½ cup rice vinegar
> 2 tbsp. granulated sugar
> 4 medium-sized peeled cloves garlic, crushed
> Salt

OPTIONAL ENHANCEMENTS:
> 2" piece gingerroot, peeled and slivered
> 2" strips fresh orange or tangerine zest

1. Carefully halve the chile peppers, removing most of the ribs and the seeds if you prefer a less piquant blend. (After handling the chiles, wash your hands carefully after rubbing with a bit of salt to remove the hot oils from your fingers. Rub the knife and cutting surface with salt before washing in plenty of soapy hot water.)

2. Place chiles in a glass jar with a tight-fitting lid. Add the vinegar, sugar, garlic, and just enough salt to enhance the flavors. (At this point, add the gingerroot or citrus peel, as desired.) Cover the jar and shake the jar to mix thoroughly. Let stand in the refrigerator about a week before using. As you use the chiles and vinegar, replace with more of the same to refresh the mixture.

Date-Lime Vinegar
Makes 1 pint

It would be hard to find two flavors that are farther apart than intensely sweet fresh dates and intensely sour fresh limes. But when combined in the presence of vinegar, a magical kind of chemistry takes place, resulting in a hybrid that tastes like neither. I like to make this in small batches and store it in the refrigerator to retain the most delicate fruity/flowery essence. Try to find dates that are soft and juicy. (See Superb Sources, page 290.) Choose limes that have a taut, brightly colored skin and feel heavy for their size.

Use this sparingly in sauces or as part of the acid in a well-balanced vinaigrette made with a combination of walnut and olive oils. It also lends a bright pungency to marinades, barbecue sauces, and condiments.

1 cup white wine vinegar
1 cup pitted dates
Zest of 2 well-washed fresh limes, removed in strips
Pinch of salt

Bring the vinegar to a boil in a nonaluminum saucepan. Place the dates and lime zest in a stainless steel or crockery bowl and pour the hot vinegar over them. Allow to stand until cool. Using a fine sieve lined with a piece of dampened cheesecloth, sieve out the solids and pour the liquid into an impeccably clean glass jar with a tight-fitting lid. Stir in salt. Stored in the refrigerator, this remains at its peak for about 1 month.

Pickled Ginger
Makes 1 quart

Although commercially made bottled versions of pickled ginger are readily available in Asian markets, the do-it-yourself kind is infinitely more satisfying to have around. It's easy to make (there are but five ingredients in all), keeps well, and seems like a treasure that inspires new uses each time I remove it from the refrigerator. Both the ginger and its liquid are indispensable flavoring agents, just right for adding a last-minute touch of slightly sweet piquancy to salad dressings, marinades, soups, and sauces. In hot weather, I like to spike freshly squeezed lemonade with a dose of the pickling liquid for a refreshingly astringent drink.

More elaborate but worth the effort is a Burmese-style salad made from thin strips of the ginger, well-drained, combined with toasted sesame seeds, roasted crushed peanuts and fried yellow split peas (fried *chana dal*, available in Indian markets) with a shot of garlic and shredded dried shrimp. Deliciously different picnic fare, indeed.

Store the pickle in a large old-fashioned canning jar (the kind with a rubber gasket ensures a tight seal). No need for artificial colorings to sully the purity of the pickle— its rosy glow comes naturally. Check to see that the ginger is well covered with its pickling liquid. Add more vinegar as needed if the level gets too low.

If young gingerroot is available, snatch up a supply to turn it into a tender, virtually stringless pickle. Though equally aromatic, the more common variety has a coarser texture. Look for firm "hands" of the rhizome whose papery beige skin is unbroken and unblemished.

1½ lbs. gingerroot, peeled and sliced into very thin diagonal coins
½ cup granulated sugar
2 cups rice vinegar
1 cup water
1 tsp. salt

1. In a stainless steel or crockery bowl, cover the prepared ginger with boiling water. Allow to steep for 1 minute and then drain. Pack into a sterilized glass jar with a tight-fitting lid.

2. In a 1-quart sauce pan, bring the sugar, vinegar, 1 cup water, and salt to a boil, cooking just until the sugar dissolves. Pour this liquid over the ginger in the jar. Allow to cool and then cover tightly. Refrigerate. This keeps in the refrigerator indefinitely as long as the ginger is well covered with liquid.

Candied Lemon Peel

Makes 1 cup

What could be easier than making this mellow golden confection? Patience and sugar are all you need to produce a versatile jewel from the part of the lemon that is usually discarded. Outshining that old '60s Chinese restaurant cliché lemon chicken, Gilded Chicken with Lemon Confiture (page 13) gains a sparkling clarity of lemon flavor with a hint of homemade candied peel. A side dish of steamed bitter greens also benefits from a surface gilding. Fragile, buttery shortbread is enlivened with a generous scattering of the peel. Delicate scones served with tea also take on new vibrancy when flecked with some of the fragrant peel.

Use lemons that are firm, with clean, brightly colored skin and preferably untreated with chemical sprays. Take care to remove only the merest amount of bitter white pith when peeling the fruit. A thin layer lends shape to the final candied peel but too much only contributes excess bitterness. To be sure that no bitterness remains, don't cut down on the preliminary repeated blanchings.

When using the peel as a true confection, a crust of coarse crystal sugar lends a professional touch. For an after-dessert dessert, serve some swathed in bittersweet chocolate (dipped on the day you wish to serve it). The peel from grapefruit, limes, oranges, and tangerines works equally well. Always taste after the last blanching to be sure all of the bitterness has been removed. If not, blanch again in fresh water.

Peel from 6 large lemons (organic, unsprayed fruit is preferred)
2 cups granulated sugar
1 cup water
Coarse-textured crystal sugar for a professional-looking coating (optional)

1. Remove the peel from the lemons in long strips about ½" wide, leaving only the thinnest layer of white pith attached. Bring 2 quarts of water to a boil and add the peel. Boil for 5 minutes and drain. Refresh the peel with cold water. Bring another pot of water to boil and add the peel. Boil again, repeating the same boiling, draining, and refreshing in cold water three more times. When you have finished the last blanching, drain the peel and dry on absorbent paper.

2. Bring the sugar and 1 cup water to a boil in a heavy 1-quart saucepan. When the liquid is clear, add the peel and cook over low heat without stirring until the peel is

well coated with the sugar syrup. Remove from the syrup and place on a cooling rack to allow excess syrup to drain from the peel. When dry, coat with the crystal sugar, if desired. Store the peel at room temperature in a tightly covered metal container lined with parchment paper, using more parchment to separate the layers of peel, if necessary.

How to Dry Citrus Peel

To lend a concentrated citrusy flavor to marinades, sauces, dressings, and sweets, homemade dried peel is infinitely preferable to the bottled, commercially prepared variety. It practically makes itself and you can't beat the price. Here's how:

Choose any citrus with brightly colored peel. (I find that honey tangerines and navel oranges make particularly fragrant dried peel.) Wash well and dry. Remove the peel in large pieces. With a small sharp knife, scrape the white layer of pith from the skin. Place the prepared peel on a metal rack, cover lightly with cheesecloth, and allow to dry at room temperature until crisp. This can take as long as several days in a warm environment. If the weather is particularly humid, you may dry the peel overnight in a gas oven using the warmth of the pilot light. If you have an electric oven, you may dry the peel in it, set at the lowest temperature setting. Watch carefully. It may take several hours. Do not allow to brown. (An electric dehydrator, of course, would provide the most direct route.)

Store the dried peel in an airtight metal or glass container in a cool, dark place. It will keep indefinitely.

How to Smoke Foods on Stovetop in a Wok-Turned-Smoker

With a well-seasoned, roomy wok at hand, regardless of the type of foods I am cooking, I need look no further to find the utensil of choice in my kitchen. Whether it's a buffet-size batch of vegetables that need stir-frying or blanching or a whole fish that benefits from a moist steaming, the wok answers the call. And the most fun bit of culinary magic that you can perform with a wok is to transform it easily into a smoker with only slight modification. A few words of advice before you begin:

Remember that foods at room temperature will acquire the deepest smoky flavor.

Don't crowd the wok with too much food to be smoked. For best results, smoking no more than a pound of foods at a time allows for a free circulation of smoke inside the wok.

Be aware also that the bone structure and leanness (or fattiness) of the meats, poultry, or fish being smoked will influence how much further cooking will be required before serving. The ingredients used to create the smoke in the wok will most likely incinerate before most foods are fully cooked. Remove the incinerated mixture and replace with a new supply and continue smoking, or simply finish the cooking in the oven, steamer, sauté pan, or grill, as you wish if after the initial smoking the food has been sufficiently smoked to your taste.

Be sure to use the exhaust fan over your stove before, during, and after the smoking process. If the season allows, open some windows as well.

Ingredients for imparting a light or medium smoke to about 1 lb. of boneless meat, poultry, fish, vegetables, or pasta:

1 cup raw white rice

¼ cup brown sugar

1 cup fragrant loose tea (Lapsang Souchong or jasmine works especially well)

1 cinnamon stick

6 whole star anise

6 cloves

1 sweet apple, cut into 8 wedges

1 strip of orange peel, about 4" long

1. Line the inside of the bottom of the wok with a crisscross of heavy-duty foil, allowing a 3" overhang on all sides. Similarly, line the inside of the lid. Outfit the wok with a wire rack with legs that lift it at least ½" off the bottom surface.

2. Combine all the ingredients for smoking and spread evenly in a thin layer on the foil in the wok. (Depending on what you are smoking, you may wish to add fragrant herbs like fresh rosemary, thyme, or oregano to the blend [for example, see recipe on page 219] or increase the quantity of whole brown aromatics to sweeten the smoky flavor the food will acquire.) Tightly cover the wok, tightly crimping the foil that extends from the base and lid.

3. Heat the wok over high heat. When the first wisps of smoke emerge from the wok, place foods to be smoked on the rack inside the wok and count 5 minutes for a light smoking and 10–15 minutes for a medium smoking. To smoke foods longer than 15 minutes, it will be necessary to replace the original batch of smoking ingredients with successive batches. Therefore, for each successive smoking, after the initial one, remove the foods from the wok, keeping them warm, as necessary. Place a new batch of smoking ingredients in the wok and then heat as directed above. After the first wisps of smoke again emerge from the wok, return the foods to the wok for as long as 15 minutes more. Repeat process as desired.

To fully cook bone-in chicken breasts, for example, will require about 25–35 minutes of high heat in a fully smoking wok. (Test with a knife inserted into the thickest part of the breast; the juices should be clear.)

How to Clarify Butter

For dishes where the inimitable, rich sweet flavor of unsalted butter is desirable and where foods are sautéed over high heat, clarified butter is the cooking medium of choice. Clarifying removes from the butter the protein and milk solids that cause it to burn when cooked over moderate to high heat. What remains is pure fat. A little goes a long way in flavoring delicate vegetable, rice, or grain dishes. Sautéing in a tiny amount of it (or in combination with flavorful oils such as olive or sesame) is pure luxury. Here's how to clarify butter:

1. Over low heat, melt 4 oz. or more butter in a heavy saucepan until it foams. Then, watching carefully, cook further over low heat, until a whitish crust forms on the surface of the melted fat. Continue cooking until the crust turns a light golden brown. Remove from heat and allow to stand for a few minutes.

2. Carefully lift off the crust and discard. Then pour the remaining liquid through a fine sieve lined with dampened cheesecloth. Only the clear golden liquid should drip through. If any of the milk solids get through the sieve, repeat the sieving process until the resulting liquid is clear. Store, refrigerated, in a glass jar with a tight-fitting lid.

2-4-6-8 Dough–Sweet Short Pastry Dough for Cookies and Tarts

Makes 1 1/2 lbs.

This is a foolproof buttery dough that gets its name from the weights of sugar, butter, and flour, and the number of eggs that compose it. It's easy to handle, keeps well frozen for about a month, and because of its relatively high proportion of fat, will not toughen even with merciless handling. The recipe may be halved or doubled as you wish. (To clearly see the proportions, one needs to look at the original recipe, designed for commercial baking, which calls for eight times the amounts of each ingredient shown below, producing a yield of approximately 12 lbs.)

You may manipulate the final texture of the baked pastry by rolling it thinly (less than 1/4") and baking it more quickly in a hotter (375°) oven for a crisp and almost flaky result, or more thickly and baking in a slower oven (275°–325°) for a pleasantly mealy texture and evenly pale color, like some shortbread.

    8 oz. unsalted butter, softened at room temperature
    1/2 cup granulated sugar
    1 whole large egg
    2 cups all-purpose flour mixed with 1/3 cup cake flour
    Flour for kneading and rolling the dough

In a food processor or in the bowl of an electric mixer, cream butter until light and smooth. Add the sugar and beat until dissolved, about 5 minutes. Blend in the egg. Add the flour and process just until the flour disappears. Remove to a lightly floured surface and knead into a rough ball. Flatten into a disk about 1/2" thick and refrigerate, covered, until cold, about 1 hour. Remove from refrigerator and soften by kneading. Roll to desired thickness, cut and shape, chill until once again firm, and bake per desired recipe.

CITRUS VARIATION:

Citrus zest from lemons, limes, oranges, grapefruit (about 1 oz. per the above recipe) can be added to the dough by combining it with the sugar and processing in a food processor until finely chopped, or by grating on a hand grater and adding to the sugar before it is added to the creamed butter.

NUTTY VARIATION:

Finely ground walnuts, lightly toasted almonds, toasted and skinned hazelnuts, toasted pecans (or a combination of any of the foregoing) can be added to the butter during the creaming to replace as much as one-quarter of flour by weight.

Roasted Red Pepper Ketchup
Makes 2 cups

Who can resist those lipstick-red thick-walled peppers from Holland? Particularly in winter, when homegrown varieties are sorely missed, these Dutch treats always inspire me to make a batch of this quick condiment. As a sweet smoky alternative to tomato ketchup, this bright chunky sauce will grace anything from grilled turkey burgers to simply steamed cauliflower or red cabbage. And what's best of all is its ease of preparation, thanks to *ketjap manis*, the thick sweetened soy sauce from Indonesia, which has come to occupy a central place in my pan-ethnic pantry.

    1 large red bell pepper (about 10 oz.)
    1 cup fresh tomato puree (canned will do when schedule or season dictates)
    ⅓ cup *ketjap manis* (or ¼ cup reduced-salt soy sauce combined with 2 tbsp. dark
        molasses)
    Salt and freshly ground black pepper (optional)

1. Using tongs, char red pepper over an open flame until uniformly blackened. Immediately plunge into a bowl of ice water. When cool, carefully rub off the blackened skin. Cut in half. Remove ribs and seeds and cut into ½" dice.

2. In a heavy 1-quart saucepan, combine the pepper, tomato puree, and ketjap manis. Cook over medium heat, stirring constantly, for about 3–4 minutes, or until sauce has thickened somewhat. It should barely coat a spoon. Let cool. Adjust seasoning with salt and pepper as needed. When refrigerated and stored in a covered glass jar, the sauce will keep at least a week.

CHAPTER 8
• • • • • • • • • • • • • • • • •

Even Healthful Eating Can Be Habit-Forming

There's no need to sacrifice flavor or enjoyment at the table even when watching calories or fat and salt intake. There is no such thing as a bad food; usually immoderate use of it is the villain. Balance is the key; everything in moderation. So if you're conscious about calories, percentage of fat, or sodium in your daily menu, refer to the following lists for help. If you adhere to the serving sizes, cooking techniques, and ingredients described in the recipes, you may be assured that you are obtaining the amount of calories, fat, and salt listed below. And since fiber is considered to be a benefit to a healthy diet, I have also included a separate list of recipes with 5 grams or more per serving.

LOW-FAT RECIPES (3 GRAMS OR LESS PER SERVING)

Starters

Fennel-Orange Salad

White Bean Potage with Sorrel Swirl

Poblano Pepper Pilaf

Onion Crème Brûlée

Malaysian Melange

Witloof with Love—Braised Endive with Roasted Carrot Sauce

Pasta Agrodolce

Roasted Rootatouille

Soothing Salmagundi Soup

Currying Flavor Three Ways—A Southeast Asian Lasagna

Sesame Mucho—A Fragrant Toss-Fry of Fennel and Artichoke Hearts in a
    Sesame Glaze

Slightly Smoked Eggplant and Company with Roasted Shallot Yogurt Sauce

Steamed Rice in Bamboo Leaves with Shiitakes and Smoked Salmon

Sides

Bittersweet Bouquet—Sweet-and-Sour Greens with Quince and Pomegranate

Poblano Pepper Pilaf

Heavenly Scented Couscous with Crisped Chapati

Onion Crème Brûlée

Ovenroast of Jumbled Grains with Tomato-Chile Coulis

Seurat's Cauliflower

Warm Compote of Sweet Potato and Tart Apple in a Tamarind Sauce (omit
    hazelnut garnish)

Pasta Agrodolce

Roasted Rootatouille

Sesame Mucho—A Fragrant Toss-Fry of Fennel and Artichoke Hearts in a
    Sesame Glaze

Fennel Gratin with a Red Pepper Ribbon

Mixed-Grain Pilaf with a Hint of Smoke

Stars

Grilled Chicken Piccata with Lemon Times Three
Red-Hot and Orange—Halibut Harissa
Malaysian Melange
Pasta Agrodolce
Currying Flavor Three Ways—A Southeast Asian Lasagna
Bird in a Bag—Aromatic Roasted Chicken in a Haunting Sauce (remove chicken skin
    before proceeding with the recipe)

Not-So-Sweets

Blushing Bartletts
Suite of Pears in a Zingy Ginger Dunk (reduce yogurt to 1 cup)
Star Anise-and-Lemon Poached Apples (without cookie accompaniment)
Prickly Pear Sorbet (without cookie accompaniment)
Grilled Fruit Salad with Fresh Berry Coulis
Broiled Oranges with Brown Sugar-Lime Glaze

LOW-SODIUM RECIPES (140 MG OR LESS PER SERVING)

Starters

Pale Perfect Poached Celery (when preparing, limit salt to taste)
Thai-Dyed Seafood Soup
Rally of the Dals
Fennel-Orange Salad
White Bean Potage with Sorrel Swirl
Syrian Fire—Fiery Red Pepper and Walnut Spread
Sharply Minted Cucumber Salad (omit salt when preparing)
Witloof with Love—Braised Endive with Roasted Carrot Sauce
Soothing Salmagundi Soup
Muncha Buncha Mungs—Crisp Bean Sprouts in a Lime-Ginger Marinade
Sesame Mucho—A Fragrant Toss-Fry of Fennel and Artichoke Hearts
    in a Sesame Glaze
Warm "Salad" of Watercress, Arugula, and Roasted Red Pepper

Sides

Rally of the Dals
Bitter Greens in a Honey-Lemon Drizzle
Bittersweet Bouquet—Sweet-and-Sour Greens with Quince and Pomegranate
Heavenly Scented Couscous with Crisped Chapati (when preparing, omit salt)
Sharply Minted Cucumber Saslad (omit salt when preparing)
Seurat's Cauliflower
Sesame Mucho—A Fragrant Toss-Fry of Fennel and Artichoke Hearts
    in a Sesame Glaze
Sizzled Shiitakes (limit or eliminate salt when preparing)
Mixed-Grain Pilaf with a Hint of Smoke

Stars

Pan-Grilled Pressed Cornish Hens, Cuban-Style
Grilled Chicken Piccata with Lemon Times Three
Pan-Seared Bass with a Searing Melon Coulis
Practically Persian Turkey Fesenjan (omit salt when preparing)

Not-So-Sweets

Grilled Fruit Salad with Fresh Berry Coulis
Broiled Oranges with Brown Sugar-Lime Glaze

LOW-CALORIE RECIPES (APPROX. 80 CALORIES OR LESS
    PER SERVING)

Starters

Pale Perfect Poached Celery
Thai-Dyed Seafood Soup
Roots Revisited
White Bean Potage with Sorrel Swirl
Onion Crème Brûlée
My Fave Favas
Witloof with Love—Braised Endive with Roasted Carrot Sauce

Pasta Agrodolce

Sweet-and-Sour Braised Fennel with Roasted Tomato Sauce

Indian Potato Salad, Street-Food Style

Roasted Rootatouille

Can't Be Beet Borscht

Soothing Salmagundi Soup

Warm "Salad" of Watercress, Arugula, and Roasted Red Pepper

Birds in the Bush—Smoked Capellini Nests

Steamed Rice in Bamboo Leaves with Shiitakes and Smoked Salmon

Sides

Bitter Greens in a Honey-Lemon Drizzle

Bittersweet Bouquet—Sweet-and-Sour Greens with Quince and Pomegranate

Nutty Chiffonade of Crunchy Cabbage

Heavenly Scented Couscous with Crisped Chapati

Onion Crème Brûlée

Afghan Aubergines (see Charbroiled Chicken with Afghan Aubergines)

My Fave Favas

Pasta Agrodolce

Sweet-and-Sour Braised Fennel with Roasted Tomato Sauce

Indian Potato Salad, Street-Food Style

Roasted Rootatouille

A Caper of Oven-Roasted Beets

Sizzled Shiitakes

Stars

Broiled Trout Aegean

Gilded Chicken with Lemon Confiture (remove skin of chicken before proceeding)

Pan-Grilled Pressed Cornish Hens, Cuban-Style

Grilled Chicken Piccata with Lemon Times Three

Pepper-Crusted Turkey Steak

Orecchiette Vegetale

Smoky Chicken Packets Steamed in Banana Leaves

HIGH-FIBER CONTENT RECIPES (5 GRAMS OR MORE PER SERVING)

Starters

Rally of the Dals

Fennel-Orange Salad

Roots Revisited

White Bean Potage with Sorrel Swirl

Poblano Pepper Pilaf

Five-Flavor Eggplant

Southwest by Southeast Saté (vegetarian variation)

Sharply Minted Cucumber Salad

My Fave Favas

Malaysian Melange

Witloof with Love—Braised Endive with Roasted Carrot Sauce

Sweet-and-Sour Braised Fennel with Roasted Tomato Sauce

Indian Potato Salad, Street-Food Style

Golden Melting Moments—A Late Summer Soup of Yellow Tomato and Yellow
    Pepper

Roasted Rootatouille

Can't Be Beet Borscht

Muncha Buncha Mungs—Crisp Bean Sprouts in a Lime-Ginger Marinade

Sesame Mucho—A Fragrant Toss-Fry of Fennel and Artichoke Hearts
    in a Sesame Glaze

Warm "Salad" of Watercress, Arugula, and Roasted Red Pepper

Napa-Kasha Nests Afloat in Cabbage Essence

Slightly Smoked Eggplant and Company with Roasted Shallot Yogurt Sauce

Sides

Bitter Greens in a Honey-Lemon Drizzle

Bittersweet Bouquet—Sweet-and-Sour Greens with Quince and Pomegranate

Nutty Chiffonade of Crunchy Cabbage

Poblano Pepper Pilaf

Heavenly Scented Couscous with Crisped Chapati

Ovenroast of Jumbled Grains with Tomato-Chile Coulis

ING 287

Sharply Minted Cucumber Salad
My Fave Favas
Seurat's Cauliflower
Sweet-and-Sour Braised Fennel with Roasted Tomato Sauce
Indian Potato Salad, Street-Food Style
Warm Compote of Sweet Potato and Tart Apple in a Tamarind Sauce
Roasted Rootatouille
Carrots Slow and Sweet
Sham Spaghetti Anti-Pesto
A Caper of Oven-Roasted Beets
Sesame Mucho—A Fragrant Toss-Fry of Fennel and Artichoke Hearts
   in a Sesame Glaze
Fennel Gratin with a Red Pepper Ribbon
Mixed-Grain Pilaf with a Hint of Smoke

Stars

Southwest by Southeast Saté (vegetarian variation)
Practically Persian Turkey Fesenjan
Malaysian Melange

Not-So-Sweets

Grilled Fruit Salad with Fresh Berry Coulis

For more information on healthful eating, contact:

American Dietetic Association
216 W. Jackson Blvd.
Chicago, IL 60606-6995

or your local chapter of the ADA (listed in the white pages of your phone book).

Superb Sources–
Mail-Order Sources

The idea of ordering foods by mail at first seemed to run counter to my need to see, smell, touch, and even taste foods before I buy them. But part and parcel of the process is also an alluring sense of adventure. Will the product live up to the expectations created by the sometimes glossy brochure? Will the merchandise arrive in good shape? Is the pricing competitive? With all of the following suppliers, both large and small, my hesitations dissolved and yours will too. And there *are* some very special foodstuffs whose extremely limited supply, relatively small audience or small-scale production (often by hand) precludes wider distribution. Therein lies their charm and many of these are available only by mail. So dip into the world of mail-order foods even gingerly, and as I was, you, too, will be rewarded. The pleasures turned out to be many, the perils few.

ADRIANA'S BAZAAR
317 West 107th Street
New York, NY 10025
(212) 877-5757

Strictly mail-order, a movable feast of ethnic ingredients, often otherwise hard to find outside of ethnic neighborhood stores in large cities. If she doesn't stock it, Adriana will get it for you. "Starter kits" of ingredients for particular cuisines are increasingly available. Another plus is highly personalized customer service.

APPLESOURCE
Route 1
Chapin, IL 62628
(217) 245-7589

A fun way to taste some of the 90 varieties of apples, many of which never make it to supermarkets due to their perishability and relatively small production. Grown in orchards from Indiana and Illinois to Michigan and California, peak harvesting times are from October through December.

COVALDA DATE COMPANY
51-392 Harrison Street
Coachella, CA 92236-1563
(619) 398-3551

A supremely accommodating and long-established mail-order source for fresh organic dates and date products. Late fall and early winter are the peak times when they pick, process, pack, and ship most of their new crop.

D'ARTAGNAN INC.
399-419 St. Paul Avenue
Jersey City, NJ 07306
(800) 327-8246

Reliably fresh, high-quality duck breasts, foie gras, prepared dishes, and wild game are available shipped overnight air.

FRIEDA'S FINEST

P.O. Box 58488
Los Angeles, CA 90058
(800) 241-1771

For more than thirty years, this specialty produce house has been selling exotic fruits and vegetables to supermarkets and will send mail orders of case lots as well as gift baskets and samplers of unusual fruits and vegetables anywhere in the country.

KING ARTHUR FLOUR BAKER'S CATALOGUE

P.O. Box 876
Norwich, VT 05055-0876
(800) 827-6836

A full line of hard-to-find flours, grains, flavorings, baking tools, and Australian crystallized ginger makes this source worthy of note.

SHEPHERD'S GARDEN SEEDS

30 Irene Street
Torrington, CT 06790
In CT, (203) 482-3638; in CA (408) 335-6910

Need that final impetus to plant a vegetable garden? This source for unique seeds should push you over the edge. They offer a wide selection of European and Asian seeds for numerous varieties of vegetables, herbs, and flowers (some edible) with encouraging how-to advice on cultivation. I particularly like their "Salads from the Continent," which offers easy-to-grow seeds for greens that will add color and crunch to your salad bowl, at least three seasons of the year, in most areas of the United States. For chile-heads, their incendiary assortment can't be beat.

TAHITIAN IMPORTS INC.

1007 Alvira Street
Los Angeles, CA 90035
(213) 655-4895

An exclusive source for soft, moist, fat, fresh vanilla beans and extracts of incomparable purity of flavor.

TOUCHED SELECT
15999 Avenue 232
Tulare, CA 93274
(800) 255-7039

Brilliant color, soft texture, and bright flavors are what distinguish these dried fruits from those produced by giant conglomerates. The secret is in the drying, which is accomplished at a lower temperature than commercially, thereby retaining moisture and true fruit flavor. You just can't miss with their apricots.

WHISTLING WINGS FARM
427 West Street
Biddeford, ME 04005
(800) 765-8989

Lower-sugar-content fruit spreads, syrups, honey, and berry vinegars have built the reputation of this small producer. Take note, raspberry-philes.

WORLD VARIETY PRODUCE INC. (MELISSA'S PRODUCE)
P.O. Box 21127
Los Angeles, CA 90021
(800) 588-0151

This comprehensive mail-order house features a full line of exotic produce, authentic Latin and Oriental ethnic ingredients, Middle Eastern, South American, and Indian grains, sulphur-free dried fruits, ground and whole spices, and dried mushrooms.

YERBA SANTA GOAT DAIRY
6850 Scotts Valley Road
Lakeport, CA 95453
(800) 499-8131

A 73-acre dairy founded in 1977 raising Alpine goats and producing a wide range of soft, ripened, and well-aged goat cheeses, herbed and plain. A particular personal favorite of mine is Shepherd's Cheese, Private Reserve, which is sold in 8-oz. wedges and 4-lb. wheels (it keeps). Excellent for grating or flaking over soups, pastas, in sauces, or simply as part of a cheeseboard.

Recommended Reading for Further Explorations

Here is a selective list of sources, old and new, each of which has provided me with thoughts for foods and food for thought and many an hour of calorie-free armchair dining.

Alejandro, Reynaldo. *The Flavor of Asia*. New York: Beaufort Books, 1984.

Anderson, E. N. *The Food of China*. New Haven: Yale University Press, 1988.

Andoh, Elizabeth. *An Ocean of Flavor: The Japanese Way with Seafood*. New York: William Morrow, 1988.

Cusumano, Camille. *The New Foods*. New York: Henry Holt and Company, 1989.

deGroot, Roy Andries. *Esquire's Handbook for Hosts*. New York: Grosset & Dunlap, 1973.

Editors, Sunset Books. *Fresh Produce*. Menlo Park, CA: Lane Publishing Co., 1987.

Foster, Nelson, and Linda S. Cordell. *Chilies to Chocolate*. Tucson: University of Arizona Press, 1992.

Hansen, Barbara. *Taste of Southeast Asia*. Tucson: HPBooks, 1987.

Harlow, Jay. *Southeast Asian Cooking*. California Culinary Academy Series. California: Chevron Chemical Company, 1987.

Jaffrey, Madhur. *Indian Cooking*. New York: Barron's Educational Series, 1983.

Johnson, Hugh. *The World Atlas of Wine*. New York: Simon and Schuster, 1971.

Margvelashvili, Julianne. *The Classic Cuisine of Soviet Georgia*. New York: Prentice Hall Press, 1991.

Marks, Copeland. *The Exotic Kitchens of Indonesia*. New York: M. Evans and Company, 1989.

McGee, Harold. *The Curious Cook*. San Francisco: North Point Press, 1990.

Ngo, Bach, and Gloria Zimmerman. *The Classic Cuisine of Vietnam*. New York: Barron's Educational Series, 1979.

Parry, John W. *Spices,* Vol. 1. New York: Chemical Publishing Company, 1969.

Roden, Claudia. *A Book of Middle Eastern Food*. New York: Alfred A. Knopf, 1968.

Schneider, Elizabeth. *Uncommon Fruits and Vegetables: A Commonsense Guide*. New York: Harper & Row, 1986.

Solomon, Charmaine. *The Complete Asian Cookbook*. New York: McGraw Hill Book Company, 1976.

Index